Fruitbearer

What Can I Do For YOU, Lord?

Candy Abbott

*An urgent call to grassroots believers—
The harvest is ripe!*

FRUITBEARER: WHAT CAN I DO FOR YOU, LORD?
Copyright © 1994, 2006 Candace F. Abbott
First printing 1994
Second printing 1995
Third printing 2006, revised
Fourth printing 2017
Ebook published 2014

ISBN 978-1979303231 paperback

Library of Congress Control Number: 2001012345
Holy Spirit · Christian Life · Religious and Inspirational
Personal Growth · Faith · Self-Help

Published by Fruitbearer Publishing
P.O. Box 777, Georgetown, DE 19947 · (302) 856-6649 · FAX (302) 856-7742
www.fruitbearer.com • info@fruitbearer.com
Graphic design by Candy Abbott; cover photo from shutterstock.com
Edited by Diane Cook and Marlene Bagnull

Passages from *The Helper* by Catherine Marshall are used with the permission of Marshall-LeSourd L.L.C.

By author preference, pronouns for the persons of the Trinity are capitalized throughout, including all Scripture quotations from NIV, KJV, and NRSV translations.

Unless otherwise noted, Scripture is taken from the *HOLY BIBLE, NEW INTERNATIONAL VERSION*, Copyright © 1973, 1978, 1984 International Bible Society. Used by permission of Zondervan Bible Publishers. All rights reserved.

Other Scripture references are from the following sources:

The Amplified Bible (AMP), copyright © 1986, Grand Rapids, Michigan: Zondervan Bible Publishers. Used by permission.

The Good News Bible: The Bible in Today's English Version (TEV), copyright © 1992 by the American Bible Society.

The King James Version of the Holy Bible (KJV), public domain.

Tne New King James Version (NKJV), copyright © 1982 by Thomas Nelson, Inc. Used by permission. All rights reserved.

New Revised Standard Version of the Bible (NRSV), copyright © 1989 by the Division of Christian Education of the National Council of the Churches of Christ in the USA.

The Living Bible (TLB), copyright © 1971 by Tyndale House Publishers, Wheaton, Illinois. Used by permission.

The Message (MSG), copyright © 1993. Used by permission of NavPress Publishing Group.

Printed in the United States of America

DEDICATED

To Mom
who always liked a good puzzle

To Dad
who never wavered

"This book is extremely powerful and practical. My mom read it and said, 'It's the first book that ever compelled me to have my Bible open and ready to read suggested verses.' I tried the journaling—God really spoke! In slowing down and writing out what I thought I heard, I was able to hear more clearly and to distinguish 'me' from 'He.'" —*Kim Eckman, Coatesville, PA*

"*Fruitbearer* is a clearly written, challenging book inviting Christians to faithful discipleship. I believe that it can help many find their way on the Christian journey." —*Ben C. Johnson, Professor of Spirituality, Columbia Theological Seminary*

"I like how *Fruitbearer* reads; it is open and transparent and the reader feels very safe. I think my favorite part is where the author records the words of prophecy the Lord has given her. These are extremely powerful and will speak volumes to Christians not yet acquainted with the works of the Holy Spirit. The 'Seeds for Thought' give the book the individuality it needs to be remembered. And the prayer at the end of every chapter allows time for personal reflection. Indeed, God's Spirit seems to have breathed upon the pages." —*Linda Eckman, Kennett Square, PA*

"*Fruitbearer* is an intimate, revealing account of one woman's incredible spiritual journey as she asks the question, 'What can I do for You, Lord?' As the Holy Spirit reveals Himself, Candy Abbott shares her personal discoveries and provides an in-depth guidebook to fruitful living. For those of us who dare to accept His challenge as we enter a new millennium, she provides not only instruction, but inspiration." —*Gail Black Kopf, Author of* Rubicon

"Candy Abbott is a superb storyteller. Her writing style is truly professional. I admire Candy's strong faith and her candid sharing. Her section 'Love in a Medicine Cabinet,' on page 203, should be prerequisite reading for all loving couples. Spiritually strong and inspiring!" —*Tom Lagana, Wilmington, DE*

"Reading *Fruitbearer* has been like carrying on a heartfelt conversation with an intimate friend. Candy tells the story of her spiritual journey in such a way that any of us can relate to the trip. In reading the book, you will feel more comfortable with your own spiritual journey, knowing you are not alone in the bumps, ruts, scenic views and comfort-stations that you will encounter along the way. For those seeking a closer relationship with the Lord, or for those who already have a close relationship and simply want to review the trip, this book is a must-read!" —*Chris Swim, Sorrento, FL*

CONTENTS

Foreword .... *vii*

Preface .... *ix*

Acknowledgments .... *xi*

Letter from Candy 13

Chapter 1 Wake Up to God's Alarm Clock 17

Chapter 2 Report for Vineyard Duty 43

Chapter 3 Surrender to the Vinegrower's Touch 73

Chapter 4 Recognize the Master's Voice 99

Chapter 5 Grow, Blossom, Share What You Believe 119

Chapter 6 Plow Up Untilled Ground 137

Chapter 7 Receive the Fullness of God 165

Chapter 8 Pruned to Flourish 193

Chapter 9 Explore Your Calling 225

Chapter 10 Stand Firm! 253

About the Author 271

Recommended Resources 275

Order Information 279

SEED FOR THOUGHT

A new convert expressed the confidence he had in Christ, "I feel much better now when I feel badly than I used to feel when I felt good."

—*Anchor Baptist Church Bulletin*

FOREWORD

My garden calls me as soon as the ground thaws and is dry enough to turn over. Although the work of planting and maintaining my 7' x 10' patch of vegetables (and weeds) seems harder with each passing year, the promise of home-grown tomatoes compels me to keep on keeping on despite my aching back.

After several years of less than bountiful harvests, I concluded the soil was worn out and needed a boost. So this spring, I enlisted my son's help to roto-till peat moss and manure into the soil. He did not share my enthusiasm that these "nutrients" would make a difference, but he knows me. When I've made up my mind, I don't let anything stop me. I expect he also figured I'd never be able to handle the roto-tiller. Doing it himself was preferable to rushing me to the hospital if I cut off my toe!

Shopping for plants was a painstaking process. Should I go with a new disease-resistant variety of tomatoes or stick with the tried and true Big Boy or Early Girl? I carefully read the tags (what if someone had switched them?) and compared the size of the plants—putting down one pot and picking up another. My husband said he'd wait for me in the car!

My plants thrived for the first month as I faithfully watered them and kept watch with an eagle eye for any weeds. But the flowers I expected to see didn't appear even though the plants kept growing taller. Out came the fertilizer. The plants, minus the needed flowers, grew still taller.

Then came drought and outrageously high water bills. The cost in time, work, and money for a garden that was not producing was just too high. Disappointed and frustrated, I gave up.

I am so grateful that God never gives up on me. Even when my life was barren of fruit, He valued me. In fact, as my pastor's wife told me years ago, "If I were the only person on this earth, He still would have sent His only Son to die for me."

While nothing is more precious than the gift of salvation Christ purchased for you and for me on the Cross, it is just the beginning of what He wants to do for us and in us. Patiently He begins to till the soil of our hearts, convicting us of those things that separate us from Him and helping us to pull out the weeds that would choke our relationship with Him.

He adds just the right things to our lives at the right time to help us grow and blossom. There's no indecision on His part. He knows the plans He has for us, and they are good plans (see Jeremiah 29:11). And even when we disappoint Him, He does not abandon us.

The Master Gardener's purpose is unwavering. He wants us to grow increasingly closer to Him. As we obey His command to "take care to live in Me, and let Me live in you," our lives will produce fruit (see John 15:4–5). While He doesn't say "when," He also doesn't say "maybe." It's a given. The more we choose to allow our roots to grow down into Him, the more Kingdom fruit our lives will produce.

I've walked with the Lord for more than 40 years and know that His Word is true. But I needed the powerful reminders in the pages of *Fruitbearer* to rekindle my passion to know Him better and serve Him more faithfully. So thank you, Candy, for sharing your heart. Thank you for challenging me to stay on that growing edge and to bear fruit for Him. And thank You, Father, for the countless lives I *know* You will touch through this book which so clearly bears the imprint of being written under Your anointing. May we all feel a new sense of urgency to live for You that others may come to know You through our witness.

—*Marlene Bagnull, Litt.D.*

$\mathscr{P}$REFACE

This is *Fruitbearer's* third visit to the printing press. For those who have read it before, I hope you will find the updates fresh and the design even more conducive to the Holy Spirit meeting you between the lines. I expect your spiritual growth has accelerated over the years as mine has; if so, you will understand my strong compulsion to get this book back into circulation.

If you are new to *Fruitbearer*, I am presenting these pages to you with assurance that the truths the Lord showed me in the '90s are even more relevant and life-changing today. But first, a word of caution: One reader described it as "a book that can only be taken in small chunks, one chapter at a time. It's meaty, and there's so much to be gleaned from it." It is common for readers to tell me that they have read the book at least twice—first for enjoyment, and then as a study guide or "workbook" where they looked up the Scriptures and actively journaled in their search for a more intimate walk with the Lord.

I believe history will prove that we are living in the harvest years. May *Fruitbearer* be to you a gift from the Master's hand that will stir up your gifts and callings for a bountiful crop. I wait on tiptoe to see how the Lord will use *Fruitbearer* this time.

Candy Abbott
Fruitbearer Publishing

SEED FOR THOUGHT

"The Bible that is falling apart
usually belongs to someone who isn't."

—*Vance Hanver*

Acknowledgments

Thank you, thank you . . .

To Drew, for the consistent balance you provide as my ever-ready helpmate, fun-loving playmate, and emotion-stabilizing soulmate. Of all the husbands in the world, surely you are the best!

To my children: Kim, for understanding your mom's preoccupation with the keyboard during your teenage years—and for the indescribable joy you give me as a wife and mother who fully relies on God. To my stepdaughter Dana, for being such fertile soil; for suggesting the subtitle; and for the godly example you have established for your household. To my stepson Troy, for clinging to God while it seems all the forces of hell compete for your soul. Never give up.

To my Sisters in Christ, for your faithful prayer support and encouragement to keep on writing when it would have been easier to hide my journals on a shelf and stuff my manuscript in a drawer. Malorie, Wilmetta, Helen, Lynn, Pat, Linda, Wilma, Jean, and all the rest, including the 275 intercessors on my e-mail list—what would I do without you?

To the faithful and candid writing mentors I have in Linda Windsor, Nancy Rue, Dan Hayne, Sara Lewis, Chris Ann Waters, Gail Kopf, Marianne Leavitt, Fran Lowe, Delmarva Christian Writers' Fellowship, and the Writeen Crue. A *very* special thank you to Marlene Bagnull and Diane Cook for your prayerful editing and valued friendship.

And to my grandchildren—Natalie, Trevor, Kade, and Saige—for the sheer delight you give me. Truly, I am blessed.

$\mathcal{L}$ETTER FROM CANDY

Dear Friend,

May I call you friend? We may not have met in person, but the Lord put you on my heart more than twenty years ago when He directed me to write this book, a task I approached with fear and trepidation. I didn't see myself as a writer, but He did. Actually, I didn't see myself as worthy of much of anything. My finances were in shambles, and my life was nowhere near where I wanted it to be. And God saw me as a fruitbearer?

No way!

Yet, my heart's cry was for something better. Something bigger. So the Lord took me on a journey that, to this day, offers new insights, inroads, revelation, and adventures at every turn. All because I prayed, "Yes, Lord!"

Have you ever felt like shouting, "Yes, Lord!"?

Has your heart-cry been, "Use me, Lord!"?

Have you ever asked, "What can I do for You, Lord?"

Then this book is for you. Through the story of my calling and faith journey, we will look at priorities—God's, mine, and hopefully yours.

Who am I? *Nobody* in the world but a female fruitbearer in the kingdom of God (despite my mistakes, wrong turns, and poor choices). This is my account of how I met the Holy Spirit and have come to enjoy and rely upon Him.

So, why should my story be of interest to you? Where do you fit in? If you're a grassroots believer who hungers to hear the Holy Spirit, this is an urgent call from above. After all, we are nearer now than ever before to Christ's return, and we need to be ready. Besides, you wouldn't want to miss the personal instructions the Lord has for You!

Onward and Upward

Christianity is so much more than a ticket to a heavenly destination; it's a daily adventure, a journey to be enjoyed moment by moment. Come along with me, and you will find that your faith walk is not a chore where we "strive to arrive," but an opportunity to grow daily into the image of our Lord.

There is definite progress in my own life. I used to worry a lot about what people thought of me. Now I'm more concerned about what God thinks. I once considered my beliefs "private," but I recognize that as a flimsy excuse for not sharing the Gospel. The Lord has plucked me out of my comfort zone and put me in a place where I know what I believe and have the courage to say so. During the ten years it took me to write this book, and the ten years the previous editions have been in circulation, the Lord has used me to plant godly ideas in fertile soil and to pull up a spiritual weed here and there. He can do the same with you.

Consider this: What would happen if every steadfast believer allowed the Lord to stir up his or her gifts and callings? What if we all were truly sorry for the many ways we have fallen short of His glory? What if God linked us together, with all of our unique differences and opportunities, in a fresh commitment to clearly hearing and heeding His call? Revival!

History shows that genuine revival began at a grassroots level where the Spirit of the Lord moved in the hearts of everyday people like you and me. Often, it starts with a curiosity or perhaps a nagging dissatisfaction of sorts, accompanied by a yearning to better understand the deep things of God. True spiritual awakening always includes honest soul-searching and heartfelt prayer. The presence of God has a way of drawing people to their knees!

Let's look at the deep things of God.

My personal objective is simple—to sow seeds. Hopefully, these tiny seeds of faith will grow into fruit you can taste for yourself: Seeds you can plant for others that will make them want to pull the weeds out of their own spiritual gardens and seeds that will get us all thinking about how we can respond to the Lord, to one another, and to the foreboding rumblings that threaten to unnerve our generation.

Check It Out!

Please, don't take my words at face value. Test the things I say! Discuss them with your pastor, your friends, and your family. Get some discussion going. Probe. Dig. Dig deeper.

Please note that you don't have to read this book straight through. If you run into a section that needs more time than you have to give, that opens a door you wish to keep closed for the moment, then move on and go back to it later. If you find you need to put the book down for an hour or a day, you're not alone. While writing the manuscript, I had to do the same thing. In returning to it, though, I've been blessed and challenged. I trust that you will be, too.

Be sure to use the personal pages at the end of each chapter entitled, "What can I do for YOU, Lord?". Invite the Holy Spirit to meet you there.

"May God Himself, the God of peace, sanctify you through and through. May your whole spirit, soul, and body be kept blameless at the coming of our Lord Jesus Christ. The One who calls you is faithful and He will do it" (1 Thessalonians 5:23–24).

Grace and peace,

Candy

"Stir up the gift of God
which is in you."

—*2 Timothy 1:6 NKJV*

CHAPTER 1

WAKE UP TO GOD'S ALARM CLOCK

 SEED FOR THOUGHT

"Don't worry about tomorrow. God is already there."

—*Carol Hamblet Adams*

"You did not choose me, but I chose you . . .
to go and bear fruit—fruit that will last."
—John 15:16

Listen Up, Lazybones—God Needs You! That was the original title when I began writing this book in 1984, but I realized I couldn't insult the reader and expect to make any sales. Not only that, but in reality, God doesn't need anything from anybody. Today, as in 1984, Jesus is calling all believers. Do you hear Him?

> "Wake up! Strengthen what remains and is about to die, for I have not found your deeds complete in the sight of My God" (Revelation 3:2).

Do you see these words flashing as if they were written with neon ink on this page? His call is more urgent today than ever before. God is fairly begging us to wake up, hear His voice, and respond to it.

I can wake up all right, but who am I to strengthen what remains of the church? That's what I wondered when this Scripture first revealed itself to me when the Lord began nudging me to chronicle my faith journey. As the years went by and I saw God's grace and power manifest itself more and more in my own everyday life, it occurred to me that if I did nothing more than heed Christ's voice daily and point Christians in the direction of the Holy Spirit, the church *would* be stronger. I became convinced that every believer has a vital role to play in the global drama that is unfolding before our eyes. This is an exciting time for us!

Like so many of us do when we reach a certain comfort zone in our faith walk, I developed the easy habit of devotions on the run as

I focused on my daily tasks. I hit the snooze alarm on my spiritual clock and went about the Father's business in my own way and on my own timetable. Then, on September 11, 2001, the alarm jumped out of snooze and rang loud and clear.

My husband Drew and I were vacationing in Bermuda. We snapped some great pictures of the Twin Towers as our cruise ship left from New York Harbor three days earlier. Little did we know when we floated joyfully past the towers that the New York skyline would be forever changed.

I was standing knee-deep in the clear water of John Smith's Bay, and Drew was strolling along the pristine beach when we heard the news. Stunned, I flopped on my beach towel where moments before I sat without a care in the world. The reality of the terrorist attack washed over me, draining me of energy, peace, and joy.

Then my eyes fell on the cover of the book I was reading. There, in eerie shades of red, orange, yellow, and black was the artist's prophetic rendering of the Twin Towers in flames! The alarm clapper was ringing loud and clear through the "light reading" I had chosen for my vacation. It was Dr. David Jeremiah's *Escape the Coming Night*, a commentary on the prophecies of Revelation (see Recommended Resources).

Despite the spiritual alarm sounding over the earth, in the surreal surroundings of crystal clear skies, turquoise water, and pink sand, peace flooded my soul. I flipped through the pages to re-read the part where I left off that said in the last days terrorism and other evils will increase, but we should not be afraid as these things must come to pass.

The Pendulum Swings

If you read this prophecy aloud to the church, *you will receive a special blessing from the Lord*. Those who listen to it being read and do what it says will also be blessed. *For the time is near when these things will all come true* (Revelation 1:3 TLB, emphasis added).

For decades, I have had an intense curiosity about Bible prophecy and the last days. My search began in 1975 with my new copy of *The Living Bible*. Its easy reading attracted me to the book of Revelation—territory I had previously avoided as being too weighty and too theological. But I was hooked by the promised blessing and intrigue of the first chapter.

I devoted a night to reading the whole book straight through. Although much of it seemed cryptic, overwhelming, and far beyond my comprehension, I kept on going, right to the final Amen. It left me with one distinct thought—*More than ever, Lord, I want to be right with You.*

Not long after that, Charlie came into my life. Well, he came into my office at the community college where I worked as the executive secretary. Every morning, this easygoing instructor would pour a cup of coffee and spend a few moments talking with me. One otherwise ordinary day, his conversation took an unexpected turn when he introduced me to new words like rapture and tribulation, Antichrist and Armageddon.

"What do you think about the rapture?" he asked.

"The what?" I frowned.

"You know, the rapture of the church. The catching away of the believers in the twinkling of an eye when Christ comes for His bride." The Lord was using Charlie to wind my personal clock and equip me for one incredibly important journey in my faith walk.

"I hate to sound ignorant. I've never heard these terms before."

"Well," he said, "you won't find the word 'rapture' in the Bible." It's a word the church uses to describe the prophecies mentioned in Corinthians and Thessalonians. According to the Scriptures, there will be a generation of believers who won't experience physical death. Instead, their earthly bodies will be changed, in a flash, in the twinkling of an eye. When the angel sounds the trumpet, all who trust in Christ will be caught up into the clouds to meet Him in the air."

"I know the Lord will be coming back." A shiver ran up my back. "But this is a real eye-opener for me. I guess I have a lot to learn."

When I asked for Scriptures to look up, Charlie sent me to 1 Corinthians 15:51–52 and 1 Thessalonians 4:16–18.

From that point on, our coffee was served with heaping teaspoons of biblical insight. It seems Charlie's pastor was teaching classes on Bible prophecy, and their correspondence course turned out to be just what I needed—just when I needed it.

My Bible got a workout like never before with highlighted passages and scribbles in the margins. Immersing myself in the writings of John F. Walvoord, Billy Graham, and Hal Lindsey, I became better acquainted with Christian bookstores and couldn't get my wallet out fast enough to buy tapes, novels, and commentaries—just about anything that had to do with the last days.

At about the same time, I discovered the television prophecy teaching of Howard Estep. He was an endearing man of small stature whose broadcast, "The King Is Coming," presented difficult words and concepts in familiar, everyday language. Although I haven't seen his show in years, I still have his booklets and fond mental images of his sincerity as he taught from a translucent podium that was almost bigger than he was.

God's tape measure isn't marked in inches or centimeters but in increments of faith. Little folks with big faith—that's what counts.

Tick–Tock, He Set the Clock

There was a Man from Galilee who said and did things that raised more than a few eyebrows. Many of the first followers who were attracted to Jesus found themselves asking the same questions we ask today.

"Who is this man?"

"What are we to make of these miracles?"

"How are we to react to His strange teachings?"

Some of the people in Jesus' day who grappled with these questions scoffed and rejected Him. Others believed and followed

Him for a while, but then they drifted away. Only a small handful of faithful believers took the Savior at His word.

Those disciples were ready and waiting when the Spirit's winds blew through the upper room on the day of Pentecost. At the appointed hour, on the appointed date, in the appointed place, the church was born. What began as expectant obedience ended in soul-stirring power as the disciples prayed together in one mind and one spirit.

The church has changed since then. While the Gospel has spread around the globe, the church suffers from splits, complacency, and theological debate. What happened to the unity, joy, and conviction that used to be the rule of the church rather than the exception?

We may well be seeing the end times. Some in the body of Christ are becoming concerned about the role of the church. Perhaps you are among those asking, "What if Christ returns in this generation?" "How can I be sure I'm ready?" and "What can I do to help others prepare?"

So, why have we changed? What's made the difference? It boils down to eschatology, which Webster's dictionary defines as "a doctrine or theory or conclusion concerning the ultimate destiny or purpose of mankind and the world." I don't pretend to comprehend all of the various doctrines involved in the biblical study of the last days, but I do have some conclusions of my own from what I've read and what I believe the Holy Spirit is revealing to me.

Jesus says He's coming back, and I believe Him. God's timetable is perfect. Just as Christ Jesus was born in Bethlehem when every last prophetic detail was in place, He will return at the precise moment that was ordained before the beginning of time. When the heavenly clock strikes twelve (figuratively speaking), the trumpet will sound, and every living person will feel the impact. Life as we know it never will be the same.

Since we are told "no one knows the day or hour" (Matthew 24:36), the important thing is not so much *when* Jesus will return but that we be *ready* for His return at any given moment. Jesus urges and implores us to be ready, and He means what He says.

As I understand it, Christ's return will come in two stages—first, in secret, when born-again believers will see Him, and then, seven years later, in power, when every eye will behold His glory.

Many well-respected Bible scholars think the next big item on God's agenda will be the removal of all Christians from the earth. According to the Scriptures, there will be a generation of believers who will not experience physical death.

> For the Lord Himself will come down from heaven, with a loud command, with the voice of the archangel and with the trumpet call of God, and the dead in Christ will rise first. After that, *we who are still alive and are left will be caught up together with them in the clouds to meet the Lord in the air.* And so we will be with the Lord forever. *Therefore encourage each other with these words* (1 Thessalonians 4:16–18, emphasis added).

Before the terrorizing reign of the Antichrist (that will come during the Great Tribulation), I expect Jesus will make a private visitation to gather those of us (His bride, the church) who are "still alive." Eugene Peterson's Bible version, *The Message*, paints a beautiful picture of believers who watch for His return:

> The word has gotten around. Your lives are echoing the Master's Word, not only in the provinces but all over the place. The news of your faith in God is out. We don't even have to say anything anymore—*you're* the message! People come up and tell us how you received us with open arms, how you deserted the dead idols of your old life so you could embrace and serve God, the true God. They marvel at how expectantly you await the arrival of his Son, whom he raised from the dead—Jesus, who rescued us from certain doom (1 Thessalonians 1:8–10).

This is not passive faith. It is active faith. These are the people who will be caught up to meet our Lord in the air.

I have a dear friend who lovingly scoffs at the whole idea. She winks and asks, "You really *believe* this crazy stuff?" And I say to her, "With every fiber of my being."

The question is not "What *if* this happens?" but "What will happen *when* this happens?" The simultaneous disappearance of so many Christians will be more than a curious mystery to those left behind. The people of the world will be confused and thrown into chaos as they try to cope with a loss of this magnitude. Those who have closed their ears to prophetic warnings won't be able to understand. They'll be easy prey for the deception of a charismatic ruler who'll appear on the scene. This "benevolent" leader, the Antichrist, will promise restored order and peace, but he will deliver tyranny and torture instead.

By contrast, we who place our trust in the Lord, not in ourselves, have hope. Though the quicksand of society tries to draw us in and drag us under, we can look forward to a dramatic deliverance from this earthly mess. One spectacular day, the same Spirit that raised Christ from the grave will lift us up to meet Him in the air. In light of our supernatural escape, Paul's admonition to "encourage one another with these words" makes sense.

Some call this event the rapture, some prefer the term "translation." Regardless of terminology or hair-splitting doctrine, the apostle Paul teaches us that we are to be encouraged, not afraid.

The apostle Paul teaches us that we are to be *encouraged*, not afraid.

Of course, the pretribulation rapture of the church I have described is only one of many theories. Some believe that Christians will be caught up after the tribulation. Still others believe that this translation will occur in the middle of the tribulation. Each of us must decide for ourselves which teaching to embrace, just like deciding which church to attend.

Are we in the tribulation now? Well, consider this. It's a fact that Christians are experiencing persecution today, especially in foreign lands, and they are clinging to their faith in Christ with supernatural strength. How can they do that? Because the Scriptures consistently point to hope and protection for those who place their trust in God.

How much trust did Moses' mother have when she placed her infant son in a basket and sent him floating down the Nile River (Exodus 2:1–10)? How strong was his faith in the promise of God when he bore witness to the Red Sea splitting on each side so the Israelites could escape from Pharaoh (Exodus 14:21–30)? What level of faith did Daniel have when he sat among the hungry lions (Daniel 6:16–22)? And don't forget Hananiah, Mishael, and Azariah, better known by their Babylonian names, Shadrach, Meshach, and Abednego—the ones who danced in a blazing furnace and came out not only unharmed but unsinged (Daniel 3:1–26)!

> The LORD is near to all who call on Him, to all who call on Him in truth. He fulfills the desires of those who fear Him; *He hears their cry and saves them.* The LORD watches over all who love Him, but all the wicked He will destroy (Psalm 145:18–20, emphasis added).

Snooze Alarm

> *"As it was in the days of Noah,* so it will be at the coming of the Son of Man. For in the days before the flood, people were eating and drinking, marrying and giving in marriage, up to the day Noah entered the ark; and they knew nothing about what would happen until the flood came and took them all away. *That is how it will be at the coming of the Son of Man.* Two men will be in the field; one will be taken and the other left. Two women will be grinding with a hand mill; one will be taken and the other left. *Therefore keep watch, because you do not know on what day your Lord will come"* (Matthew 24: 37–42, emphasis added).

Are you a morning person? One who jumps out of bed when the alarm first rings? Or do you hit the snooze button, hoping to get a few more minutes of precious sleep before starting another hectic day? I think Noah must have been a morning person who responded to God's first call.

Note that God didn't say, "Now, Noah, I want you to stand in your front yard every day and peer into the sky until I send the flood. I want you to spend every spare minute speculating about when the storm is going to hit. When you finally see the rain clouds gathering, I want you to rush around and throw a shelter together."

What God *did* say was, "Noah, build an ark!" And He gave him blueprints. Noah didn't procrastinate or panic; he heard and *obeyed*. Methodically, with patience and perseverance, he built that ark, one gopher wood board at a time. Faithfully, he carried out the Lord's instructions *to the letter* in spite of a scoffing society.

And Noah was saved. Granted, he might have been tossed and heaved around during those 40 unpleasant days afloat and confined in the ark for 300 days (150 days until the wind blew and another 150 days until the waters receded enough to get out of the boat), but Noah and his family were saved (Genesis 8:7–11; 9:6). To say that Noah and his loved ones were "uncomfortable" would be an understatement. But what happened to the scoffers?

God may put us through what seems like torture, but He gives us second chances. He always sends a warning before He sends His judgment. Unfortunately, Noah was the only one who had ears to hear and a heart to respond to God's voice.

> God saw how corrupt the earth had become . . . [and] said to Noah, "I am going to put an end to all people . . . So make yourself an ark . . ." (Genesis 6:12–14).

The people who mocked God and Noah perished. They didn't think they needed to listen to the ramblings of a prophet. They didn't have ears to hear. But the Lord promises to strengthen those who do listen and heed His call.

If we take our Lord's commands seriously, we are offered a comforting reminder in Matthew 28:20 (KJV), "Lo, I am with you always, even unto the end of the world."

Jesus wants us to be just as dedicated to preparing people for His sudden return as Noah was about building a refuge from the flood. The Lord still gives practical, specific assignments to those who have ears to hear Him. It's not our *efforts* that count but our *obedience* and *reliance* upon the One who calls us.

Getting ready for the rapture is like building a modern-day ark. Noah may have personally guided each animal into God's safety zone, but it was the Lord who rounded them up. Today, the Spirit of the Lord is moving across the face of the earth, guiding believers to a place of refuge.

The more I study the mystery described in 1 Thessalonians 4:14–18, the more I marvel at God's eternal grace and mercy. Yet, imperfect as we are, we might find ourselves obsessing over the silliest things. At one point, my biggest concern about being raptured was whether or not my bed would be made should I disappear unexpectedly. The Holy Spirit gently led me to 1 Thessalonians 5:6–9 and adjusted my focus to "be alert and self-controlled" (v. 6), to "put on faith and love as a breastplate, and the hope of salvation as a helmet" (v. 8), and to hold onto the confidence that "God did not appoint us to suffer wrath but to receive salvation through our Lord Jesus Christ" (v. 9). He showed me that there is work to be done, not just cloud-watching.

Some believers have spent an incredible amount of time and energy debating the time of Christ's return. Although no one can really know the day or the hour, we are given lots of clues about the signs of the times and a clear mandate to *"keep watch"* (Matthew 24:42).

As in the story of the five foolish virgins who ran out of oil (Matthew 25:1–13), it's possible to be caught off-guard. My friend, Kay, said what motivates her to be ready and watchful is not so much that Jesus is *coming* but that Jesus is *here now*! We don't have to wait for His return to be in His presence. We can experience Christ today.

These are intense days. Whether they're exciting or frightening depends on our perspective. While the world groans in chaos, the Holy Spirit moves in fresh, unprecedented ways to counter intensifying evil during these millennium days. It's not unusual to overhear conversations of believers and non-believers alike buzzing about the signs of the times. Nobody knows exactly what lies ahead, but the body of Christ is being prepared, tested, strengthened, and equipped to handle victoriously whatever may come, whenever it comes.

While the Bible doesn't paint rosy pictures of living conditions just before our Lord's return, Christ assures us that "he who stands firm to the end will be saved" (Matthew 24:13 and see 2 Thessalonians 2:13–17). Repeatedly, He instructs believers to be alert, saying,

> "Therefore keep watch, because you do not know the day or the hour" (Matthew 25:13).

Fruit Alarm

We can see many of Jesus' predictions (recorded in Matthew 24 and Mark 13) being fulfilled before our very eyes.

> "Now learn this lesson from the fig tree: As soon as its twigs get tender and its leaves come out, you know that summer is near. Even so, when you see all these things, you know that it is near, right at the door" (Matthew 24:32–33).

Here are a few examples:

1. *False christs and false prophets deceiving many* (Matthew 24:5, 11). Cult leaders like Charles Manson, Jim Jones, and David Koresh and "New Age" authors like Shirley MacLaine are luring sincere seekers away from family pews and biblical teaching into a mystical realm where spirit guides lead them astray. Others walk in delusions of greatness either by design or by their own mental instabilities. I actually received a mass mailing from some con artist who said, "Beloved, it is I, the Christ, bringing you greetings." The letter went on to ask for money.

2. *Wars and rumors of wars, nation rising against nation, and kingdom against kingdom* (Matthew 24:6–7). Daily we hear about Middle East turmoil, South African racial

violence, nuclear threats from emerging nations, or political upheaval. The Iraqi situation has been referred to as the "restoration of latter-day Babylon." Visit *www.countdown.org/armageddon/war.htm* if the nightly news isn't convincing enough. The twentieth century witnessed the escalation of wars unlike any other century. The Red Cross estimates that more than a hundred million people have been killed in wars since the beginning of the twentieth century.

3. *An increase of famines and earthquakes in various places* (Matthew 24:7). Who hasn't been touched by pictures of mothers and children with distended stomachs starving in Bangladesh or Ethiopia? And what of the United States? As I write this, the Gulf states are still reeling from the devastation of Hurricanes Katrina and Rita. Earthquakes in Mexico and California are more frequent, with tremors in unlikely places such as Delaware—not to mention the increase in volcanic eruptions, floods, hurricanes, fires, and tornados. Consider the tsunami of December 2004 that took more than 10,000 lives in southeast Asia. Matthew 24:8 says, "All these are the beginning of the birth pains." Just like when a woman approaches childbirth and her contractions steadily increase in frequency, so the birth pangs of Matthew 24 will increase. Here are some interesting statistics I found by visiting *www.propheticrevelation.com/quake.htm*—

> 16th century . . . 253 (2 major earthquakes)
> 17th century . . . 378 (2 major earthquakes)
> 18th century . . . 640 (5 major earthquakes)
> 19th century . . . 2119 (9 major earthquakes)

The 20th century alone saw the greatest number of earthquakes rocking the earth. There were some 91,000 of them (ranging from a magnitude of 0.3 to 6.99 on the Richter scale) and 198 major earthquakes (of 7.00 to 9.99). This pattern is likely to continue in the twenty-first century.

4. ***Christians being persecuted and put to death*** (Matthew 24:9). I awoke on a summer's day in 1992 to live coverage of Christians in Peru being shot in the streets in front of their children because they refused to renounce their faith. The "Persecuted Church" in our day is widespread. According to *www.christianfreedom.org*, "The holdout Communist states of China, North Korea, Laos, Cuba, and Vietnam still bear down heavily on Christians who dare to hold another master higher than the state." In 2004, I received an e-mail with this "breaking prayer request:"

Iraq—Pray for safety for the Christians living in Iraq and that violence in the country may come to an end.

North Korea—Pray for thousands of Christians in North Korea's labor camps and for the estimated 400,000 Christians who worship God in secret.

Colombia—Pray for the over two million internally displaced refugees in Colombia and for courage and hope in the midst of relocation, violence and intimidation.

Eritrea—Pray for hundreds of Christians who have been arrested, interrogated and tortured in this small African country over the last year for meeting in unregistered churches.

Tragically, Christians in Islamic-dominated countries such as Nigeria, Sudan, Turkey, Egypt, Libya, Saudi Arabia, Pakistan, Iran, Iraq, and Indonesia live in constant danger. It is unthinkable that Al-Jazeera, the Arabic satellite channel with "updated news and views," would air live footage of beheadings of those they consider infidels, but they do. For comprehensive, up-to-the-minute information on what the church is doing to help, visit Dan Wooding's ASSIST News (Aid to Special Saints in Strategic Times): *www.assistnews.net.*

5. ***Former believers turning from their faith, exhibiting betrayal and hatred toward Christians*** (Matthew 24:10). Islam, one of the fastest growing religions in the world, is converting Christians. One web site (*www.thetruereligion.com/priests.htm*) showcases Christians who have embraced Islam: a former minister (deacon) of the United Methodist Church who holds a master's degree in divinity from Harvard and a doctorate in psychology from the University of Denver; a former pastor and missionary who was fired from her job as teacher in two Bible colleges; a former Lutheran archbishop; and a former Catholic priest. In an attempt to enlighten those of us who "continue to walk in darkness," they claim, "Islam is the solution to the problems plaguing the world of Christianity, as well as the problems facing the so-called world of religion as a whole." Some converts even go so far as to pray, "O Allah, destroy the usurper Jews and the vile Christians."

6. ***Wickedness increasing, sin running rampant, with evil parading its filth*** (Matthew 24:12). Satanic churches, occult literature, and witches' games dominate bookstore shelves and are infiltrating public schools. We have pro-choice activists who think it's the mother's *right* to be able to terminate the life of her unborn child, even in the last month of pregnancy. Sexual perversion leers at us from every corner. Increased drug abuse and violent crimes are reported daily. Child abuse, pornography, abortion—need I go on?

7. ***The love of many people growing cold*** (Matthew 24:12). Terrorism at home and abroad, prison riots, epidemic teenage suicides, hatred toward parents, drive-by shootings, babies found in trash cans, apathy in churches, and divorce. Who would believe that in 2005, rescue helicopters in New Orleans would be shot at by looters and already-traumatized hurricane victims would be raped and murdered in shelters? The tragedy of Columbine High School in 1999 is beyond understanding. Some of our schools are battlegrounds, with metal detectors and police patrolling the corridors; yet, murders still happen, the latest being in Red Lake, Minnesota, on March 22, 2005.

8. ***The Gospel of the Kingdom being preached to the ends of the earth*** (Matthew 24:14). We are living in the days of worldwide Bible distribution; Christian schools, bookstores, and publishers; evangelistic crusades; religious broadcasting via TV, radio and video; Jesus films; underground prayer groups; and missionaries. More and more Jews in Israel (the Promised Land) and around the world now recognize Jesus as the Messiah and are leading others to Christ.

9. ***A faithful remnant standing firm in their faith*** (Matthew 24:13). That's us, folks—the faithful few. We are the overcomers who can know what it means to have peace in the eye of the storm. Our attitudes, actions, and testimonies provide evidence of God's goodness, strength, and mercy in the midst of mounting evil.

Of these nine examples, notice that the first seven were bad fruit, while only the last two were good fruit. Although the odds may look overwhelming, the faithful few have God on their side, and no matter how ugly things may look in the end, God wins!

Supernatural Fruit

So many things are happening in our world these days that we can't explain—not only chaos but supernatural mysteries like the appearance of angels and demons. Understand this: The supernatural is real.

I used to be a skeptic about things like visions until I heard firsthand accounts of people who said they'd actually seen and talked with supernatural beings. Then I had some hard-to-explain encounters of my own. I'm no longer skeptical and secretive about my conclusions.

It seems perfectly natural to me that the Lord will use every available means at His disposal to awaken His people—to get us on our feet and prepared for His return. By using willing believers as *receivers* to transmit heavenly signals around the globe, those who have eyes to see and ears to hear will not be caught off-guard at the crucial moment. Conversely, our enemy Satan will use similar tactics to derail God's children.

What if an Old Testament angel appeared to you in modern-day clothes and confided that you had only a couple of months to get ready for the Lord's return? What would you think? What would you do about that encounter?

My daughter and I both have had to answer these questions. I'll share two stories for you to mull over. Kim's story first . . .

Kim's Story (Dateline 1990)

"Mom, Mom!" my daughter called, her voice charged with electricity as she rushed through the door, returning home from a college class. "You've got to hear what this girl told me today."

I sat down to give her my undivided attention.

"She's not somebody I know very well—in fact, we only have one class together—but we had a few minutes to kill and struck up a conversation. She said from watching me that she thought I must be a Christian."

"That's great, honey! She could tell from watching you? Your faith must be showing."

"Yeah, but that's not it. This girl told me the most incredible thing. She said she had to tell somebody or she would burst. I still have goose bumps thinking about it. Her mom and her aunt were driving along, talking about the signs of the times. They're deep Christians, the kind who like to talk about the Lord more than anything. Well, they passed an old, dilapidated car by the side of the road. When her mom looked in the rear-view mirror, she saw a man—an average-looking, humble sort of guy, medium height and build, wearing everyday work clothes. He wasn't hitchhiking, just walking along with a gas can."

"Where was this? Locally? Or in some other state?" I asked.

"Somewhere near here—Seaford, Salisbury, Milford, somewhere like that—I can't remember. But local, yes. Please don't interrupt, Mom. This is important.

"They pulled over and asked if that was his car back there. When he said it was, they told him the next gas station was miles away and offered him a lift. Normally they wouldn't have dreamed of picking up a stranger, but this was different. Something told them it was the 'right' thing to do. So he got in the back seat. Her mom said he had the kindest blue eyes.

"'We were just talking about the signs of the times and thinking that the Lord might be coming back soon,' she told him.

"'When do you think He might return?' the man asked.

"'Oh, twenty years, maybe?'

"'Sooner,' he said.

"'Sooner than that? Well, there's a lot of discussion about the year 2000.'

"'Sooner.'

"'You mean you think the Lord will come back *before* 2000?'

"No answer. They turned to look at him, and Mom," Kim exclaimed, "nobody was in the back seat! He was gone!"

I asked Kim to get the young lady's phone number so I could interview her mom or aunt to clarify some of the details. Several weeks later, when I reminded her, Kim said, "You know, it's funny, but I only saw her a couple of times after that, and then from a distance. I haven't seen her around campus in weeks."

Like Kim, I thought this must surely have been an angel. In fact, in the early '90s I heard numerous versions of this same mysterious man appearing in Georgia, Ohio, and other states. But something didn't ring true. In the first and second editions of *Fruitbearer* I noted a disclaimer, citing Matthew 24:36, "No one knows about that day or hour, not even the angels in heaven, or the Son, but only the Father."

So, was this an angel sent to prepare believers for Christ's return? Surely not! I can't recall a single biblical instance where God sent messengers of misinformation to His children. In fact, according to 2 Corinthians 11:14–15, Satan himself masquerades as an angel of light. It is not surprising, then, if his servants masquerade as servants of righteousness. Like the little boy who "cried wolf," we need to be careful to not let our guard down when the real thing comes along.

Although I couldn't find this particular incident listed, urban legends and e-mail hoaxes are rampant these days. Before passing along a story you've heard, you may want to check with *www.hoaxbusters.ciac.org* or *www.snopes.com*, etc.

I don't believe in setting dates. Too many well-intentioned believers have brought discredit to the church by attempting to predict the day of the Lord's appearing. But the Word of God clearly tells us to be ever watchful and ever ready. All signs clearly indicate that the time is short.

Trumpet Call (Dateline February 1994)

It happened at 11:35 a.m., the day before a crippling ice storm hit our community in southern Delaware. I remember the hour because Jeri, who shared an office with me, had just left for lunch. It was a hectic day, as usual, and I was busy collating a report at top speed. I held a fistful of papers in my left hand and was propelling my right hand toward the stapler when—*flash*—it happened.

"Suddenly" isn't a strong enough word to describe how unexpectedly the episode occurred. I guess you could call it a vision.

There was an eerie absence of sound, as though I had gone deaf. I couldn't hear the hum of the computer, the printer, or the copier. The only thing I "heard" was the distant sound of a trumpet—not exactly a blast, but several distinct musical notes that seemed to come from high above the ceiling on my left. Instinctively, I cocked my head in that direction to hear it better. There were three or four clear but faint notes echoing in my left ear.

As the silence in my office continued, I stood mesmerized in thought, contemplating the significance. *Could this be a practice run? Could it be that the Lord's return is so near that angels are beginning to rehearse their roles? That's how it will be,* I realized, *just like that! The rapture will come when we least expect it, when we're all doing normal things, going through everyday motions.* I needed to pray—on my knees.

Concerned that somebody might come through my doorway at any moment and think my behavior strange, I realized that the papers I still held in my hand could serve as a good cover. *If somebody comes in, I'll just get up from under my desk as though I were looking for these,* I decided.

"Oh, Lord. Help us. We're not ready! Have mercy on us . . ." I prayed. At the sound of someone entering my office, I said "Amen," came up from under my desk with the papers in my hand, and said "hello" to the woman who had entered my office. With that, the vacuum lifted and the normal office sounds returned.

I didn't share the incident with Jeri until the following week after the ice storm had devastated the East Coast. The worst was over, and some of us had managed to make our way to work even though power lines were still loaded down with ice and roads were detoured. Then the lights went out. It was then, as we stood near our desks waiting for our eyes to adjust to the dark, that I described my vision to Jeri.

"That's how it sounded," I explained, "just like this, as silent as though there were no electricity."

"I *believe* you," she said. "Everything you've ever told me has been true. Besides, it's eerie standing here in the dark. Look how dependent we are on electricity."

"You're right," I agreed. "Some of our own neighbors, forced from their homes because of no heat, are living in temporary shelters with total strangers. Others who have heat but no appliances will stick it out, with makeshift arrangements for meals. It's been five days now since the ice storm, and people in Milford still don't have power."

"How quickly things can change from normal to disastrous," Jeri said. "It's almost like the ice storm was a sign to show us that God means business. He can snap off the tops of trees with one wave of His hand."

"If you think *this* is quick and powerful," I said, "it's nothing compared to the rapture."

"And we think this inconvenience is bad." She gave a visible shiver. "We get so wrapped up in ourselves."

I shook my head in sad comprehension. "I'm afraid we forget how powerful God is and that it *is* possible that His patience with us has a cut-off point."

"But we're a Christian nation, aren't we?"

"Are we? Polls show that somewhere around 95 percent of the people in America say they believe in God. That sounds good until you realize that 62 percent of those people don't think it matters what god you pray to."

"Yeah. People think they can make up their own religion as they go along, picking up this part and that part of spirituality, smorgasbord style, to suit themselves. I guess it doesn't work that way."

"You're right," I nodded. "That's like playing God. There is *one true* God, and He tells us He's a jealous God. The people of America and the world have put too many other gods before Him. There *will be* a day of reckoning."

When the Trumpet Sounds

Regardless of how accurate my own perception turns out to be, when the heavenly trumpet sounds, we want the Lord to find us being "about our Father's business" (see Luke 2:49 KJV). Maybe we'll be speaking kind words, sitting with a lonely senior, scribbling a note of encouragement, serving as a peacemaker, helping someone in secret, spending time in prayer. Whatever we're doing, hopefully we'll be doing it with all our hearts *as unto the Lord*—in short, bearing fruit!

If our earnest desire is to please God each day and follow our calling as we understand it, there is security in the knowledge that we're storing up our treasures in heaven.

"Do not store up for yourselves treasures on earth, where moth and rust destroy, and where thieves break in and steal. But store up for yourselves treasures in heaven, where moth and rust do not destroy, and where thieves do not break in and steal. For where your treasure is, there your heart will be also" (Matthew 6:19–21).

Yea, though we walk through the valley of the unknown, He leads us to passages like Ezekiel 37. I get excited as I read Ezekiel's instructions from the Lord to prophesy to the bones he saw before him.

"Dry bones, hear the word of the Lord! This is what the Sovereign LORD says to these bones: I will make breath enter you, and you will come to life" (vv. 4, 5).

With God, anything is possible! As you work with your first "What can I do for You, Lord?" page, you'll notice that the section entitled "God's Call" is written in the first person, as though God were speaking. He is. The Holy Spirit is calling us to sit up, take notice, and get our bones moving to get ready for Christ's return.

Shall We Pray?

Lord, use these pages in some small way to strengthen the precious souls who read them. Help them to recognize it is Your Spirit who quickens their hearts. Exchange any confusion they may have about these troubled days for a clear vision of what You want them to do. Oh, Lord, wake us up to Your voice and to Your will. Give us eager ears to hear and hearts to obey.

WHAT CAN I DO FOR YOU, LORD?

DIG INTO SCRIPTURE

Look up Jesus' words and read them for yourself, as though He were speaking them only to you:
- Matthew 24:36–44
- Mark 13:32–37
- Luke 21:34–36

GOD'S CALL—KEEP WATCH

"When the angel sounds the trumpet, My coming will be swift and sudden. On that day, there will be no opportunity for afterthought, last-minute repentance, or bargaining. It is written that today is the day of salvation. Come to Me, dear one, and do not delay, for you are the one in whom I delight. Come into the refuge of My presence where you will find peace and hope and joy."

YOUR RESPONSE TO GOD

I choose to follow You, Christ Jesus. Today, by signing my name on this line or in a special place in my Bible, I pledge to You my sincere allegiance in preparation for Your expected but unannounced return. Help me to be alert and obedient to Your call.

_____   _____

Name   *Date*

 SEED FOR THOUGHT

"The safest hiding place in the world
is in the center of God's will."

—*CPT Struecker*

 SEED FOR THOUGHT

"The best thing about the future
is that it comes only one day at a time."

—*Abraham Lincoln*

CHAPTER 2

REPORT FOR VINEYARD DUTY

 Seed for Thought

Keep on sowing your seed,
for you never know which will grow—perhaps it all will.

—*Ecclesiastes 11:6* TLB

"Still other seed fell on good soil, where it produced a crop—
a hundred, sixty or thirty times what was sown.
He who has ears, let him hear."
—Matthew 13:8–9

Today's believers have a responsibility, a *calling* many of us never fully realize or understand. Anyone who is God's child can make a difference. It's an exciting prospect to consider that you and I can play a part in preparing others for Christ's return. How wonderful to see the Lord motivating and inspiring everyday people. But how much more thrilling it would be if all of us who consider ourselves Christians would respond *wholeheartedly* to that small inner voice that whispers, "Follow Me."

When we embrace our calling, every new day becomes a spiritual adventure! Although our own faith journeys are distinctly different, any God-given role is fruitful and fulfilling.

To be effective for the kingdom, Christians do not need to be flashy or make a lot of noise. I was recently reminded that the farm wagon that clatters the loudest and moves the fastest is usually empty; it is the full load that moves along quietly, slowly but surely, toward its destination.

In flower gardens there are many big, showy flowers that are breathtaking to behold. But the less conspicuous bluebells and buttercups or the sprawling ground cover that complements the landscaping are just as precious.

At a grassroots level, which are you? A sunflower or a buttercup? Maybe a wayward sprig of ivy? An oak tree or weeping willow? Or, perhaps . . . a lily pad?

Water Frog

"Would you feed my fish while I'm gone?" Kim was sixteen and about to leave for a week of cheerleading camp. How hard could it be? You open the lid, sprinkle the food, close it, and go about your business.

My duties started the day after she left for her trip. Walking quietly into her bedroom, I approached the aquarium on her dresser, not far from the window. Slivers of color glided through the aquatic world in front of me, unaware of the life outside their own domain. Lifting the tank lid, I sprinkled the food around—manna to them perhaps, but an easy task for me. How peaceful I felt watching the feathery fins fan their way toward the surface. And then I saw it.

What's that? A frog? I stared at a half-inch, sickly pale, motionless amphibian on the coral in the middle of the tank.

"Are you dead?" My words danced along the rim of the twenty-four-gallon tank and must have assaulted the ears of the fat goldfish swimming nearby. A casual bump spurred the frog to life. Jolting his little arms out straight, he spanned his fingers like the folds of a fan.

"You're alive!"

As his colorless, translucent body settled again on the rock, I wondered for how long. Then, in slow motion, he began to stir.

A sliver of food floated down beside him.

Can he see it? Do frogs even eat fish food? His fragile right arm inched toward the delicacy which floated to the left. Sluggishly, he engaged his puny left arm, sending the morsel straight into the mouth of a neighboring fish.

With great effort, he began to climb the rock. It took forever, but eventually he reached the top and then stood up! Swaying from the swish of the water that I thought would knock him over, he stretched his body to its full height of almost an inch. His frail arms strained toward the water's surface, and he stood as if on tiptoe with his nose and chin barely at water level. His skeletal fingers were extended as far as they could go. Food floated everywhere around him—except into his mouth which he opened and closed futilely.

You poor little fellow. You're going to starve before my very eyes.

He and I stayed like that for the longest time—the frog stretching, gaping, and looking hungry; me crouching, staring, and feeling sorry for him. At last, he got a flake of food. But . . . as he closed his mouth, *trouble!* His body went rigid.

Spread-eagle, arms extended toward heaven, frozen in position, his legs started to slide along the ridge of the rock. *He's doing a split,* I marveled as his stiff back drifted lower and his legs slid out from under him. Then, when he was completely horizontal, he just sort of bent forward at the hips and disappeared head-first behind the rock, somehow still hanging on. All I could see were his outstretched legs, his tiny bottom, and his webbed toes sticking straight out.

Eyes watering from laughter, I couldn't watch any longer. This was too good to keep to myself! I raced down the hall.

"Drew, Drew! You've got to come see this crazy frog. I don't know if he's alive or dead, but it's the funniest-looking thing I've ever seen." Pulling my husband by the hand down the hall to check on the fate of the frog, we found him swimming merrily around, full of life!

Learning from the Frog

I returned to Kim's aquarium often after my encounter with the frog and learned an important lesson from him for the church. Every time the frog took a bite, he stopped everything else he was doing to give total concentration to receiving his nourishment. He rested a lot, *really* rested. Like the frog, we need to be still once in a while, really still, and savor our daily bread.

When the Lord God says it's time for His people to be fed, His hand moves, and a morsel of spiritual food floats down from heaven, meeting us right where we are. For sleepyhead believers, He may send a big fish (a trying circumstance, a singed conscience, a hint of divine revelation) to "bump" us into an awareness to wake up and eat. At first, this may startle us.

Then we begin to grope around in our circumstances, unaware of the joy that is set before us. Just when things look hopeless, some mysterious inner prompting causes us to look upward, encourages us to keep moving, and motivates us to climb higher—even to the point of stretching ourselves on tiptoe to seek the nourishment we need.

But the food doesn't come quickly. Straining and pleading with outstretched arms and aching hearts, we wait. And then the morsel comes—a mouthful of biblical truth that tastes sweet but is sometimes difficult to swallow. Even a small taste of what it means to be a devoted follower of Christ can stiffen every fiber of our being. Yet, as we begin to comprehend what Christ endured for us on the cross, His Spirit stirs within us, prompting us to action or convicting us of sin, and we find ourselves moving.

As we chew on what it means to receive forgiveness and count the cost of discipleship, our legs start to slide out from under us. We digest questions like, *What will be required of me as a believer who has tasted the Good News?* Weighed down by our own attempts to please God and frustrated by our own weakness, we find ourselves spread-eagle, with arms extended toward heaven, and immobilized.

Like the frog who hung tenaciously to his coral rock, we cling to Christ, the Rock of our salvation. We begin to appreciate the wisdom and importance of waiting on God. Our food is His written Word which nourishes our hungry souls.

> "He who has an ear, let him hear what the Spirit says to the churches. To him who overcomes, I will give the right to eat from the tree of life, which is in the paradise of God" (Revelation 2:7).

Things are not always as they appear:

- The church, like the frog, may look pale, immobilized, even dead. *But it isn't.*

- Spiritual depth enjoyed by others who seem swifter and stronger in the faith appears beyond our reach. *But it isn't.*

- Observers might think today's body of Christ is small and weak. *But it isn't.*

Inconspicuous People Count

History shows us that God uses inconspicuous people to do His greatest works. His pattern is not to call forth the self-made man but the humble servant.

He picked a quiet-natured, spunky young shepherd to put that big bully, Goliath, out of commission. He called on an innocent maiden to give birth to His Son. He discipled a handful of inexperienced laymen to take His Gospel message to the ends of the earth. Even Jesus began His earthly ministry as an infant.

In the eyes of the Lord, the ninety-year-old prayer warrior who cannot leave her bed yet continues to intercede could be doing as mighty a work as the popular television evangelist. If only the residents of our nursing homes and assisted living communities could grasp this truth.

We're not all called to build an ark or to lead a family through the wilderness for forty years, but each believer has some significant work to do for the Kingdom. Any commission God gives will be accompanied by an extra measure of His grace to bring it to fulfillment in His perfect time.

Over the years, the Lord has given me both big and little jobs to do. Without exception, the little ones have always come before the big ones. And it's a good thing, because the little assignments are the ones where I've learned how to trust in His strength and not my own. I'd like to say that whenever He calls me I always respond with an enthusiastic, "Yes, Lord," but the simple truth is that I tend to gulp and squirm in my seat with, "Could I have a few days to think this over?" I guess it's my way of counting the cost before making a commitment.

But I've come to appreciate the Lord's confidence in me. If He believes in me, who am I to say that I can't? During those times when I totally abandon myself to His will and spontaneously say "yes," I am rewarded by a deep sense of personal fulfillment. Besides, can I in all honesty call Him Lord if I insist on picking and choosing which of His commands to obey?

It is clear to me that spiritual growth can never occur unless God initiates it. Let me hasten to emphasize that any progress I make is due to God, not Candy Abbott. Even the slightest *desire* to seek a closer relationship with the Lord didn't originate with me but with Him.

> For we are God's workmanship, created in Christ Jesus to do good works, which God prepared in advance for us to do (Ephesians 2:10).

It's not what I can do *for* Him that counts, but what He can do *in* and *through* me. Someone once said, "When I try, I often fail, but when I trust God, I always succeed."

Divorced and Miserable

I thought I was trusting God during my six years of marriage that finally ended in divorce in 1972, but in reality, I was only trusting myself. It took a book by Merlin Carothers to help me see how selfish my prayers were.

Anticipating my need years in advance, God made arrangements to reach me through my coworker, Ellen. She is a good example of how the seemingly insignificant things we do out of obedience to God's leading may carry huge blessings. I doubt if she even remembers placing that yellow paperback in my hand—a book that, when I read it and applied the principles, changed the course of my life and revealed the concept of praising God in all things.

Shortly after my divorce, Ellen said to me, "I don't know why I'm giving you this, but it's like a little voice inside said, 'Give this to Candy,' so here it is."

I thanked her and glanced at the title, *Power in Praise*. After she left, I hastily leafed through the pages, then put it on a shelf where it stayed until an evening in the spring of 1975, two and a half years later.

That night, frustrated and discouraged from struggling as a single parent playing the "I-seem-to-be-getting-nowhere-fast dating game," the Lord found me nestled under the covers in my apartment. He reminded me of the book Ellen had given me years before. Surprise of surprises, I knew right where to find it. I opened the first few pages and read Merlin Carothers' words:

As long as we praise God with an eye secretly looking for the expected results, we're only kidding ourselves, and we can be certain that nothing will happen to change us or our situation.

Praise is based on a total and joyful acceptance of the present as part of God's loving, perfect will for us. Praise is not based on what we think or hope will happen in the future. This is an absolute "law," clearly observable in the practice of praise.

We praise God, not for what we expect will happen in or around us, but we praise Him for what He is and where and how we are *right now.*

Praise is not a bargaining position. We don't say, "I'll praise you so that you can bless me, Lord."

To praise God is to delight ourselves in Him. The psalmist wrote, "Be delighted with the Lord. Then He will give you all your heart's desires" (Psalm 37:4).

Notice the order of importance here. We don't make a list of our heart's desires and then delight ourselves in the Lord in order to get them. We're first to be delighted, and once we've experienced being really delighted with God, we'll discover that everything else becomes secondary. Still, it is true that God does want to give us all our heart's desires. Nothing short of that is His wish and plan for us.

Learning to Praise

"Oh, Lord," I prayed, "I've been doing it all wrong. I am ashamed. Even my motivation for prayer has been self-centered. Forgive me for trying to manipulate You into giving me what I thought I so desperately needed. I see now that all I really need is to learn how to praise You no matter how bad things may seem or how low I may feel. The Bible says I should give thanks in all things, even for how miserable and confused I am.

"This is not easy to say, but well, thank You, Lord. Thank You for the mess I've made of my life. You've seen it all." A shudder went through me as I realized the things He had seen me say and do.

"And yet You still love me." Tears of remorse and repentance trickled down my face. My nose started to run.

"Thank You for Your patience. Thank You for bringing me to this point of honest soul-searching. It took all this time for me to understand how much I really need You. Now I see that without Your help even my best intentions stink. Thank You for not giving up on me and for teaching me that I need You as my Savior as much in this life as I do for eternal life. Until now, I always thought of myself as a fine person, yet You have shown me that I'm just as much a sinner as the people I criticize."

A calming sense of forgiveness flooded over me. Somehow I knew He understood and that I was accepted—just as I was, with all my mistakes and poor judgments. I smiled.

"You're teaching me how to trust You and not myself, aren't You? Only You know what's best for me. It's clear I don't."

I began to feel more optimistic. Appreciation flowed as my attention shifted from how much I *didn't* have to how much I *did* have.

"Thank You for my precious three-year-old daughter, sound asleep in her room across the hall; for a full-time job with good benefits; food in the refrigerator; and a roof over my head—such a nice apartment!" I opened my eyes and looked around the bedroom. "Thank You for these ruffled curtains and matching bedspread, for the yellow wicker rocking chair, and for a decent paycheck that, with a little help from my tax refund, should cover the bills. Oh, Lord, You've given me so much!"

My thoughts shifted back to what I didn't have.

"Now, about my love life, Lord, I give up. I've dated just about every man who's asked me out. Most of them are nice, some of them are jerks, but nobody seems to be a perfect match. Is there anybody out there just right for me? Could it be that no such man exists? Only You know. Father God, You can look down from Your heavenly throne across the face of the earth and see every eligible bachelor. You know me and what I need in a mate. If You want me to be married, then help me to find a husband. And . . ." I hesitated, then continued with renewed resolve. "If You want me to be single, help me to like it. Amen."

I awoke the next morning absolutely *thrilled* to be single! Convinced that the Lord had answered my prayer by giving me an awareness of His forgiveness and a contented heart, I danced around the kitchen with a sense of freedom. *I don't have to share a closet with anybody. Things stay where I put them. Nobody else's toothpaste messes up my sink. I don't have to answer to anybody if I want to get up in the middle of the night and clean out a closet or read a book. I have Kim to love and enjoy and share my affection with.*

Overnight, I had relinquished my own expectations, and I was happy, actually joyful, to be single. Little did I know that my newfound joy was only part of the answer God had in store for me.

Within two weeks, Kim's babysitter struck up a conversation that literally sent me along a new path. I can still hear Fannie's words as she met me at the door.

"You're always in such a rush. Do you have a minute to chat? There's something I've been meaning to talk with you about for some time now, but I never seem to get a chance."

"You caught me at a good time," I said. "It would do me good to relax and visit awhile. Is it about Kim? Is anything wrong?"

"No, she's fine. I've been wondering about you and how you're doing. It seems like you should be remarried by now, and I wondered if you've been dating anybody special."

"Oh, that. No, well, I went with a guy for a year or so but we broke it off, and there hasn't been anybody in particular since then."

"I've been thinking for some time that you and my nephew have a lot in common," Fannie said, her eyes sparkling. "He lives just across the street, and he's not dating anybody special either. I thought you two might be good for each other. Would you like to meet him?"

"Well, I don't know," I hesitated. The joy of being single was still fresh in my spirit.

"Of course, you would," she countered. "Come with me, it'll only take a moment. His car's there, so I'm sure he's home."

The rest of her words blurred together as she walked me, with Kim in tow, across the street to Drew's house. A shaggy collie met us at the driveway, startling Kim who jumped up for me to carry her.

"Oh, don't worry about Ginger," Fannie said. "She wouldn't hurt a fly. Come on, we'll just go in the back way."

The next thing I knew, she had marched us through the back porch and into the kitchen where she introduced me to her nephew and his two children, fifteen-year-old Dana, and ten-year-old Troy. We had come at an inopportune time as they were perched on bar stools eating dinner. Drew's knife and fork stayed suspended over his steak during the introductions. I was mortified at what he thought of our barging in that way and concluded that I'd never hear from him again.

Drew called me that night. Three weeks later, he surprised himself and me by proposing on my birthday, June 7, 1975. We were married twenty-two days later.

Drew and I do not believe in love at first sight, but we do believe in answered prayer. Drew is a fine Christian man who had been saying some prayers of his own. We celebrated our thirtieth anniversary on June 29, 2005, and are more deeply in love today than we were when we took our vows. If ever a marriage was "made in heaven," ours qualifies.

Looking back on my years as a single parent now seems actually painless (yes, it's true). The agony has slipped into the Sea of Forgetfulness, extinguished by a pattern of praise, relinquishment, brokenness, and childlike trust. I've tried using praise as a "formula" on other occasions to get what I wanted from God, only to experience silence. But those times of waiting and wondering and not seeing any relief as I poured my heart out to the Lord were times when I grew the most in character and faith. I am learning when I pray, "Thy will be done," to really mean it. God really does give His best to those who leave their choices with Him.

Ruth Myers, in her book *31 Days of Praise* (see Recommended Resources), articulates it perfectly:

> True praise is unconditional. It's not an attempt to manipulate God into producing the precise results we hope for. Instead, it helps us accept our situation as it is, whether or not He changes it. Continued praise helps us reach the place where we can say, "Father, I don't want You to remove this problem until You've done all You want to do through it, in me and in others."

Hear Him Knocking?

Jesus is concerned about our intimacies and relationships, especially our intimate relationship with Him. As we become more sensitive to His voice through reading the Bible and listening to the still, small promptings within, I hope that each of us will recognize without question and respond without reservation to His imploring call:

True praise is unconditional.

> "Here I am! I stand at the door and knock. If anyone hears My voice and opens the door, I will come in and eat with him, and he with Me . . . . He who has an ear, let him hear what the Spirit says to the churches" (Revelation 3:20, 22).

Taken in context, these words of our Lord were written not for the unsaved but for believers. They are words of rebuke and discipline for those of us whom Jesus loves. "Be earnest and repent," He says in verse 19. I can see Him standing there with holy patience, knocking on our doors, waiting to be invited in for some two-way, heart-to-heart conversation. Unfortunately, too many of us are distracted by the noise of the world to even hear the knock. And for those who do hear, too many are apprehensive about letting Him "in" for fear of what He might require.

If you are apprehensive about what God may ask of you, remember that He knows just how much you can handle. What He requires may be as simple as telling your four-year-old that God made the dandelions.

I once heard a minister say, "God doesn't want our ability; He wants our availability." When God looks at our hearts, what does He see? Our attitude. The depth of our sincerity. The level of our commitment. Some of us are responsive to God, while some of us are resistant. To quote my friend, Shelia, "Father God, make me willing to be willing."

Willingness for me took on a new meaning in 1976. It began with a heartfelt desire and a tiny, three-word prayer: "Use me, Lord."

Canterbury Road

It came as I drove along Canterbury Road, a winding country road half an hour from home. I was all by myself on a bright, crisp autumn day. Caught up in a sudden burst of gratitude as I reflected on the beauty of the day and the tremendous things God had done to turn my life around, I was so overwhelmingly thankful that it seemed important to say the words out loud. It was a prayer of dedication, commitment, and confessed inadequacies—a prayer of appreciation so deep that the only suitable "thank you" was to offer my life back to God as a living sacrifice, "warts and all."

"I realize there's no way I can repay You, nothing I can give You except myself. Use me, Lord. I'm all Yours. I guess I've always been Yours. After all, You created me. I've known and loved You from the first time I prayed, 'Now I lay me down to sleep.' But now I give myself fully to You—my will, my time, my talents and insecurities, my everything. If there's ever some small way You can see fit to use me—my hands, my feet, my voice, anything—then I would consider it an honor to serve You, to let Your will be done through me. Just let me know what and how, some way."

Even now, many years later, I can still vividly recall the intense gratitude that bubbled out of me in the form of that "use me" prayer as I drove along the quiet back road.

God wasted no time testing my sincerity. What appeared to be my first "job" came within the hour.

As soon as I got home, Drew and I headed for the tennis courts. We had barely begun playing when our game was halted by a piercing scream. A five-year-old girl had fallen off the handlebars of her brother's bike. We dropped our rackets and ran to see if we could help. As I knelt by the girl to inspect the nasty gash on her head, Drew asked her brother some questions.

"Where do you live?"

"On the other side of town."

"Where's your mother?"

"At home."

"She lets you ride your bike this far by yourself?"

"Sometimes."

"Your sister needs a doctor. Want us to take you home?"

"Yes. But what about my bike?"

Drew put the bike in our trunk, and I scooped the sobbing child into my arms and onto my lap as we situated ourselves in the front seat. Her brother, from the back seat, directed us to their house, where we found their mother. She had Medicaid for the little girl, but no car, so we drove her and her brave but whimpering daughter to the hospital, leaving the boy at his house with neighbors. Assured by a nurse in the emergency room that the girl would be fine and by the mother that they would be able to get a ride back to town, we left the hospital.

On the way home, I told Drew about my prayer and how I saw this minor emergency as a confirmation from God that He had actually heard my "use me" prayer. Then we noticed a fascinating coincidence. Not only was I "useful," but so was Drew.

God knows that some women are independent trailblazers who work well alone. And He knows that there are others, like me, who work better in tandem to get the job done. Drew is my ballast—the one who tempers my spiritual zeal, quietly working in the background with a ready hand or a helpful word. When God yoked us together, He called us as a team.

More Helpers, Please

Drew and I may be good teammates, but it takes more than just a couple of people earnestly praying "Use me, Lord!" to meet the needs of the hurting people of our time. The job is too big. The Scriptures say lots of laborers are needed and that we should ask the Lord to send in more help.

> "The harvest is plentiful, but the workers are few. Ask the Lord of the harvest, therefore, to send out workers into His harvest field" (Luke 10:2).

The cry is for more recruits, more workers, more "sowers" for the kingdom. Is God stirring your heart? Is the Lord Himself nudging you to abandon yourself more completely to Him?

One great thing about kingdom work is that it isn't designed to be accomplished single-handedly by any of us. When God calls us to action, remember that the task He delegates to me in my hometown is somehow connected to the one He's giving to you and all the other Christian sowers around the globe. Fortunately, we're only responsible for completing our own small part of the larger picture.

It's human nature to compare ourselves with others. But comparisons can either leave us feeling puffed up or put down. A better way is to measure our own progress. If we compare where we are in the Lord right this minute with other times in our lives when we felt the closest to or farthest away from Him, this lets the Holy Spirit tutor us into being our "best selves."

In one of Larry Tomczak's speeches, he said, "God loves to take people who seem like flops, fill them with resurrection life and power, and use them to turn the world upside down."

God has methodically and systematically planted believers in every community around the globe, often in low-key positions. There you are in your corner of the world, and here I am in mine, with lots of other everyday Christians sprinkled in between. You can reach people that I've never seen, and I may be marching across a spiritual bridge that you may not even know is there. I used to tiptoe around, but the Lord has told me lately to stop that—to be brave and strong and march. Although we may be in different places, at various levels of growth with assorted talents, resources, and opportunities, we're tied together by an invisible bond: the Holy Spirit.

Jesus insists that we come to Him as small children. Just as each child is unique and learns at his or her own pace, one stage of spiritual development is as important and precious as another. It is written that Jesus called a little child to His side and had him stand among His disciples. Then He said:

> "I tell you the truth . . . whoever humbles himself like this child is the greatest in the kingdom of heaven" (Matthew 18:4).

Baby Jane

Consider Baby Jane. She's only three months old but is already well-acquainted with her new crib. Lately she's been working her infant arms, legs, and tummy muscles overtime—reaching, pulling, and stretching. And then on Tuesday, at 10:00 a.m., she rolls over, all by herself.

Mommy and Daddy run to get the camera. Balancing Jane on her side, they hope to get her to do it again so they can capture the momentous occasion on film.

Are they disappointed that Jane didn't get up and run around the room a few times, or do a few jumping jacks? Of course not. Her parents are thrilled that their baby just turned over. That's all they expected her to do at twelve weeks of age. Baby Jane has acquired a new skill—a skill which she will need to practice over and over again. A skill which, when properly exercised and developed, will serve as a foundation for many other precious moments of growth.

And so it is with us. If our heavenly Father is delighted with each stage of our spiritual progress, why shouldn't we be? Our walk of faith requires many steps—some stumbling, some tottering, some on tiptoe or maybe even some stubbed toes. But don't babies have to bump their noggins a few times if they're going to learn to walk? Each level of spiritual growth, no matter how insignificant it may appear, is packed with trial-and-error value. Let's appreciate and treasure the journey, not just tolerate it or try to hurry through it.

Babes in Christ

Kids can get away with asking the silliest questions. They aren't embarrassed to admit when they don't know the answer. They don't try to impress anyone with their sophistication. Their egos aren't too big for their intellectual britches. Total innocence. Complete openness. Absolute trust. Childlike faith.

Just as children who grow up to be well-adjusted adults share many quiet moments learning about values, priorities, and love from their parents or guardians, we who want to mature as Christians need to spend quality time with our heavenly Father. Some of us, like children, need to be told to "sit down and be still." We run at such a fast pace and juggle so many responsibilities, it's easy to lose our perspective. Childlike humility is a rare virtue in our society. There seem to be too many big shots barking orders, and far too few regular fellows listening for the still, small voice of the One whose commands really count.

I'm always fascinated by the breath of fresh air that a brand new Christian brings to our women's Bible study. She comes in childlike faith, eager to **"Every adult needs a child to teach. It's the way adults learn." —Frank A. Clark** sit under the teaching of seasoned Christians. But the benefits are mutual. As the newcomer bubbles over with enthusiasm for who God is and what He is doing and hungers for a deeper understanding of the Scriptures, the longtime believer who has moved into the perseverance stage is reminded of the joy of the Gospel. In this setting, faith blossoms, creating an atmosphere of "fertile ground" where spiritual seeds, balanced living, and effective service are planted.

Good Roots

Before we dig any deeper, let's take a minute to think about the groundwork necessary for spiritual growth to occur. We must be

1. *Rooted in the Scriptures.*
   The Scriptures are the foundation and proving ground for all spiritual progress. (Stop and read 2 Timothy 3:14–17.)

2. *Nurtured by faith.*
   Without faith it is impossible to please God. (Visit the "faith chapter," Hebrews 11.)

3. *Cultivated through obedience.*
   God, who is not pleased by those who shrink back, rewards the ones who do His will. (Comprehend the straight talk of Hebrews 10:35–39.)

The inner voice of the Spirit will never contradict the Word of God or the character of Jesus Christ. Faith is essential in seeking God and hearing His call. He promises to reward those who place their confidence in Him and persevere along His course. Regardless of how far we've come or how wobbly we may be in our faith walk, the Word of God speaks to believers individually, calling and encouraging us.

Whether we wilt or flourish as Christians depends on where our roots are planted. Are we really rooted in Jesus Christ? Or are we rooted in tradition or self-effort as we minister in His name? In other words, do we have religion or a personal relationship with Jesus Christ?

Assurance of Salvation

Is your salvation genuine? To grow and flourish in a wilting society, we must be absolutely sure of our salvation. For many, awareness of their new birth isn't something they can pinpoint because God has been at work gradually, quietly, gently over the years, without fanfare, renewing their minds. For them, there is no specific time and date or bells and whistles. Others are born into the kingdom of God so dramatically and with such a shocking conversion that they can remember the very hour or minute of their born-again experience.

Because they have grown up hearing it, some people believe it's impossible to be sure of our salvation—that we will only be able to know our eternal destiny after we die. But the Scriptures urge us to be assured of our salvation now. It is a matter of *faith*.

Take a minute to read Jesus' own words on this important issue in John 5:24. Then look up the words recorded by John, the beloved disciple and a firsthand witness that Jesus is who He claims to be, in 1 John 5:1, 10–13 (especially v. 13).

According to the book of Romans, there are only two basic requirements for eternal life: (1) to believe, and (2) to say so.

> If you confess with your mouth, "Jesus is Lord," and believe in your heart that God raised him from the dead, *you will be saved*. For it is with your heart that you believe and are justified, and it is with your mouth that you confess and are saved (Romans 10:9–10, emphasis added).

But what does the word "believe" really mean? The foreword of the *Amplified Bible* explains:

> There is no one English word that adequately conveys the intended meaning. Actually, the Greek word used here for believe is "pisteuo." It means "to adhere to, cleave to; to trust, to have faith in; to rely on." Consequently, the words, "Believe on the Lord Jesus Christ . . ." really mean to have an absolute personal reliance upon the Lord Jesus Christ as our Savior.

So how do we know whether or not our salvation is genuine? The answer lies in the Great Commission and what we do with it (Matthew 28:16–20). Notice that even some of His closest disciples doubted at first. But oh, the joy that comes when we embrace the truth of Jesus' words and follow His teachings:

Then the eleven disciples went to Galilee, to the mountain where Jesus had told them to go. When they saw Him, they worshiped Him; but some doubted. Then Jesus came to them and said,

"All authority in heaven and on earth has been given to Me. Therefore go and make disciples of all nations, baptizing them in the name of the Father and of the Son and of the Holy Spirit, and teaching them to obey everything I have commanded you. And surely I am with you always, to the very end of the age."

Contagious Joy

The contagious joy that makes a good Christian witness doesn't come from anything we generate ourselves: It comes from the grace of God. It comes from the love and power of Jesus coursing through our lives, verifying who He is—the Lamb of God who came to take away the sins of the world, the Lion of Judah who alone is worthy to open the seals of God's judgment scroll (Revelation 5).

The Jesus *in us* is the same Jesus who tangibly fulfilled every prophecy regarding His first coming. To name a few:

- Jesus' mother was a virgin, and He was called Immanuel which means "God with us" (Isaiah 7:14; Matthew 1:18; Luke 1:26–35).

- Jesus was born in the small, unlikely Judean village of Bethlehem (Micah 5:2; Matthew 2:1; Luke 2:4–7).

- He was a descendant of the tribe of Judah (Genesis 49:10; Luke 3:33; Matthew 1:2–3).

- He was despised and rejected by His own chosen people, the Jews (Isaiah 53:3; John 1:11; 5:43; Luke 4:29; 17:25; 23:18).

- His triumphal entry into Jerusalem was predicted, right down to the donkey He would ride (Zechariah 9:9; John 12:13–14; Matthew 21:1–11).

- He was betrayed for thirty pieces of silver (Zechariah 11:12; Matthew 26:15; Matthew 27:3–10).

- He was crucified with sinners (Isaiah 53:12; Matthew 27:38; Mark 15:27–28; Luke 23:33).

- His hands and feet were pierced (Psalm 22:16; Zechariah 12:10; John 20:27).

- He was mocked, insulted, and challenged to save Himself (Psalm 22:6–8; Matthew 27:39–40; Mark 15:29–32).

- He said He was thirsty, and they gave Him vinegar (Psalm 69:21; John 19:29).

- His garments were divided by casting lots (Psalm 22:18; Mark 15:24; John 19:24).

- He was resurrected from death to life (Psalm 16:10; Matthew 16:21; Luke 24:36–48).

- He ascended to heaven (Psalm 68:18; Luke 24:51; Acts 1:9–11).

For those of us who long for His appearing, there is hope and joy in this knowledge and an excitement in the challenge of being prepared, with less than a moment's notice, to meet the Lord face-to-face at His second coming. Even now, we have the privilege of knowing Him Spirit to spirit.

But here's something to think about—our Lord's promise of true joy, the infectious kind, doesn't come to the puffed-up person who thinks he or she is a real asset to God, but to the humble believer who takes Him at His Word.

I struggle with pride. Who doesn't? Excuses aside, pride needs to be dealt with. So periodically I make an intentional effort to yield to God's searchlight, allowing the Holy Spirit to probe the hidden recesses of my mind and will. Since pride is such a sneaky and deceptive characteristic, I have learned the value of asking the Lord to show me any pride I might be harboring that I'm too blind to see on my own.

Recently, I discovered I've been guilty of false humility with regard to my priorities. Since I retired from my secretarial job three years ago, I have wholeheartedly thrown myself into writing, speaking, and publishing—all part of my calling. The problem is, I have been spending more and more time on the tasks before me and less and less time with the Lord.

Interestingly, my return to morning devotions coincided with the first day of Lent. After four days of uplifting journaling, I awoke late on Sunday and had to rush to get ready for church. I grabbed my journal and wrote, "Lord, You said I should meet with you every morning. Does that mean I need to write in my journal every day?"

I'm still chuckling at His answer: ***"What I said was, 'Come to Me daily.' I did not say let us have a meeting and you take minutes."***

Whoa! I was even turning my devotions into a job! I'm rediscovering the freedom, conviction, and equipping that come from communion with God. He is telling me—telling us all—***"Come. Release your burden and receive the grace."***

As my eyes scan the words of an open Bible, the following passage of comfort, assurance, and joy captures my attention.

He who began a good work in you will carry it on to completion until the day of Christ Jesus (Philippians 1:6).

Suddenly, I'm no longer wilting but flourishing! His Word speaks hope. The Lord will do the work, and He'll do it through us, His flawed but willing followers, as we submit ourselves to His searchlight.

The fact that you are reading this is a good indication that God has begun a good work in you. And what He starts, He finishes. Our responsibility is to see that our ego, pride, or other characteristics like complacency don't hinder His work in us. I feel a prayer welling up within me.

"Please, Lord, don't let our ego, pride, or independent nature hinder our relationship with You. We don't want to be spiritual wallflowers that never bloom for lack of light. We want to be the real thing—like a rosebud, created by Your loving hand, whose petals open ever so slowly, but surely, to receive the strengthening rays of Your Son's light. Help us, Lord God, to venture out from among the wallpaper patterns of imitation faith, leaving self behind and moving ahead to a place where others will notice the sweet-smelling fragrance of Your love as we pass by."

The Contrast

My tender prayer stands in stark contrast to the terrible stench that infiltrates our world today. Sweet, timid, pious Christians must have steel at the core, for we face an aggressive force that will stop at nothing to gain control of our world. Second Timothy 3:1 tells us, "But mark this: There will be terrible times in the last days." I believe those terrible times are upon us. But remember, Jesus entrusted the keys of heaven into the hands of His people—ordinary, everyday people like Peter the fisherman, saying,

"I will build my church, and the gates of Hades will not overcome it" (Matthew 16:18).

The true church is not one that boasts, cowers, cringes, or stammers hollow words in the face of evil; it is one that steadfastly overcomes. You and I can stand together, unruffled and unafraid, with a peaceful countenance, elegant as a long-stemmed rose whose thorns serve as a reminder of the crown our Lord wore at Calvary. The true church is made up of godly, praying people who reflect the confidence of Jonathan (1 Samuel 14). Jonathan was not concerned about the overwhelming odds. No, he was focused on how he—one dedicated believer—could make a difference.

David Wilkerson preached, "Indeed, if God had a large army of faithful servants, He would use them. But God doesn't need a great army—He can use one or two committed soldiers!"

Whether we see ourselves as soldiers in God's army or as flowers growing under His tender care, we can measure the extent of our loyalty to Him by the way we respond to His call.

I see our Christian journey as a spiral, illustrated by the map on the following page of how a "Little Sower's" faith journey might look. I hope you'll be able to identify with this fellow enough to see your own spiritual growth, even if in a different sequence. I've saved this exercise for the end of the chapter because I'm hoping it will be a visual resource as you use the worksheet.

Shall We Pray?

Father God, pour out Your grace on my friends as they join me in seeking an ever-deepening awareness of Your love. Help us to bear fruit that is pleasing to You. Strengthen us as sowers, with all power according to Your glorious might so that we may have great endurance and patience, joyfully giving thanks to You, Lord Jesus, for qualifying us to share in the inheritance of the saints. Teach us to know the power of Your indwelling Spirit.

Little Sower's Journey

1. There you stand, a believer indwelt by the Holy Spirit. Grateful for who God is and how He has affected your life, you eagerly await an opportunity to plant good seeds in the unique set of circumstances He has given you.

2. You're drawn to the Scriptures. In searching through the pages of your Bible, you find yourself joining hands with Jesus and entering into a partnership with Him.

Design by Kylie Westlake

3. Looking to Him for guidance, you pray *sincerely* to hear His voice as you seek His personal direction for your life. Two words, "Yes, Lord," are on your lips. As you practice exchanging your will for His, you begin to depend more on the Holy Spirit and less on yourself.

4. Somewhere along the way, you become curious about the Holy Spirit. As the third person of the Trinity reveals Himself to you, there comes an inner explosion, a "power for service." You are filled with enthusiasm and a love you've never known before.

5. You realize that Jesus is more than Someone you know *about*, He's Someone you *know*, Someone you're willing to follow *no matter how great the cost*. Suddenly, the Gospel is more than an important story or a ticket to heaven; it's dynamic Good News that you just can't seem to keep to yourself! Reaching out to others, you begin to find new, natural ways to share your faith as the love of God radiates through you.

6. This is only the beginning. In your mind's eye, you see tiny new spirals forming around the people whose lives have been touched by the Lord through your witness. They, in turn, reach out to countless others whose hearts are stirred by the Spirit of the living God.

7. Picture, too, an invisible blanket of prayer covering every step of the journey. With that in mind, I'll be praying Colossians 1:10–12 for those of you who want to continue the journey:

May you live a life worthy of the Lord and please Him in every way: bearing fruit in every good work, growing in the knowledge of God, being strengthened with all power according to His glorious might so that you may have great endurance and patience, and giving joyful thanks to the Father, who has qualified you to share in the inheritance of His holy people in the kingdom of light.

WHAT CAN I DO FOR YOU, LORD?

DIG INTO SCRIPTURE

Read the following passages slowly. Ask God to point out the parts He wants to bring to your attention.

- Psalm 139
- Romans 8:35–39
- 1 Corinthians 1:26–31

GOD'S CALL: RECOGNIZE YOUR WORTH

"Today you may not realize what I am doing, but later you will understand. Every step you have taken, and every breath you have drawn has been recorded. All of the experiences of your life work together to help you see your calling. Not only the good things you have done, but your secret sins, even the sins committed against you, have a purpose. Remember, I choose the foolish things of the world to shame the wise; the weak things of the world to shame the strong; the lowly things of this world and the despised things . . . so that no one may boast. Trust Me. And know that the same One who laid the foundations of the earth has fashioned you for a great purpose."

YOUR RESPONSE TO GOD

Write here, or highlight in your Bible, the words of Scripture that had the most impact on you. Meditate on those words. Memorize them.

_____

_____

 SEED FOR THOUGHT

"The trouble with some of us is that we've been inoculated with small doses of Christianity which keep us from catching the real thing."

—*Leslie Dixon Weathehead*

SEED FOR THOUGHT

Faith isn't nervous.

—Author Unknown

CHAPTER 3

SURRENDER
TO THE VINEGROWER'S TOUCH

 SEED FOR THOUGHT

"The world stands aside to let anyone pass
who knows where he is going."

—*David Starr Jordan*

"The world cannot accept Him (the Spirit of truth),
because it neither sees Him nor knows Him.
But you know Him, for He lives with you
and will be in you."
—John 14:17

Do I truly know my Lord? Do I know the power of His indwelling Spirit? It was a question raised during my morning quiet time as I was reading Oswald Chambers' classic devotional, *My Utmost for His Highest* (see Recommended Resources).

Mary Magdalene knew Jesus. In fact, she was desperately looking for Him outside the tomb when He spoke to her saying, "Woman . . . who is it you are looking for?" Even as intimately as she knew her Lord, she didn't recognize Him until He spoke her name, "Mary." Before that, she mistook Him for the gardener (John 20:15).

Maybe there's something to that gardener business. Christ reveals Himself to us in many ways. I like to think of Him as the "Head Gardener" of our souls, the One who cultivates our desire to know Him better. It was the voice of Jesus, silently calling my name, that helped me discover the power of the Holy Spirit.

I knew my Lord—or so I thought. Happily married to Drew, I was enthusiastically serving God. I sang in the choir, taught junior high Sunday school, and even led a women's Bible study. But the Lord used Pam in 1983 to open my spiritual eyes to what it means to have a *truly* personal relationship with Him.

Enter Pam

The new part-time secretary intrigued me, but I found her presence disquieting. Outspoken and quick to talk about the Lord, she appeared to have a definite sense of meaning and purpose to her life as though she'd tapped into a source of spiritual depth I didn't know existed. She had something I didn't, and I wanted it.

Looking back now after twenty-plus years, I can see that the Lord knew just what it would take to draw me into a closer walk with Him. At the time, all I knew was that Pam's glow shook my confidence as a Christian. I moseyed around the office, going through the motions of unlocking the filing cabinets and situating a coffee cup by the papers on my desk. Suddenly, the faith that had served me well for so many years seemed pale and meager. Sitting squarely in front of my IBM Selectric typewriter (before the day of personal computers), I wondered what it was about this new secretary that agitated me. She was nice enough, but her frankness about Jesus unnerved me. I guess I felt, well, threatened in my faith. But it wasn't like me to be intimidated.

I have an easygoing personality. As a rule, I float through life, bobbing contentedly along—kind of like a duck. Concerns just seem to bead up and roll off my back. Usually this is good, but there are times when the Lord has to ruffle my feathers in order to get through to me. Pam became my official feather-ruffler.

It didn't take us long to warm up to one another. I could hardly wait for our workload to cooperate so we could get into some real conversation. Our chance came that afternoon. Instinctively, I knew small talk was already a thing of the past.

"How long have you been a Christian, Candy?" she asked.

"All my life." I felt good about being able to say that.

"Oh? All your life?" She raised an eyebrow.

"Sure. I was baptized as an infant, have loved the Lord ever since I learned to pray, 'Now I lay me down to sleep,' and have been active in church for years."

"No, I mean, how long have you been living for the Lord and serving Him—doing things for Him?"

"All along. In fact, just last year I taught a seminar on biblical principles in marriage. How about you? How long have you been a Christian?"

"I accepted the Lord in 1977, the summer after that wild New Year's Eve party where we first met."

Until then, I hadn't realized that Pam and I had crossed paths before. The party wasn't one I wanted to remember, but it started coming back to me. *She does look familiar*, I admitted, searching the recesses of my mind.

"Oh, I remember you now," I said, as scenes from the party came dimly into view. It was a time when I was between marriages and alcohol flowed freely. *Did I do anything out of line that she might remember? No, I don't think so.*

"We've come a long way since then, haven't we?" Pam said. "Those were foolish days of darkness, but now we're living in the light. That party was a real turning point for me. Looking back, it seemed shallow and empty. Now, instead of being filled with wine, I'm filled with the Spirit!"

Pam told me of her dynamic conversion and pressed me to identify a "moment in time" when *I* had been "saved." Unable to pinpoint a specific day, she wasn't convinced that I was born again. Our conversation accelerated as she challenged my salvation. There was a competitive air between us like a tennis game where we volleyed beliefs and batted opinions back and forth. Pam slammed the point home with her next words that were like arrows in my heart.

> "Instead of being filled with wine, I'm filled with the Spirit!"

"Isn't it a thrill to be used by the God to lead others to Him?" she asked. "When it comes down to what really matters, how many people have you led to the Lord?"

Gulp. Until then, I'd maintained a pleasant and fairly smug opinion of myself, secretly viewing Pam as the culprit with a holier-than-thou attitude. Suddenly, the tables were turned. As she talked of bringing lost souls into the kingdom, I retreated into some soul-searching of my own. The more she talked about leading the unbeliever to Christ, the more inadequate I felt.

Confronted by my own insecurities about evangelism, I blurted out, "Oh, Pam, I haven't actually led *anyone* to the Lord. I'd like to, but I can't go out and tell strangers about Jesus!"

"I'm not talking about knocking on doors and handing out tracts," she explained. "It's just a matter of telling the people you know and love about what Christ has done in your own life and what He can do for them."

"Y-you don't understand," I stammered. "As important as the Lord is to me, I can't even bring myself to share the plan of salvation with my own family." My throat constricted, my eyes filled up, and without warning, a flood of emotion broke loose within me. "If Troy, my own stepson, walked up to me today and said, 'Candy, I've made a mess of my life and want to become a Christian,' I wouldn't know what to do, what to say, or how to pray!"

"Come here." Pam wrapped her arm around my shoulder and led me to a back office where I wouldn't be seen blubbering.

Away from the threat of observers, I continued, "Oh, this is silly. I don't know why I'm crying like this. I feel like such a baby." Later, I learned that tears are often evidence of the Holy Spirit at work. "It's just that winning souls is so important, and I feel so unqualified! It's hard enough for me to pray out loud. And this is such a major thing, such a big responsibility. What if I pray wrong and botch it up?"

"You won't," she assured me. "Any heartfelt prayer gets through to the throne of grace, no matter how rough it might be around the edges. You have everything you need. You love the Lord and want to serve Him. There's just one thing missing."

"What's that?" I blinked.

"The power," she replied. "The problem is that you lack confidence, and the confidence you need only comes from God. All you need is the power of God!"

God's Power

"The power of God?" I echoed weakly.

"Yes," she said. "Only the Holy Spirit can convince people that they need God. Converting souls is *His* responsibility, not ours. All we have to do is yield to the Holy Spirit and trust Him to work through us. The fact that you acknowledge Christ as your personal Savior is proof that the Holy Spirit is within you, because it's only by the Spirit that anyone can believe in the first place. And if you have God's Spirit, then you have access to His power. It just needs to be *released*."

"You're right." My heart started yearning for more. "If there's one thing I don't have, it's power!"

She took my hands in hers and handed me a tissue. "It's like you're wired to do God's work but haven't plugged into the power source."

"No wonder I feel so overwhelmed," I said through a half-smile as I cleaned off my smeared make-up. "I've been trying to do God's job *for* Him instead of letting Him do it *through* me." The tidal wave of pressure was gone. Left in its wake was raw curiosity and a deep yearning. "Tell me, Pam, how do I get this power?"

"It's all the work of the Holy Spirit," she said. "You just need to get better acquainted with Him. I have a couple of books that might help. If you want, I'll bring them in tomorrow."

"If I want?" the words gushed out. "Yes! The sooner, the better!"

The next day, true to her word, Pam arrived at the office with two books: *The Helper* by Catherine Marshall, and *In His Steps* by Charles M. Sheldon. She suggested that I read *The Helper* first.

To Read or to Be Sidetracked

I could hardly wait to get started. After a hectic day at work, I rushed home to pick up my then eleven-year-old daughter for her voice lesson. We drove the half hour to Milford, where I wheeled into the church parking lot and hustled Kim upstairs to her classroom. I sighed with delight as I eased myself into an overstuffed chair in a sitting room, to wait . . . and to read. I turned on the soft light at a nearby table, grateful to be alone.

Perfect—a few minutes of solitude, I thought as I opened *The Helper*, trying to tune out the trombone and piano warm-ups that wafted through the wall behind me.

Somewhere around the fifth word of the third sentence, the door flew open, and a lively three-year-old bounced in, accompanied by her big brother who was early for his saxophone lesson.

"I'm Audrey," she announced. "Look at me-e-e!" With a grin, she began twirling around in circles, faster and faster. "I can dance!" she sang, flopping herself dramatically on the floor in a lopsided grand finale.

"That's wonderful!" I chuckled, and turned back to my reading. *Now where was I?*

"Want to see what else I can do?" Audrey continued, not about to forfeit the spotlight. "Look! I can take my shoes off." And she did.

"Very good," I acknowledged, which was just what she needed to do it again. Audrey could unbutton her sweater, too, and by the time her talent show ended, so had Kim's voice lesson.

So, I'll read later tonight. I firmly closed the book and headed for home, just in time to dash off to choir practice. Stuffing a banana in my mouth, I waved a cheerful hello/good-bye to Drew and called out to him over my shoulder, "Honey, can you take care of Kim's dinner?"

"Sure," I heard him say as the door closed behind me.

Home by 9:00 p.m., I helped Kim finish her homework, threw a load of towels in the washer, scanned the mail, cleaned up the dishes, donned my nightgown, hopped into bed, and reached for *The Helper*.

I glanced up for a second. There sat Drew, next to me in his recliner. Mr. Patience.

"He's your husband," an inner voice reminded me.

The only conversation we'd exchanged since our good-bye kiss 14 hours earlier was Kim's dinner request. As eager as I was to read, I opted to give him my full attention. Although it was difficult to pull my eyes away from the page in front of me, the good communication and intimate moments that followed gave me assurance that I had done the right thing. Drew is always there for me. As his helpmate, companion, and friend, I want to be there for him, too.

In my eagerness to learn more about God's power, the Holy Spirit had a couple of preliminary lessons:

1. *Patience.* When Alexander Pope said, "Fools rush in where angels fear to tread," he knew what he was talking about. Spiritual power cannot be grasped quickly like plucking an apple off a tree. It's a fruit of the Holy Spirit which buds, blossoms, and grows slowly. Spiritual maturity takes patience which comes in direct proportion to how fully we yield ourselves to God.

2. *Priorities.* God first, yes! And when we truly give our relationship with the Lord top priority, He will help us attend to our families.

The Holy Spirit had carefully arranged the circumstances of my life so I wouldn't plunge carelessly into holy matters without including Drew in my search for a closer walk with the Lord. Sleep, deep and restful, came quickly that night.

Up Early

I awoke the next morning at 5:30 with the words, **"Draw near to God and He will draw near to you,"** running through my mind. Peace and quiet and solitude. I was refreshed and as eager as ever to dig into *The Helper.* Without the slightest hesitation, I slipped out from under the covers, put on a fresh pot of coffee, and hopped into the shower before reality hit me. *I've never voluntarily gotten up this early in my life!*

Coveting each moment of undisturbed silence, I quickly patted myself dry and settled down at the kitchen table. *At last, I'm going to find out about the Holy Spirit and the power of God.*

I flipped the book open to the first chapter. My hungry heart ate up each word. Every line bombarded me with new awareness.

I learned that the Holy Spirit is not a feeling, an influence, or some ghostly supernatural thing that warrants the impersonal pronoun "it," but a person—one of the three persons of the Godhead.

"Forgive me for my ignorance," I prayed. "I see now that You're He! Not an 'it' or a 'thing' but my Lord and my God." Eager to learn more, I read on and ran headlong into this prayer:

> Lord, I need the Helper today because I need to have the greatest gift of all, that You become real to me. There is not a single part of my life where I do not need Your help, Lord Jesus. Forgive me for those days when I haven't taken the time to talk things over with You. When I ignore You, I am the loser. Sometimes I tell myself that I am too busy to pray. That is self-deception. The truth is that I have a strange resistance to face You and to be honest with You. Lord, I give You permission to melt that resistance . . .

Moved to Repentance

Catherine Marshall's words stung my conscience. How rarely I prayed. The year before, I had attempted to get into a prayer routine, but it was short-lived. Although my commitment was sincere, there had been too many interruptions and too little understanding of the importance of prayer and perseverance. When interferences mounted, my devotions fizzled. I was about to discover how much I needed the Holy Spirit's help to combat obstacles that threatened my prayer time.

My self-defeating pattern was clear. I was chronically "busy" and easily sidetracked. Quickly distracted from entering fully into the reverence, the awe, and the vulnerability that His holy presence warrants, I knew firsthand what that "strange resistance" felt like. It was one thing to enthusiastically present myself to be used by God in a moment of heartfelt gratitude while driving 40 miles an hour along Canterbury Road. It was quite another to meet Him privately, personally, in the quiet of the morning while sitting absolutely still at the kitchen table.

In this "go-go-go" society, a moment of stillness can be an unfamiliar—even uncomfortable—sensation. The hectic pace of the previous day was fresh in my mind. I never had enough time. Meeting myself coming and going, I typically scurried from one place to another. Even now, with *The Helper* in front of me, my thoughts raced at breakneck speed. In shame, I bowed my head.

"Oh, Lord," I cried out softly, "I'm so sorry for running away from You in my mind, for being too busy to sit quietly in Your presence. I confess my reluctance to face You. This must be how Adam and Eve felt when they hid from You in the garden. I am spiritually and emotionally naked before You, Lord. Forgive my puny efforts at prayer. I surrender myself to You again, more completely this time. Mold me. Shape me. Teach me . . ."

A pervasive and awesome quietness blanketed the kitchen. It was as though a holy, invisible presence had come quietly into the room. I prayed earnestly to experience the nearness of the living God, and He honored my prayer. Right there in my kitchen, the Holy Spirit revealed Himself to me.

My prayer ceased in mid-sentence as I basked in the love that enfolded me. I wondered at this *presence* I was encountering. Who is it? What does it mean? And in that instant of near-comprehension, I opened my eyes! Why? Not in an attempt to see Jesus but to regain control—to bring me back to the reality of tangible things. The book in front of me was something I could control; the awesome presence I had sensed was not. It was a mental tug-of-war for me to do what the Scripture says: "Set your minds on things above, not on earthly things" (Colossians 3:2).

The intense tranquility that had settled upon me moments before lifted. My awareness of the presence of God lasted only briefly, for a fleeting moment, because it was all I could handle.

Now, where was I? I retreated mentally to a lighter note, but I couldn't concentrate. While I was desperately trying to comprehend what I was reading, two penetrating words that were not on the page pierced my thoughts: ***"SLOW DOWN!"***

The Voice of God

I stopped, all right. The words were so unexpected and so startling, that I not only slowed down, but I froze! Sitting there, wide-eyed and barely breathing, I was acutely aware of the hum of the refrigerator and the ticking of the clock. I found myself staring at empty space, not daring to read even one more word. The nerves in my fingertips reminded me that I still held the book in my hand which, slowly and deliberately, I closed and placed on the table.

If the words had been audible, they would have rung in my ears. They might as well have been because, like a broken record, they replayed in my thoughts, *"SLOW DOWN . . . S L O W D O W N . . . S L O W   D O W N . . ."*

Realizing it was absolutely essential for me to "slow down," I closed my eyes again and ordered my pounding heart to be still like the rest of me. Then, and only then, completely quieted inside and out, did I discover what it meant to practice the presence of God and to simply enjoy His company. The Holy Spirit had not left. He was right there with me. It was I who had retreated. *What was happening? Had He spoken to me?*

Aware again of His closeness, I was fearful, yet I wasn't afraid. The air was electrified. I wanted to get up and run, but I couldn't and wouldn't move. I was unsettled, while completely at peace. It didn't make sense. But I didn't have to understand, because I was a little girl again, snuggled in her heavenly Daddy's arms, being rocked and affirmed and loved. Safe and secure. Time was meaningless. Moments stretched into minutes which somehow were suspended into a realm where there is no time. I was consumed by His majesty, His holiness, His tenderness, His magnitude, and His unconditional love.

Truly, I tried to comprehend, *I am in the presence of God*. At that realization, the Holy Spirit spoke clearly to the inner recesses of my mind.

"Good. Now you are still. Candy, you must slow down if you are to know Me. I have known you before you were conceived in your mother's womb. I have monitored your every move from infancy to adulthood. I have watched you falter and have seen

you stand firm. I know you, My child. I know everything about you. There is nothing about you that is hidden from Me. And as fully as I know you, that is how intimately I desire for you to know Me.

"You must go slowly, though, for things quickly learned are quickly forgotten. It is important that you walk leisurely, hand-in-hand with Me daily. Do not run, My child, lest you fall. But stroll quietly in My company that we might become better acquainted. Cherish and savor each moment. There is much I have to teach you, enough for a lifetime. Slow down. Enjoy our time together."

Gradually, the awesome presence lifted, and I became aware of my surroundings once more. Humbled beyond description, I was filled with an intense desire to please the Son of God, the risen Lord, my Jesus.

Overwhelming reverence drew me from the kitchen chair to my knees. I spoke no words in prayer. No more thoughts pierced my mind. It was just a precious time of oneness—the Spirit of my Lord and me, alone together. Eventually, I lifted my head, opened my eyes, and pulled myself up from the floor.

> "As fully as I know you, that is how intimately I desire for you to know Me."

Feeling strengthened and refreshed, I reached for *The Helper* again. This time it was with gentle respect, aware that the Holy Spirit would meet me between the words and teach me through the pages. I not only slowed down, I started over—right from the beginning. I even read the Foreword and How to Use This Book and discovered some crucial pointers.

The 40 chapters (only a couple of pages each) were recommended as a daily devotional guide. The idea of reading a single "help" a day appealed to me. It was a good way for me to slow down and develop a habit of regular Bible reading. Besides, I would have a good twenty-four hours to put each small, but mighty, teaching to practical use. God was teaching me how to practice His presence. It was as though I'd been given a prescription for good spiritual health that read: "Take one chapter every morning for 40 days; do not overdose by reading ahead."

Developing Listening Skills

The first big lesson the Holy Spirit had for me was how to stop talking long enough to listen to what He had to say. Which reminds me of a story about a husband who found himself in front of a marriage counselor:

"Hmm . . . ," the counselor contemplated after listening intently to the wife's long-winded complaint. He leaned back in his chair, his hand on his chin. Peering over the rim of his glasses and into the eyes of the little man, he said, "Your wife claims that you have not spoken a single word to her in the past five years. Is that true?" he asked incredulously.

"Yes, sir. That's true," the man admitted meekly.

"This is highly unusual," the counselor stated. Leaning forward, he pressed, "Would you care to offer an explanation? In your own defense, is there some good reason for your behavior?"

"Yes, there is, sir," the gentleman responded.

"Go on," the counselor urged.

"Well, your honor," the man replied, "I didn't want to interrupt her."

The Lord didn't interrupt me, either. He, too, is a gentleman. All those years, He had stood faithfully by, protecting and sustaining me, waiting to be acknowledged. I pledged to become a better listener.

If it takes twenty-one days to make or break a habit, then forty days of pulling away from the obstacles of noisiness to enjoy a private audience with the Holy Spirit was just what I needed. Drawing near to God is a privilege, an honor, and a gift—one chapter a day for forty days was a meager investment for life-changing results. Suddenly, I was enthusiastic about the very thing I had previously avoided: a consistent, disciplined time of private devotions.

My adventure had begun! I could hardly wait to get out of bed every morning to see what the Lord had in store for me. Learning to recognize the Holy Spirit's subtle presence actually became great fun. I discovered His ways to be endearing, surprising, personalized, and well-ordered. I never cease to marvel at how the Spirit meshes a number of elements into a finished product. It seems as though He has entered into a kind of partnership with me, helping to gather together the things I need the most—in this case, the ingredients that went into establishing a regular and deeply fulfilling prayer walk.

The Main Ingredients

Desire. My desire to be alone with God came only because of His gentle call, a yearning He created in my spirit. He instilled the desire. My simple role was—and is—to respond.

Commitment. Committing the time is my department. If I don't take the initiative, it won't happen. As an act of will, I *made* time to be alone with my Lord. I started out with five minutes, a contracted portion of time that I knew I could live with. Soon I decided I needed fifteen. Within a matter of weeks, an hour didn't seem long enough. While the idea of scheduling God into your day may sound tacky, it works!

Time. This is a matter of trial and error. I tried praying at night, but I fell asleep. I tried praying during lunch, but there were too many distractions. It seemed that the time that worked best for me was after my morning shower, freshly scrubbed and bright-eyed. In the serenity of the early hours, there is a certain hope for the new day that no other time frame seems to capture. For me, 5:30 a.m. is "prime time." Some mornings, the Holy Spirit and I enter into a friendly tug-of-war to get me out from under those covers, but whenever He lets me win and oversleep, I am the loser, for I've lost an opportunity that can never be regained.

Place. It's no easy task to find your secret prayer closet. At first, my refuge was the bathroom. It was more than private and humbling to kneel in front of the toilet. Although bathrooms are good places for privacy, if your devotional time happens to stretch into an hour, it can be uncomfortable. So, I moved to the kitchen which proved to be too conspicuous as other members of the household began to stir. Finally, I discovered my upper room—the attic! With Drew's help, mountains of junk were climbed, tamed, and claimed. Voila! My own private place at last.

Resources. I had my Bible and *The Helper*—everything I needed. Or, so I thought.

Taking Stock

Bright and early the next morning, settling into my cozy corner of the attic, I took stock of my environment. The gray metal chair was cold but much more comfortable than it looked. My elbows rested lightly on Drew's old oak desk. My Bible, *The Helper*, a highlighting pen, and a steaming mug of coffee were at my fingertips.

But something was missing. I could feel it. An attitude of prayer evaded me. *Oh, well*, I decided, *it must be that my new "prayer closet" will just take a little getting used to.* I opened the book and reviewed the guidelines Catherine Marshall had outlined:

For individual use, I recommend setting aside the same time each day, in the same quiet place, for reading, checking Bible references, and personal prayer. [*So far so good*, I congratulated myself.]

It helps to be very specific in one's prayer requests. This can become an exciting experiment by the keeping of a Prayer Log in which each petition is jotted down by date, with space left to record the date of the answer as well as details about how it came.

So something was missing, after all. *Now, where can I find a prayer log—a notebook, a diary or journal of some sort at this hour?* The Holy Spirit triggered my memory. Many months before, I had received a *30 Day Prayer Diary* from *Guideposts*. At the time, I had tucked it away on a shelf. Now, it was just what I needed. My feet propelled me down the attic stairs and into our bedroom to find it.

"What are you doing?" Drew asked sleepily as I rummaged around in the dark.

"Oh, just looking for something. Sorry, I didn't mean to wake you."

There it was, right where I had put it. Grasping my prize, I bounded back up the stairs feeling as buoyant as a girl on her fifth birthday. What a great coincidence!

Coincidence?

As I leafed through the pages, I was startled to find an uncanny number of similarities between *My 30 Day Prayer Diary* and *The Helper*. Not only were the style and subject matter almost identical, but the diary had the very same layout Catherine recommended. It was almost as though the same author had written them both. They seemed like custom-ordered companions.

With keen interest, I read the introduction in the diary. "My husband, Peter Marshall, died so suddenly . . ." I stopped short. *Who did write this thing?* I flipped back to the copyright page: Catherine Marshall and her husband Leonard LeSourd, *My 30 Day Prayer Diary*. Carmel, NY: *Guideposts*, from *My Personal Prayer Diary*. Lincoln, VA: Chosen Books, 1979.

Coincidence, or providential circumstance? I could almost see the fingerprints of the Holy Spirit on the pages as I evaluated just a few of the conditions that had to be met in order for that prayer diary to wind up in my hands at that moment. It was written by the same author as the book that Pam had loaned me. I was astonished to catch a glimpse of the meticulous lengths the Holy Spirit is willing to go to in order to monitor the affairs of His beloved. Even me. Praise and wonder mushroomed in the core of my being. What a wonderful way to christen my prayer closet.

Faithfully, every morning, I climbed those stairs. And every day I learned something new about the Holy Spirit. The more I learned, the more I realized how little I knew. I vowed never to miss an appointment with Him.

Meanwhile

Life went on as usual around the house. I seemed to have an abundance of energy, so when Drew suggested that we paint the living room, I was ready. Down came the drapes, out came the paint brushes. By Friday night, everything was ready to put back in place, but that's our "date night," so I decided to tackle the curtains the next morning.

You have to go through the living room to get to the attic door in our house. Saturday morning, coffee cup in hand, I was about to open the attic door for my "appointment with God" when I paused, just for a moment, to put a couple hooks in the drapes that were sprawled over the chair. The trap was set. One pinched pleat led to another and, before I knew it, my coffee was cold and somebody was running water in the bathroom.

"Seven o'clock!" I gasped. "Oh, Lord, forgive me. I've stood You up!" Fear gripped me. If I could allow this to happen once, it might happen again. I desperately wanted my private devotions to continue in a consistent and predictable way. Had my prayer time started to deteriorate already? And worse, was God angry with me?

"We are flexible."

"What?"

"We are flexible."

I sat down in the chair by the television and meditated on the words that popped into my mind. *Who is "we?"* I wondered. *The Holy Spirit and I, perhaps?* I certainly wasn't being flexible. It was my every intention to rigidly adhere to my set schedule. *Who could "we" be?*

"The Father, the Son, the Holy Spirit."

I was beginning to see. The Spirit reveals Jesus. Jesus reveals the Father. The Father reveals the Spirit through His Son. The cycle continues. It was a unified message from all three Persons of the Godhead: The Lord does not promote bondage but freedom.

While the curtain hooks may have been, in fact, a trap to divert me from my appointment with God, He used the situation to teach me a valuable lesson. Devotional discipline should never be allowed to become a ritual, a technique, or something you feel you *must* do. Time alone with God is precious communion with Someone who understands the demands of daily living and says it's okay to take a break from an established pattern of worship.

What a relief! What a joy to serve a God of such liberation. He is with me and in me, never leaving nor forsaking me. There is no condemnation in Christ Jesus.

Developing a Life of Prayer

In resuming my prayer routine the next day, I saw that I must let the Spirit set the pace. Learning to recognize His inner tugs and blocks and leadings is not an easy thing. In fact, I'm still learning daily, even after more than twenty years of practice. One thing I know, though, is that God is always with me. He is my Lord, my Friend, and my constant Companion. And one of the few things He asks is that I be aware of His presence, not only in the prayer closet but throughout the day, no matter how hectic it gets.

My quiet time continues to be an important benchmark. When I miss it, my priorities can quickly get out of kilter. My peace of mind, general sense of well-being, and energy fall prey to confusion, irritability, or fatigue. I can see how Satan would like nothing better than to keep me away from a private audience with my Lord. I can picture that old devil rubbing his hands together with glee at the very thought of anything that could serve as a stumbling block to prayer.

But God is too big to be confined to a prayer closet. After years of intimacy with my Lord in the mornings, I noticed my devotions were growing dry. The Master's voice seemed distant until I asked what was wrong. Then it came to me, loud and clear, that God refused to stay in the box I had created for Him. He wanted to go with me everywhere and teach me how to make my life a prayer.

Oswald Chambers addresses this in *My Utmost for His Highest* (May 12): "Your god may be your little Christian habit—the habit of prayer or Bible reading at certain times of your day. Watch how your Father will upset your schedule if you begin to worship your habit instead of what the habit symbolizes. Love means that . . . your habits are so immersed in the Lord that you practice them without realizing it."

I take great comfort in knowing that the Lord constantly watches over me and lovingly observes how I handle each obstacle that comes my way. I know He is keenly interested in how I order my day, and He stands ever ready to help me straighten things up when they get out of whack, moving me out of my comfort zones. Once, for instance, after neglecting my quiet time, an explicit message from the Lord broke through my apathy:

"Come to Me, child, not for chastening and duty, but for joy, peace, and new direction. My love is perpetually being showered upon you, but you have been slow to come to the fountain where you may receive it in full measure.

"How long I have waited, and even now wait, for you to seek Me for no other reason than because I Am. Come apart from the distractions that separate us from one another. Seek from Me a new understanding of the depth of My affection. My love changes not, neither does it increase nor decrease. Only your awareness of it varies.

"Look not for some great emotional response from within your being, but be content to find that your heart is quickened by the reality of My presence.

"I have called you by name, and you are Mine. When you pass through the waters, I will be with you. The rivers will not overcome you, nor will the flames of the fire through which you walk consume you. For I will lift you up, high above the things of this world that seek to entrap you. Even in days of ease, keep

*your eyes on Me, for often you may wade into troubled waters
without seeing the danger therein.*

*"Delight yourself afresh in the discovery of My glory amidst
the pages of the Bible which you seldom hold upon a still lap. Come
to Me, and I will come to you. Come, and be refreshed."*

His Invitation

The Lord's invitation is compelling. He continuously reminds me
of the importance of spending time in His company. But there are
times when an hour (or even fifteen minutes) isn't feasible. Here's
what He had to say one hectic morning when I grabbed a quick two
minutes for my devotions:

*"When you have little time, be still. And simply know that I Am
with you. A few moments of appreciation are more beneficial than
an hour of obligation. True worship originates in the heart. Time is
not a factor with Me. Ritual is offensive if the heart is not sincere.*

*"Be quiet now, be still. And allow your heart to be right with
Me. Put on an attitude of praise, for I am your God."*

Then, there's the other extreme. Once, when my devotions were
unwavering, I got so pepped up about the benefits of prayer that I
started looking beyond my own prayer closet and into other people's. I
guess I poked my nose into one closet too many, unwittingly assuming
the role of "mother hen" to some friends whose prayer habits were
not as fulfilling as I thought they should be. And the Lord called me
on it. It was a time of admonition I will never forget:

*"I am the One who sounds the call to prayer. Not the sound
of your own voice or your own determination, not your schedule
or ideals. Meaningful prayer is initiated by the prompting of the
Holy Spirit. Be not dismayed by those who do not enthusiastically
follow your example of devotional discipline, for it is only I who
can motivate believers to fervent prayer. You have seen for
yourself how futile self-effort can be in this matter.*

*"Speak openly about the significance of prayer, My daughter,
but speak gently, and permit Me the prerogative of impressing
the hearts of My children."*

Spiritual Molds

The Head Gardener, the Holy Spirit, wants His workers to know Him and to follow His instructions. God has some valuable lessons to teach us in order to produce the kind of fruit that will be pleasing to Him.

Over the years, my journal has served as a trustworthy vehicle for the Lord to teach me many things. I'll explain more about how my exercise of written dialogue with God came about in the next chapter. For now, I want to share my journal entry of March 6, 1987, as an illustration of how important it is to develop and maintain a truly *personalized* relationship with the Holy Spirit that remains fresh and flexible (as opposed to cookie-cutter Christianity):

"Some people try to fit themselves into spiritual molds that were never intended for them, and what's worse, they try to fit other people into them, too. I know that role models are important for us as examples to follow, but only to a certain extent. Things that worked for the person I've chosen as my role model may or may not work for me.

"According to 1 Corinthians 12:4–6, 'There are different kinds of gifts, but the same Spirit. There are different kinds of service, but the same Lord. There are different kinds of working, but the same God works all of them in all men.' I see, Lord, that You have designed each of us to be unique and to serve You and worship You in uniquely different ways."

"Be receptive to the changing needs I place before you, My daughter. For example, there was a time when an hour of prayer every morning was critical to prepare your heart for ministry. The work to which I call you required this intimate commitment as training ground.

"You notice that your motivation for the morning hour of structured and predictable prayer time is not as strong as it once was. This is not to say that you are any less spiritual or any less committed to serving Me. It is an indication that you have

become more attuned to My Spirit's voice moment by moment throughout your day.

"Yes, for some I do require uninterrupted and sometimes quite lengthy periods of daily meditation. For them, a structured routine is necessary for a lifetime.

"You should not follow those things that have worked for others—or even for yourself in the past—so ritualistically that you miss the calling that is in front of you this day."

"It's true that I often experience the joy of Your closeness throughout the day, but Lord, I'm confused. There seems to be such a fine line between recognizing the calling of Your Spirit to a different routine and what could be laziness or disobedience on my part. How do I know if I'm in Your will or if I'm backsliding?"

"Perpetual communion between us is the first thing of importance, whether you are sitting attentively at My feet or enthusiastically engaged in carrying out an assignment I have given you. When in question, search the Scriptures and let the words test the condition of your heart. If your motives are pure, the words will not convict but comfort your spirit. However, if your heart is in rebellion to Me, the words will sting. The important thing to remember is this:

"'I am the vine; you are a branch. If you remain in Me and I in you, you will bear much fruit; apart from Me you can do nothing. If you do not remain in Me, you will be like a branch that is thrown away and withers; such branches are picked up, thrown into the fire and burned. If you remain in Me and My words remain in you, ask whatever you wish, and it will be given you. This is to my Father's glory, that you bear much fruit, showing yourself to be My disciple'" (John 15:5–8, personalized).

In other words . . .

Let us run with perseverance the race marked out for us. Let us fix our eyes on Jesus, the author and perfecter of our faith (Hebrews 12:1–2).

Shall We Pray?

Lord Jesus, how keenly aware I am of my need for You to continue to mold and motivate me. You truly are my Helper, and I am well aware that any good fruit my life produces is only because of You. I have come such a long way, but I have so far to go, with so much to learn. Keep me teachable, Lord, and use the lessons I am learning—such as my clumsy attempts to recognize Your still, small voice—to touch the searching spirit of my friend, the reader, who may be struggling with mounting pressures in these uncertain days.

*W*HAT CAN I DO FOR YOU, LORD?

DIG INTO SCRIPTURE
- James 4:7–10 (with particular emphasis on verse 8)
- Psalm 46:10
- John 14:18–21

GOD'S CALL: DRAW NEAR TO ME
"You may wish you knew the day of My return so you could prepare for it, but the Father alone has this knowledge. I have not left you comfortless but have given you all you need to know in order to be prepared. Have I not promised that I will never leave you nor forsake you? Call on Me and I will come to you. I will plant My Spirit within you and reveal Myself to you. The future is not a mystery to Me. I know what will happen and will be with you through it. Fear not. Rather, have faith in God and trust your future to Me."

YOUR RESPONSE TO GOD
To show that you are serious about your desire to draw near to God, make an appointment with Him, and be sure to keep it. Record your commitment here, in the back of your Bible, and/or in your journal, daytimer or calendar.

Date: _____

Time: _____

Place: _____

 Seed for Thought

Good listeners are not only popular everywhere,
but after a while they know something.

—Author Unknown

CHAPTER 4

RECOGNIZE THE MASTER'S VOICE

 SEED FOR THOUGHT

Time spent waiting on God is never wasted.
(Did you catch the double meaning in the word "waiting?")

—*Author Unknown*

*"Blessed are all who hear the Word of God
and put it into practice."*
—*Luke 11:28* TLB

God speaks to those who take time to listen. An intriguing concept, this statement triggers instant questions: "How do I hear Him?" "What does God's voice sound like?" "How can I tell if it's really the Lord?"

The Lord has limitless ways of speaking to His people—through the Holy Scriptures, magazine articles, poetry, books, sermons, songs and hymns, friends and enemies, natural disasters, television or radio, etc. There are numerous external avenues the Lord might use to reach us, but only one internal path—that still, small voice that cries to be heard.

The heart of every believer is equipped with sensitivity to the voice of the Master who has taken up residence within us. What a joy to recognize those precious times when His Spirit moves within our spirits to give us specific direction and personal guidance.

When God spoke to Samuel, we don't know if His voice was audible or silent, but Eli, the high priest, didn't hear it. The voice called Samuel by name, so Samuel thought it was Eli. It didn't take long for the old priest to realize what was happening, so he told Samuel to go back to bed and wait quietly, expectantly.

The next time the young boy heard, "Samuel, Samuel," he answered, "Speak, for Your servant is listening." Then, when the Lord had Samuel's full attention, He spoke at length, revealing some awesome, even alarming things. Read 1 Samuel 3:1–21 to see what these things were and how others responded. Can you relate to Samuel's initial bewilderment?

Our Master's voice is not always easy to recognize, especially when we are first learning. Over and over, I've had to ask, "Is that You, Lord?" Now, after much practice, I'm able to say with expectation, "Speak, for I am listening."

In our relationship with God, it's vital that we listen and respond. Also, we need the discernment of the Spirit to help us accurately interpret how to apply the Scriptures to our own situations. Faced with a responsibility to rightly handle the words the Lord tells us, like Samuel, sometimes it takes practice before we catch on.

One of my most memorable lessons came when God took a casual conversation with my dear friend, Lynn Fulop, and turned it into a training ground for hearing His voice. Here's the "ear-opening" account.

Insomnia

"Oh, Candy," Lynn complained as she scooped some tuna salad onto a plate in front of me. "I'm so glad you could come over. I need to talk to somebody, and I hate to bother John with something so trivial."

"What's wrong?" I asked.

"It's no big deal, I guess. It's just that I can't sleep. It's been three nights now, and I don't know how much longer I can go on like this. I'm exhausted. I've tried everything I can think of, and nothing seems to help. What do you do when you have insomnia?"

"Insomnia? Oh, I wouldn't know anything about that," I flippantly remarked with a smile. "I've never had any trouble sleeping."

Be careful what you proclaim, especially when the Lord wants to teach you something.

Less than twelve hours later, I lay in my bed, saucer-eyed, staring at the ceiling. Me and my big mouth.

What was it Mom used to tell me? I struggled to remember. *Oh, yes, "Just keep your eyes closed, lie as still as you can, breathe in and out s-l-o-w-l-y, and pretend to be asleep."* It had worked when I was a child, so why wasn't it working now?

I know. I'll count sheep like they do in the cartoons. No good. So I tried counting my blessings instead of sheep. Nice, but each recollection only woke me up more.

I rolled to the left. I rolled to the right. I bunched up my pillow, buried my face in it, forced my eyelids shut, and tossed Drew around in the process.

"You awake?" he asked.

"Sure am, for over an hour now. Think I'll get up and listen to a tape."

"Good idea," he said from deep beneath the covers. I slid out of bed, put on my slippers, and made my way to the tape player.

The cassette was soothing but not nearly long enough, so I heated a cup of milk in the microwave and curled up in the living room chair with a book. I didn't get drowsy, just bored.

Meandering restlessly around the house, I stood in the hallway and looked with admiration into the bedrooms of our three rapidly maturing children: my daughter, Kim (then eleven), and my stepchildren, Troy and Dana (who were eighteen and twenty-two). Shuffling back to the living room, I breathed in the warm, fragrant June night air through the front screen door. Filled with appreciation for my family, home, the freedom of our country, and God, I was aware of so many things, including the time: 4:00 a.m. *You'll never get any sleep this way*, I chided myself. I would need to get ready for work in a few hours. I had instant empathy for Lynn.

Back to bed I went. *I know what I'll do*, I decided as I pulled the sheet up to my chin. *I'll pray.* Before I could begin, I was struck with a piercing thought, ***"Be on your knees."***

Be on my what? My knees? That's silly. God can hear my prayers just fine from right here.

"Be on your knees," came the penetrating thought again.

That's a funny way to put it, I debated with myself. *Get on your knees would be more like it. Or, at least, that's how I would say it. Besides, why should I do that? There's certainly no danger of my falling asleep. I'm wide awake!*

"Be . . . on . . . your . . . knees," the nagging phrase came for the third time.

I was perplexed. Where was the thought coming from? "Is that You, Lord?"

"Who else would direct you to be on your knees?"

My mind raced as I considered the alternatives. *Well, the suggestion is not coming from me, I decided. The last thing I want to do is get out from under these covers anymore tonight. And it can't be the devil, because he wouldn't want me to be praying in the first place, let alone on my knees. So it must be . . .*

Besides, the voice had a familiar ring. It was much like the similar command to **"slow down"** I had heard several months before. Both times, I had a quickened awareness of God's personal attention, His tenderness, and patience. The Lord was eager to open the precious but dormant lines of communication He had placed deep within me. I was keenly aware of His willingness and desire to hear and to answer prayer.

Awestruck, yet dismayed at my own hard-headedness, I lowered myself from the bed to my knees. Names and prayer concerns gushed out of me, fluently and earnestly, until I ran out of words. With a grateful "Amen," I climbed back into bed and was asleep the moment my head hit the pillow.

Lazybones

In retrospect, it's as though a tender, smiling Jesus was nudging me, saying, **"Wake up, sleepyhead. I have something to say to you. This is no time to be a lazybones!"** That could account for my restless "lazy bones."

That night when I was roused from my slumber, I awoke to the sound of His voice. Although it was still and small, it was more than a whisper. It was a *call, a call to prayer.* And I had a choice—to respond in obedience, which takes effort and faith, or to brush aside the impulse with indifference.

The Lord had called me to prayer. I obeyed, and He answered with a resounding "yes" to the intercession I offered that night. Lynn reported that her insomnia mysteriously vanished as quickly as it came. Our friend Sue had an easy delivery and a healthy baby. Two friends who had been out of work for a long time found jobs. A coworker experienced an uncanny peace in the midst of a heart attack. Another friend's disposition improved dramatically, and her marriage did an about-face. Not to mention that, as a personal bonus, I awoke refreshed after my night of insomnia.

Would these things have happened in any case, whether I prayed or not? Skeptics might argue the point, but I'm not a skeptic—I'm a believer. It was important for me to respond to God's coaxing, especially in light of Hebrews 11:6:

> Without faith it is impossible to please God, because anyone who comes to Him must believe that He exists and that He rewards those who earnestly seek Him.

Sometimes the rewards are tangible, like God's "yes" answers to my prayers. At other times, the rewards are elusive, like the character building that comes from God's "no" or "wait" answers. At that stage in my walk of faith, I needed lots of positive reinforcement about prayer, and I got it! Still, what if I *had* tuned out those crisp, concise words and not prayed on my knees? I'll never know, because I was in the process of *tuning in.*

The Holy Spirit tutored me daily, revealing Himself through the pages of my Bible. Didn't He say He wanted me to become better acquainted with Him? Hadn't I actively sought the Holy Spirit's guidance? Wasn't I the one who had a hunger and thirst to know God's voice? Why, then, with this track record of preparation and desire, would I have so much trouble recognizing when God spoke to me? I believe it is because His voice is so quiet and sounded so much like my own thoughts.

Tuning in is an ongoing challenge. It's not something you can learn once and have down pat. Any meaningful relationship takes sensitivity to establish and nurture, and in this clamoring world, it's not easy to develop—let alone maintain—a quiet, sensitive spirit. The more I practice His presence, the easier it gets. But I suspect I've barely scratched the surface, especially when it comes to God's involvement in the practical stuff that makes up daily living—what some would call the insignificant things.

One day, for example, the Lord challenged me to allow the Holy Spirit to save me time. This time-saving experiment taught me that God not only delights in helping me with the nitty-gritty things in life, but He does it through the use of halts and nudges that are a part of His voice. I learned that nothing that touches my life is too big or too small for the Lord's attention and involvement. Not even . . .

Kim's Jeans

Kim needed new jeans for her class trip. She had grown two inches and could hardly bend over in her old ones, and I'd been promising for over a month to get her a new pair. The sixth graders were going to the Smithsonian Institute the next day, and I was down to the wire.

The chapter of *The Helper* open before me that morning was "He Saves Me Time," so I prayed that we'd be able to find Kim some jeans that fit and still get to bed on time (not only for her benefit but also for mine since I was one of the chaperones). Before leaving my attic prayer closet, my eyes rested on these words from pages 75–77:

> Lord Jesus, so often I ignore or ride roughshod over these strong inner feelings supplied by the Spirit. . . . What is willfulness in me, Lord, change. . . . Nothing could be more foolish than thinking I know better than You do. Help me this day, no matter how busy I get, to listen and to obey.

At the office, things were fairly slow, and my thoughts drifted back to the day's lesson. Could the Lord save me time if I heeded the voice of His Spirit? Around 11:00, I began to toy with the idea of using some overtime hours to make a quick run to the Salisbury Mall to look for Kim's jeans. My boss was in a meeting, so I arranged for someone to cover my desk. *I'm sure he won't mind,* I rationalized, *and it sure will save me time.* Off I went.

The 45-minute ride was, in a word, harrowing. I hardly ever speed, but I did that day. My thoughts kept time with the speedometer as I raced along. If it was difficult for me to recognize the Lord's voice in the quiet of my home, how could I ever hope to hear Him with cars and trees whizzing by my window?

My heart tugged and told me not to go, but I tried to ignore it. *Wonder if that nagging feeling is God's inner nudge? No,* I countered, *it's probably just my guilty conscience because I didn't get the official okay. Besides, I asked God to save me time, and this looks like a golden opportunity time-saver.*

"Listen. Don't go," the tug repeated. My heart thumped, but I sped on.

"Help me, no matter how busy I get, to listen and to obey."

Rounding the bend, an inner voice cautioned, **"Turn back; it's not too late."**

"Is that You, Lord?" I couldn't be sure. "If it is, please bear with me." Was I guilty of 'riding roughshod' over the strong inner feelings supplied by the Spirit? *Maybe I shouldn't buy Kim's jeans without having her along to try them on.* As I reconsidered my excursion, the internal struggle eased a bit. *My mind is made up!* I insisted. Again, something grabbed at my gut as I pressed on the accelerator.

"Turn back, turn back, turn back," the voice seemed to echo.

"Lord," I prayed, "if this is You and You're trying to keep me from having an accident or something, please make it clear."

"You're speeding."

"I know. I'll slow down."

"Go back. Don't waste your time."

"Lord, I'm sorry if I'm being bull-headed, but it's too late to turn back now; I'm over halfway there. Besides, this will be a good test. If I don't find any jeans in Kim's size, then I'll know it was Your voice after all. On the other hand, if I'm successful, then I'll chalk this up to a vivid imagination. Either way, I'll learn something. Thank You, Lord, for seeing me safely through this experiment."

I rushed into the store and before my very eyes stood a rack of 12-Slims, just what I was looking for. I scooped a pair of designer jeans off the rack and onto the sales counter where the cashier was quick to accept my credit card. I signed the form in haste, not paying any attention to the total.

An ear-splitting alarm sounded the moment my foot passed through the door on the way out. *What's that?* I jumped but kept on walking, although I could hear a distant voice calling, "Ma'am, oh, ma'am." When I turned around to see who was in trouble, the sales lady was racing toward me!

"What have I done?" My face flushed as she reached for the bag I was holding. She had forgotten to remove the security device from my purchase, and, although I was innocent of any wrongdoing, I had this eerie feeling that I'd been caught.

On the return trip, I concluded that I must not have been hearing the Lord's voice to turn around, after all. My mind must have been playing tricks on me. The jeans were easy enough to find, and there were no traffic complications. Back at the office, everything was fine. I was relieved but a bit puzzled about that inner tug. I really had hoped that it was the Lord.

But surprise, the jeans didn't fit! They were even tighter than Kim's old ones. My heart skipped wildly.

"So it was You, after all! That *is* what You sound like."

About that time, as if the ill-fitting jeans weren't proof enough, I noted the sales slip and the outrageous price I'd paid. "Thank You, Lord, for convincing me. Next time, help me not to doubt Your voice and to be more obedient."

Kim and I went shopping together that night, as originally planned. But this time, there was a difference. I was tuned in to the Lord's voice, and I wasn't racing around in a panic.

"You know where today's sales are, Lord. Where should we go?"

"Dover."

"Okay, here we are; which shopping center?"

"This one."

"Which store?"

"This one."

We drove into the parking lot and walked leisurely into the nearest store where Kim and I discovered a half-price sale and three pair of jeans that didn't pinch, pull, sag, bag, or need to be hemmed. We were home and tucked into bed that night by 9:15.

Eventually, I returned the unwanted jeans to Salisbury. Some might say, "What a waste," but I say, "What a workshop!" So many glorious lessons came out of that experience. It was almost as though God had enrolled me in a special "mobile classroom." The return trip provided valuable time for reflection. Never again will I think that God is too busy with important things to be bothered with my trivial concerns. Not only did I learn that the Holy Spirit cares enough to save me time, but I know He's big enough to pay attention to the tiniest detail and tolerant enough to deal with my clumsy experiments.

We don't need good hearing to detect the Lord's voice, just a sensitive, willing heart. I actually think the Holy Spirit delights in providing sensitivity training. Although the voice may be still and small, it is near. In fact, Luke 17:21 says, "The kingdom of God is within you"—in our very own hearts, souls, and minds.

But thoughts can be tricky. Not all inner nudges, promptings, impulses, or impressions come from God. The handcuffed, suicidal maniac I saw on the news who insisted, "God told me to do it!" as he was being thrust into the back seat of a squad car was responding to the voice of the god of destruction, not the God of heaven.

Checklist for Listening

How can we be sure it's God's voice we're hearing? Examine what the voice tells you in light of God's attributes. I compiled the following checklist as a tool to test the validity of any inner leading I may have. Let the truth of these points sink deep into your heart, soul, and mind.

1. **God will never lead me astray.**
   He won't ask me to do anything immoral, unethical, corrupt, vicious, dishonest, unkind, or unbecoming. If my morals or integrity are jeopardized in any way, the voice can't be His. *He is a God of righteousness.*

2. **God will never violate His Word.**
   He'll never ask me to do anything contrary to the Scriptures. Even if I can find a supporting passage, I must be careful not to twist it to suit my own needs but to consider the context in which it was written. *He is a God of honor.*

3. **God will never cause confusion.**
   He offers me peace, joy, and clarity of mind. If I'm experiencing anxiety or confusion, it's probably my own pandemonium, worldly pressure, or some unholy spirit—which I promptly and deliberately reject. *He is a God of order.*

4. **God will never bring condemnation.**
   He is compassionate, righteous, and just. While He insists on confronting me with my own sins and shortcomings, He'll never whip me with guilt. It isn't His desire to cripple me but to lead me in the ways of repentance and restoration. His trademark isn't incrimination but forgiveness. *He is a God of mercy.*

5. **God will never entertain discouragement.**
   He builds me up and calls forth courage. He doesn't throw in the towel, promote defeat, or look for easy escape routes. He offers power and victory, no matter how bad a mess I get myself into. *He is a God of hope.*

6. **God will never contradict Himself.**
   His message will never be in opposition to His nature which is unconditional love coupled with unwavering justice. God is love and His Word is truth. Christ's character and His law will always be reflected in the things His Spirit says. *He is a God of conviction.*

7. **God will never hurt me.**
   He is the Great Physician, the Healer, and the Restorer. He is the Good Shepherd, the Seeker of Lost Sheep, our Protector, and Guide. He is the Solid Rock, a ready Fortress and Refuge. *He is a God of grace.*

A test like this is imperative since human beings are basically vulnerable, like sheep. As believers and members of the flock of God, we need to stay very close to the Good Shepherd so we won't go astray. The Scriptures give assurance so we don't need to fret about being deceived:

> "The Watchman opens the gate . . . and the sheep listen to His voice. He calls his own sheep by name and leads them out . . . and His sheep follow Him because they know His voice. But they will never follow a stranger . . . because they do not recognize a stranger's voice" (John 10:3–5).

This whole concept of hearing the Lord's voice has its roots in *faith*. Remember, "Without faith it is impossible to please God" (Hebrews 11:6). The principle is to believe first, receive proof later.

It seems to be a "you'll-find-what-you're-looking-for" sort of deal, like a self-fulfilling prophecy. When you make a decision to believe, pretty soon you'll find that you *do* believe. If you expect to hear God's voice, the day will come when you will. But those who say, "Not me, I'll never be able to hear God's voice," somehow never do. The Lord does not reward scoffers.

The Voice with No Sound

In my early years of writing *Fruitbearer*, I was sitting in my prayer closet wondering about how to describe the "voice" of the Holy Spirit, so I asked the Lord what He would say. This is what came to me in the quiet of the morning:

"It is a language of the heart, the mind, and the soul. This kind of hearing does not involve the ears. My words are impressions sent from My Holy Spirit to your human spirit. They are more often sensed than heard. Look for a tug of the conscience, a strong conviction, a leading, or an internal halt. Sometimes My voice will come as a knowing, a keen awareness of My ways, often in stark contrast to your ways. My voice is available to all of My children, but it is heard best by the seeker who practices My presence. Are you willing to be quiet and wait for Me to reveal Myself?

"Even if you are eager to hear Me and willing to wait, you may not readily recognize My voice. Often, it will come as a single thought or phrase which will replay in your mind, over and over, like a broken record. Don't be surprised if you have difficulty separating My words from your own mental process. I expect to repeat My message several times, especially at first, in order to reach you. If you truly desire to establish a dialogue with Me, I will not tire of repeating the point until you have heard it with clarity.

"I will not tire of repeating the point until you have heard with clarity."

"Sometimes there will be no words, only a pervading sense of peace or joy or love. Sometimes I give only a strong sense of direction or a conviction of right and wrong. Do not strain for words that are not there.

"Have you embraced Me as your Savior? If so, My Holy Spirit dwells in you and is readily accessible. I, your Lord, stand ready to answer any questions you may have. My answers are reliable, sound, and comforting. And yet people run to and fro seeking

advice from every other source and from those who cannot help. Help is found in My Word, through My Spirit.

"Do you want to hear Me? Then do this: Read My Word, and seek My face. Ask Me questions. And be still. For it is in quietness that you will best learn to recognize My words as I plant them deep within your mind and heart. I will help you develop the sensitivity you need to recognize My Spirit."

Since the Holy Spirit abides within all true believers, we are already equipped with the capacity to receive communication from our Maker. He knows how to reach us and where we are; He knows what language to use and when we will be receptive. Because no two people are exactly alike, the Lord takes each unique personality and situation into consideration when He speaks to us.

Drew Gets the Message

One day Drew was stopped at a highway intersection, waiting for the light to change. A van blocked the view on his left. The light changed. Both Drew and the van hesitated.

"Something told me not to go," he said. "I could tell the traffic behind me was impatient. They were ready for me to move, but I didn't because I had an uneasy feeling, a feeling of danger. At the moment I would have crossed over, a car came flying through the intersection and ran the light! That guy had to be going 65 miles an hour or more. He never even attempted to slow down. If I had moved just ten feet, that car would have slammed into me, hitting me broadside."

What was the "something" that told Drew not to go? Was it common sense? An angel, perhaps? Or the voice of the Holy Spirit? We don't know. But it was undoubtedly divine intervention. Divine communication. Divine protection.

On another occasion, Drew detected the Lord's voice in a restaurant. We were discussing someone else's "lifestyle" from our own limited point of view. During an interval in our conversation,

Drew blinked and hesitated. Cocking his head sideways, he looked across the table at me with amazement.

"I just had the strangest thought," he said. "Out of the blue, it struck me, *'Are you the Judge?'* That's not the kind of question you go around asking yourself, is it? And yet it was so strong, so intense, so distinct. Do you think it could be . . ."

"The Lord?" I nodded. "Yes, honey, I do. It sounds just like something He might say. He doesn't mince words. During that same brief silence, a piercing thought flashed through my mind, as well: *'Judge not, that ye be not judged'* (Matthew 7:1 KJV). I think we're being called to account."

Hindrances to Hearing

Unfortunately, too many faithful, Spirit-filled Christians think that the ability to hear God's voice is reserved for only a chosen few. According to Dr. Charles F. Stanley, "When God speaks (and He does), everyone should listen." In his dynamic book, *How To Listen To God* (see Recommended Resources), he identifies ten specific hindrances to hearing:

1. Not knowing God
2. A poor self-image
3. A false sense of guilt
4. Busyness
5. Unbelief
6. God-directed anger
7. Harboring sin
8. A rebellious spirit
9. Rejecting God's messengers
10. Being untrained to listen

Regardless of how many obstacles stand between us and the voice of our Lord or how difficult they may seem, the Holy Spirit is eager and ready to help us overcome them. Those who are serious about obeying Psalm 5:3, "In the morning, O LORD, you hear my voice; in the morning I lay my requests before you and wait in expectation," are bound to encounter obstacles. Here are some strategies that have worked for me:

- *Are too many thoughts coming at once?* God is not the author of confusion (1 Corinthians 14:33). Ask the Lord to help you focus on *one* thought.

- *Are you afraid?* Psalm 111:10 says that the fear of the Lord (awe of the Lord) is the beginning of wisdom. Meditate on 2 Timothy 1:7 which assures us that God does not give a spirit of fear (or timidity) but a spirit of power, of love, and a sound mind (or self-discipline).

- *Are you distracted by thoughts of things to do?* Write them down and tend to them later. When you concentrate on developing a dialogue with God, you are seeking first the kingdom of heaven (Matthew 6:33). Go ahead—ask the Holy Spirit how to order your other priorities, and all these things will fall into place.

- *Are interruptions slowing you down?* Resist the devil's interference (James 4:7). Explain to your family how important your quiet time is to you. Ask for their help in protecting it (taking phone messages, for example). Keep experimenting to find your own private "trysting place," a place where you meet Someone Special. Your appointment is with the Author of Love.

- *Are you harboring sin in your life?* Even the sin of worry can act as a cloud that separates you from God. Confess it. Turn from it. Receive forgiveness. "If we confess our sins, God is faithful and just to forgive our sins, and to cleanse us from all unrighteousness" (1 John 1:9). Try talking it over with God.

- *Are you full of doubts?* Read James 1:5–8. Jesus is the Good Shepherd, and His sheep should know His voice. He will not lead His flock astray. Read John 10:1–16.

Becoming a good scriptural listener is an attribute well worth the effort it takes to develop. And it does take effort, especially if you want to hear the Lord's voice clearly enough to capture the words in writing.

Shall We Pray?

Thank You, Lord, for going to such great lengths to speak to each of us—through nature (the wind, earthquake, and fire); through Your Spirit (the still, small voice within); and through Your written Word. Give us wisdom in these trying times, when competing voices vie for our attention, to tune in to Your voice and Your priorities. Help us to be diligent in seeking You. And when we find You, give us courage to tell others the Good News.

WHAT CAN I DO FOR YOU, LORD?

DIG INTO SCRIPTURE

And when you turn to the right or when you turn to the left, your ears shall hear a word behind you, saying, "This is the way; walk in it" (Isaiah 30:21 NRSV).

You must understand this, my beloved: let everyone be quick to listen, slow to speak (James 1:19a NRSV).

GOD'S CALL: LISTEN AND OBEY

"Be anxious for nothing. Those who seek Me will find Me, and the peace of God, which is beyond your understanding, will keep your heart and mind attuned to My voice. Do not say, "I tried so hard to hear You, but I heard nothing." You did hear, for I spoke to your heart saying, "My grace is sufficient." Stay close to Me and I will teach you to comprehend My ways. Seek My face and you will know My voice. When you hear My voice, or even think you detect My counsel, obey it. Obey, and you will be blessed."

YOUR RESPONSE TO GOD

With the help of the Holy Spirit, I will actively seek to recognize the voice of God during the day and follow His direction. I will put a mental stopwatch on my conversations and keep track of how much I talk and how much I listen. When a good thought comes to mind, I will recognize it as coming from You and act on it.

SEED FOR THOUGHT

Manager to secretary: "I have a message of great importance
for all employees. Please connect me with the grapevine."

—*Author Unknown*

CHAPTER 5

GROW, BLOSSOM, SHARE WHAT YOU BELIEVE

"If you can't make a mistake,
you can't make anything."

—*Marva Collins*

"What I tell you in the dark, speak in the daylight."
—*Matthew 10:27*

Where would the church be if everybody kept what they believed to themselves? How would the Gospel be spread to the ends of the earth if nobody talked about it? Where would I be in my own faith journey if other believers hadn't shared their discoveries with me? Let me tell you how I learned about journaling the Lord's words in the first place.

"Sisters in Christ" was newly formed. Recently filled with the Holy Spirit (more about that in chapters six and seven), I had opened up and shared my experiences with the ladies. I was moving toward the door when a woman named Cathy pulled me aside.

"Could I talk with you for just a minute?" she asked.

"Sure," I said, glancing at my watch.

"I brought my journal along. I didn't know why at first, because it's, um, really private. I hadn't planned on showing it to anybody. But . . ." She hesitated, anxiously turning the hardbound notebook in her hand. "I know you keep a journal and, well, I want you to take a look at mine."

"Oh, Cathy," I said, trying to read the uncertainty in her eyes. "I couldn't do that. I know how personal journals can be. But thanks anyway."

"No," she said, looking almost offended. "You don't understand. I was hesitant at first because I didn't know why I brought it with me, but now I know. It's because there's something in here the Lord wants *you* to read. Please take it. Please. I would really like to know what you think about it."

"Sure," I smiled. "I'd consider it an honor. How soon would you like it back?"

"Oh, there's no hurry," she said with a smile. "Keep it as long as you like."

At home that night, I settled back to see what secrets Cathy's journal might contain. She had some poetry, some painfully honest and emotion-filled prose, a lot of prayers, some Bible verses, and carefully printed sections that appeared to be messages directly from God. Endearing salutations such as *"My child"* and *"little one"* were frequent. I'd never seen anything like it.

Journaling

My initial reaction was mixed. It seemed, quite frankly, a bit much. I mean, after all, who did this woman think she was, anyway? What audacity to actually write God's words on paper. But I couldn't deny the strong sense of awe, beauty, and peace that I felt each time I read one of those passages. There was an air of mystique about the words, but a familiar substance, too. The comfort they evoked in me outweighed my misgivings.

Could there be something to this? I wondered. *Is it okay to write in the first person as if God were speaking? Yes,* I decided. *There must be merit in capturing something so uplifting and edifying that could be read again and again.* I thought of the many times I'd felt God speaking personally to me, and I began to speculate. *Do I dare? Is it possible that I, too, might put in writing some of the things I feel God is telling me?* Tomorrow, I decided, I would ask the Helper about it.

Morning came, and with it, my search for wisdom.

"I've been learning to hear Your voice, Lord," I prayed as I ascended the attic stairs. Seated in my friendly folding chair, I continued. "You've spoken to me before, but I've never attempted to capture Your words in writing. If I'm wrong to do this, stop me now before I begin. I need Your guidance in this matter, Lord. Direct my thinking in accordance with Your will."

I sat quietly, reverently, and waited for His response. Nothing. No green light, but no stop sign either. After what seemed like an eternity, in an act of faith, I poised my pen above a blank sheet of paper.

"Here I go, I'm going to write something, Lord. I don't know what, but help me to lay hold of Your words." Instantly, my mind was flooded with thoughts. My brain propelled into high gear, spinning with a haze of words and phrases, huge amounts of wisdom, and vital insight, but in quantities too vast for me to comprehend or capture on paper. Too much to sort out. Where to begin?

"What's going on here?" I asked aloud, hoping to still my thoughts. But the mental uproar continued. *This is not right*, I concluded, and declared with authority, "My God is not a god of confusion!" With that pronouncement, one clear phrase surfaced above the whirlwind of all other thoughts.

"Candy, slow down. Relax. You're working too hard at this."

The words were comforting and distinct—a steady, persistent message. The jumble of other words faded away as this single phrase permeated my mind. It occurred to me that it might look silly, but with great diligence, I printed those very words on the page in front of me.

"Candy, slow down. Relax. You're working too hard at this."

Sounds from the kitchen below distracted me. *Only one person in this household can make that much noise fixing breakfast*, I thought as the aroma of scrapple and eggs seeped through the attic floor. *Troy sure can sling a frying pan.* I was proud of my stepson's initiative, despite my broken concentration. Struggling to regain it, I scribbled out a question for the Lord.

"But what about interruptions?"

It was a beginning. As I put my question on paper, an answer nudged forward. I started printing the concise words as they came, one or two at a time.

"I am the Father of all things, even interruptions. You are simplistic; I am . . ." (I couldn't bring myself to write the next word.)

Intrinsic?

What kind of word is that? I didn't think it should be used in that context and couldn't bring myself to write it. So, in mid-sentence, I got up from my seat and made a dash for the dictionary. My heart skipped a beat, and my eyes widened as I read the definition: "belonging to a thing by its very nature." *Just like He told Moses.* I gasped. *"I AM WHO I AM"* (Exodus 3:14).

In awe, with heightened confidence and a gigantic lump in my throat, I found my way back to the chair. As I wrote the word "intrinsic," my train of thought picked up right where it left off, as if it had been suspended in time.

"Although life is complex, you are not to focus on the outward or the external, for the kingdom of God is within you. Seek to become quiet. There is much I have to say, but I will not compete with the noise of the world. Draw closer to Me, and I will draw closer to you."

"I'm afraid," I wrote on the page in front of me.

"Do not be afraid. Have I ever hurt you?"

"No."

"I am love. Love does not seek to hurt but to cherish. You are very precious to Me."

Even so, I was tense, unsure of whether or not I should write these things.

"Relax. Go ahead, write. I will give you the words. I will also give you assignments and help you carry them out. Be aware that I am with you—and in you. Trust Me."

That was it. "That's all she wrote," as my dad would say. I was eager to share my journaling with Drew, but I was apprehensive about his reaction. With tact and timing evading me, I hot-footed it down the stairs.

"Oh, hon," I blurted out as I barged into the bathroom to find him leaning toward the mirror with shaving cream on his face. "You've got to read this!" After he put his razor down and patted his face with a towel, I handed my prayer journal to him like a hot potato and disappeared into the other room, praying that he wouldn't think his wife had gone bonkers.

He took his time reading it. When at last he spoke, his words were quiet and few. "That's really something, isn't it?" It was more of a statement than a question, and I detected a touch of astonishment, some hesitancy, but at the same time, obvious support.

Drew is my balance. He observes my spiritual growth with a protective eye, and I count on the Lord to speak through him to help me keep things in perspective. If I get off-track, Drew is the first to notice and caution me. That day, he wasn't wary, but he was intrigued.

Unworthy?

A week later, I returned Cathy's journal to her with deep gratitude that the Lord used her to open this realm to me. I continued to journal daily. In those early days, I often wondered if the words would even form complete sentences. They did. Sentences that have influenced the course of my life. Sentences that often left me in awe.

"I feel so unworthy to be writing Your words, Lord."

"Moses felt unworthy. Is it not fitting for you to feel unworthy as well? The yielded, humble spirit is of great value to Me. If you felt worthy, you would be of little use as a vessel for My purposes, for your own ego would be in the way. I do not speak through the proud but through the meek."

"Why is it, Lord, that You are encouraging me to do this?"

"To strengthen you, My beloved. The manifestation of the Spirit is always given for the common good."

"I am honored that You have found favor with me. I want to be a willing and obedient servant. Forgive my shortcomings. You know them all. I am not worthy. This seems like an overwhelming responsibility."

"Worry not about being worthy, My child, for I am your worthiness. Do not be anxious. The burden I give is light. Keep your eyes on Me, that you may know the joy of the Lord. I am your God, and I call you unto Myself for a good purpose."

Becoming Fluent

Week after week, month after month, I diligently recorded our conversations. In time, my dialogue with the Lord became more fluent. The more I journaled, the more questions I had.

"Lord," I asked at one point, "is this prophecy?"

"Seek not to name your gift but to use it wisely. You have not been given the title of prophet, but of servant. You are a mouthpiece for the Lord and will serve Me well, if you simply bring forth My words in love."

Mouthpiece, eh? I'm a mouthpiece, all right, I chuckled. But I didn't have the foggiest notion of how to "bring forth" the words He wanted me to share. In June of 1984, I received some insight.

"Seek not to name your gift but to use it wisely."

"The time for Me to speak plainly to My children is now. The messages you will be asked to deliver to My beloved must be loving, clear, and bold, for there is much to be accomplished in a brief time. You cannot lead others where you have not been, My child. So take My hand and let Me guide you more deeply into My Word. There is a great deal yet for you to learn. Come away with Me now into the deepest recesses of your prayer closet, and I will strengthen you for the task ahead. Be refreshed in My teachings."

"I come to You, Lord, with deeply mixed emotions: great honor and joy that You would call an ordinary person like me to handle such responsibility, and great anxiety about how people may react to this whole concept of hearing Your voice."

"Answer this, My child: Have you not entrusted your very life to Me?"

"Totally."

"Would I allow any life that has been entrusted into My care to suffer harm?"

"No, I guess not. Unless it has a higher purpose."

"Have I not promised to guide and to strengthen you so that you will be like a well-watered garden and a spring whose waters never fail?"

"Yes, Lord. It's in Your Word, Isaiah 58:11."

"Have I not commanded that you cast your cares upon Me?"

"Is it a command?"

"It is. Will you obey it?"

"I will, Lord. In fact, I do! Right now, in an act of will and through faith, I place my cares on Your shoulders. Thank You for lifting the fear of tomorrow from my heart today, even though I don't feel any relief yet."

"Dwell not on what you feel, dear one. Dwell only on Me. Submit yourself to My direction that I might communicate afresh with My children. Fret not over what you are to say, for I will help you write what is needed. You are not alone in this work. I have called others to similar assignments, and I am helping them, also, to be heard and respected. Trust Me. And obey. You will grow in confidence as you find My words confirmed in the mouths of other witnesses."

Other Witnesses

At the time, I knew of only one other person who could "hear God." But now I know plenty! Dozens of books have been published on the subject of hearing God's voice over the past decade. Two of my long-time favorites are Charles Stanley's best-seller, *How to Listen to God*, and Frances Roberts' prophetic devotional, *Come Away My Beloved* (see Recommended Resources).

Those of us who hear God's voice with clarity seem to have a number of common denominators:

- A curiosity about the deep things of God.

- A hunger and thirst for righteousness.

- An unwavering trust in and dependence upon the Holy Spirit.

- A personal and private relationship with Jesus Christ as Savior and Lord.

- A heart for prayer.

- An uncommon kind of love for people, even the unlovable, and a keen desire to serve others—often in secret, which gives glory to God.

- An insistence that the message ring true with the "whole counsel of God" as revealed in the Scriptures.

I was fascinated when I discovered how the Lord's words to one person will often confirm what He is saying to another. I shouldn't be surprised, though, because it is the voice of the same Spirit. Two recurring themes keep coming through loud and clear to those who hear the Lord: ***"Behold, I am coming soon!"*** and *"I love you, My child."* He cares deeply about us as individuals.

My daughter, once more, serves as a good example of how deeply the Lord cares for His children.

A Message for Kim

During a tender bedtime moment in Kim's pre-teen years, I felt it was time to share the contents of my journal with her.

"If you ask Him," she wanted to know, "do you think God will give you a message for me?"

I told her I didn't know, but I would pray about it. Although I don't make a practice of seeking messages from the Lord on behalf of others, in this instance, it seemed appropriate.

Few people know that Kim grew up with the stigma of a learning disability. From the ages of six to eleven, she was on Ritalin and enrolled in special education classes through the ninth grade. When she was in second grade, a psychiatrist told me that Kim "may never be able to read a complete sentence." That professional was wrong.

Not only did Kim earn a master's degree (with honors throughout college), but she went on to become a special education teacher at East Millsboro Elementary, where she was named Teacher of the Year in 2004.

Grateful for the Lord's help in overcoming her learning disability, she wanted me to include this account in hopes that it would encourage someone who may be struggling with a handicap like ADD (Attention Deficit Disorder).

That night in her bedroom, her struggles to cope with the normal insecurities of adolescence were compounded by a nagging self-doubt because of her learning disability and a growing tendency to think of herself as "stupid," a name she frequently called herself.

As I approached my journal the next morning, one word penetrated my thoughts, *"Kimberly."* So I wrote it down. The rest flowed:

"Kimberly, My precious. You are so very dear to Me. There are many things I have to teach you, but we must go slowly if the lessons are to last. Be not sad or disappointed if you are not able to read as well as you like, but trust Me to help you with each word. Your learning disability is not a drawback in My eyes, but rather an opportunity for you to grow closer to Me.

"You see, it is important to know that without Me it is difficult to do anything. Your own efforts are good and pleasing to Me, but there is something more I want you to do: Ask Me to help you. Invite Me to come into your mind to help you think in a new way. Trust Me to do for you what you cannot do for yourself. This is what I want all My children to know and do, and yet most do not listen and do not obey.

"I know you, because I created you, Kim. I know that you want to understand what I am saying and that you want to do what is right and good. Do not expect a miracle but look to Me as your personal Friend and Adviser. As you seek My kingdom and My righteousness, all these things shall be added unto you" (Matthew 6:33 KJV).

"When Kim reads this, dear Lord, she will probably want to know how to do what You're asking of her. Can You give her some direction when she's ready to respond?"

"Dearest Kimberly, do not be afraid, but come alone to meet Me. I am Jesus. When you were nine, you asked Me to live in your heart, remember? This is possible because of My Spirit.

"I want you to know Me better. My Holy Spirit will help you. One of the ways you can learn more about Me is by listening to My voice. It is very quiet—only a whisper in your thoughts—but you will be able to hear it.

"Here is what I want you to do: Go to a place where you can be alone. Sit there in silence until you feel calm and quiet inside. Then ask Me to come to you. You could say, 'Come to me, Jesus,' or 'Speak to me, Lord.' Your heart will tell you of My presence.

"Think on those things that come into your mind. If the thoughts are good, you can trust that I am in them. You are safe in My presence. So come, and listen to the words I have for you."

Several weeks passed, but still it didn't seem the right time to share this journal entry with my daughter.

Esther

Meanwhile, my friend Esther asked if I had any suggestions on how she might learn to tune in to the Lord's voice. I figured if the Lord thought this approach was good enough for my budding teenager, maybe it would work for Esther, too, so I shared the *"come alone to meet Me"* part of Kim's instructions with her.

"Oh, Candy!" she gushed into the phone the next morning. "I got under the covers last night and pulled them right up over my head—it was the only place I could find to be alone. Well, I got all quiet inside. And honey, when I prayed those words, 'Come to me, Jesus,' the Holy Ghost overwhelmed me so, I thought I was on my way to heaven!" Although Esther did not hear any "words" until much later, she experienced the immediate and powerful presence of a holy and loving God. For days she bubbled over.

Back to Kim

As for Kim, the right time came for me to share my journal with her, oddly enough, on a day when she got up on the wrong side of the bed. She met my cheerful "good morning" with a scowling response, "Go away."

I did. She followed me into the kitchen.

"I'm hungry," she grumbled. "Fix me some breakfast."

I answered her command with a sigh and a tolerant smile. *So this is what it's like to be the mother of a teenager.*

"Didn't you hear me?" she barked. "I said, I'm hungry!"

Nothing I said or did improved her disposition. Eventually, I retreated to my prayer closet for some insight on how to handle this tough cookie who, just yesterday, was a sweet child. Armed with a sense of direction, determined love, and my prayer journal, I decided—deep breath—the time was right. I came back downstairs.

"Remember that night we talked about my journal?" I began. "Well, I prayed like I promised I would, and there's a special message in here for you. Want to read it?"

"No." Her posture was defiant—jaws clenched, eyes riveted to the blaring Saturday morning television.

"It might help you feel better about things," I said.

Self-incrimination kept her at bay.

"It's a nice message, honey," I coaxed. "God's not going to scold you or anything like that. Here, how about reading a couple of lines?"

"How do I know you didn't make it up yourself?" she challenged.

"Well," I said, "it *was* my pen that wrote the words, but the Lord put the thoughts in my mind."

I could see she was skeptical. "Mom," she whined, "I just don't want to read it now. Do I have to?"

"Of course not," I said, "but I'll leave it right here in case you change your mind. I have a big grocery list to tackle." Giving her a parting hug, I left.

I prayed in the car. "Lord, there they are . . . Kim and that journal . . . all alone in the house. Give her an extra measure of curiosity, and when she opens those pages, meet her between the lines."

Arriving home from the store, I could tell at a glance that a transformation had taken place. Kim's gloomy frown was now a soft, sunny expression. Her disheveled hair was washed and wrapped in a blue towel. Her complexion glowed. My pre-teenager was actually serene.

"Oh, by the way," I asked as casually as I could, "did you read those pages?"

"Yes," she smiled sheepishly. "You knew I would."

"I prayed that you would," I said, turning my full attention to her and ignoring the carton of ice cream on the counter. "Did the Lord have anything to say to you after you read it?"

She paused and then whispered, "Just *'I love you. I love you, My child.'*"

"Oh, Kim, honey!" I scooped her into my arms. "That says it all! God's love for us is more important than anything."

She helped me put the groceries away, and we talked about how God's love had helped transform her bad mood into a good one. We talked, too, about where the words originated.

"Even if they do come from us," Kim reasoned, "God had to put them in our heads in the first place, because without God our brains wouldn't work at all." Childlike logic. Budding faith.

Esther's Praise Report

You may wonder how Esther eventually learned to hear the Master's voice. It began the day she asked if I would "journal" to see if the Lord might have some special insight for her regarding a certain situation. I told her I'd be happy to. But the moment those words were out of my mouth, it was as though a cement wall went up all around me.

"Esther," I said, "on second thought, maybe I'd better not. I'm getting a definite halt on that. But if the Lord gives me anything, I'll be sure to let you know."

In short order, it became clear to me that my journal was not to be used for fortunetelling. Furthermore, I felt strongly that the Lord wanted to talk with her Himself, not through me. This wasn't the message Esther anticipated, but she was receptive and even apologetic for putting me on the spot.

"Do you really think the Lord will speak directly to me?" she asked. And then she lamented in the same breath, "But I don't know how I'd ever hear Him."

I had no doubt that the Holy Spirit wanted to help her find a way to communicate more fully with Him. We talked about the importance of being reverent, expectant, quiet, patient, surrendered, repentant, open, and well-rooted in the Scriptures. Esther has a music ministry and the voice of an angel, so I suggested that she set the tone by beginning with songs of praise. Then I suggested a fill-in-the-blank approach.

I felt strongly that the Lord wanted to talk with her Himself.

"After you're in an attitude of worship," I said, "sit down and write the words, 'My child,' on a blank piece of paper and pay attention to the thoughts that come into your mind. Maybe the Lord will give you words to complete the sentence."

God honored her praises and her longing. Following a time of heartfelt adoration, as an act of faith, Esther printed *"My child"* on a blank piece of paper, hoping that the Lord might plant other words in her mind. He did. Beautiful words. Words that drew her to the foot of the Father's throne. Esther is not the flowery type, yet the language that flowed from her pen was like poetry. One sentence troubled her, though. She felt it was presumptuous to refer to herself as *"a jewel in the Lord's crown."*

"I thought I must have made up the whole thing myself," she said. "As far as I knew, there was no scriptural basis for such a thing, and I figured I'd gotten carried away. But—bolt that chair to the floor, honey—and listen to what I found in Malachi 3:17 of my King James Bible: "And they shall be Mine, saith the LORD of hosts, *in that day when I make up My jewels.*"

Take my word for it, Esther really is a gem!

But Remember

The Canon (the sixty-six books that comprise the Holy Bible) is closed. God's words to our spirits are not "in addition to" the Scriptures. Rather, they are "personalized promptings" to draw us more deeply into it. Be careful not to fall into the trap of giving the internal word He speaks to your heart *(rhema)* more attention than you do the living Word He calls you to read *(logos)*.

If we are to be successful in hearing and responding to the Lord's voice and surprised by the power of His Spirit, there's an essential quality we need to foster: a willingness to surrender our preconceived notions and personal prejudices.

Are you ready? Reflect with me for a moment on the words of James 4:10:

Humble yourselves before the Lord, and He will lift you up.

Shall We Pray?

Lord Jesus, I humble myself before You, awed by how much You care for me. Well aware of how little I truly know about the mystery of Your ways, I love You and want to make myself vulnerable to You. In my desire to walk more closely and intimately with Your Holy Spirit, I invite You to plow up patches of my soul that have not yet been tilled. In my powerlessness, I yearn for Your power. I hunger for Your spiritual gifts and, although I may receive a lesson in waiting, I know that Your gifts are good and perfectly timed. When at last, with Your help, I come to a place of complete abandonment, I count on You to meet me there and transform my life.

$\mathcal{W}$HAT CAN I DO FOR YOU, LORD?

DIG INTO SCRIPTURE

Read Mark 4:3–20.

Where do you fit in this parable?

GOD'S CALL: GROW IN FAITH

"As fertile soil, let My Word sink deep into your heart where it can minister to your innermost needs. Then, as My words take root in your life, they will grow into a mature faith, visibly blossoming so others may notice and be able to benefit many times over from what has been sown in your life. Perhaps you are still uncertain of what you believe. There is no shame in this if you are earnestly seeking the truth. Be patient with yourself and ask My Holy Spirit to open your mind and heart, for you cannot expect to understand the things of the spiritual realm through human reasoning."

YOUR RESPONSE TO GOD

Record your feelings and/or observations in a spiritual journal. Notebook paper will do for starters, or you might want to purchase a bound journal from your local bookstore. If the Lord were to respond to what you have written, what would He say? Do you dare to write down the words He speaks to your heart?

 SEED FOR THOUGHT

"Each time we ask more of ourselves
than we think we are able to give
and we manage to give it, we grow."

—*Bert Decker*

CHAPTER 6

PLOW UP UNTILLED GROUND

If God is your co-pilot,
switch seats.

—*Author Unknown*

"Sow for yourselves righteousness,
reap the fruit of unfailing love,
and break up your unplowed ground;
for it is time to seek the LORD, until He comes
and showers righteousness on you."
—Hosea 10:12

Someone once told me, "Don't be afraid to go out on a limb—that's where the fruit is." I'm out on a limb now. So how did I get here?

- First, God brought me to my knees in prayer.
- Through prayer, He taught me to commit time to Him in private devotions.
- Devotions led me deeper into the Scriptures which came to life as the Holy Spirit quickened my heart to the truths I read.
- Then He instilled within me a keen desire to hear His voice and spoke to me through my prayer journal.
- Motivated by the things the Lord spoke to me, I began to share my beliefs and discoveries with others.
- Now He wants to encourage you to break up some unplowed ground in your own heart.

Notice this was all God's doing, but it required a response. Grab hold as I inch my way along this fruit-laden limb and reflect on what was required in order for me to discover God's power.

I had to follow Him to untilled fields I didn't know even existed and tromp around in soil where the gifts of the Spirit grow. I had to allow Him to instill in me a curiosity about what it might be like to cultivate such tough turf as "tongues." I had to invite Him to plow through some misconceptions and irrigate every crevice of my being with streams of living water.

What I'm talking about is my own personal Pentecost—my mountaintop experience of March 31, 1983—when the fullness of Christ Jesus surged through my body, flooding me with peace, joy, and the love of God. This experience is referred to as the "baptism in the Holy Spirit." Consider the words of John the Baptist:

> "I baptize you with water for repentance. But after me will come one who is more powerful than I, whose sandals I am not fit to carry. He will baptize you with the Holy Spirit and with fire. His winnowing fork is in His hand, and He will clear His threshing floor, gathering his wheat into the barn and burning up the chaff with unquenchable fire" (Matthew 3:11–12).

The same One who baptizes with the Holy Spirit is the One who decides what is "wheat" (to be gathered into His barn) and what is "chaff" (to be burned with unquenchable fire). I want to be wheat, which is why I'm so intent on studying the Word of God and applying it to my life. We all have wheat and chaff within us. The wheat in us bows in humility, while the chaff stands up in the form of pride, vanity, ambition, jealousy, and so forth. This spiritual chaff must be burned out of us so we can draw closer to the Lord and walk in the fullness of His call on our lives. He nourishes us. Then, as our wheat matures, He causes the seed from our field to nurture others.

As I became better acquainted with the Holy Spirit in 1983, I realized how little I knew about God's power and righteousness. As He instructed, I went s-l-o-w-l-y that first month. I saturated myself with Scripture by meditating daily on the lessons the Holy Spirit gave me, and basked in moments when the Lord stilled my heart and stirred my soul. With every passing day, my hunger and thirst for "something more" deepened. It seemed unquenchable, yet the Bible promises,

> "Blessed are those who hunger and thirst for righteousness, *for they will be filled*" (Matthew 5:6, emphasis added).

Filled. Filled with the power of His righteousness. That's what I needed! To know for sure that I had given myself totally, without reservation, to Jesus and that He, in turn, had released in full measure the power of His Holy Spirit within me.

I wasn't looking for a mountaintop experience; all I knew was I had an aching void in my life that only Christ could fill. In my search for the Holy Spirit, I discovered some vital things.

Preliminary Lessons

Proper motives. The whole point of the Holy Spirit releasing His power in us is not so we can enjoy an emotional high (although emotions are often involved), but that He might empower us for service and witnessing (Acts 1:8). The focus is on the Baptizer, not on the baptism; we seek the Giver, not the gift.

Skeptics. Some people are skeptical of spiritual gifts such as prophecy, tongues, miraculous healing, and so forth. This may be due to a lack of personal knowledge (consider Hosea 4:6 that says, "My people are destroyed for lack of knowledge"), or erroneous teachings they receive in church. Or perhaps these skeptics have had a spiritual experience and it wasn't good. Unfortunately, the gifts of the Spirit, entrusted to imperfect human beings, are sometimes misused or distorted.

Is there such a thing as demonic tongues? Probably. After all, the devil is in the business of imitating and distorting the things of God. Should that keep us from pursuing godly gifts? No, a thousand times no! Beware of mystical counterfeits, yes. But, as the Scriptures warn, "Do not put out the Spirit's fire; do not treat prophecies with contempt. Test everything. Hold on to the good" (see 1 Thessalonians 5:19–21). We are known by our fruit.

In the book of Acts, the believers reacted with doubt when they heard that the Gentiles also had received the Word of God. They were convinced it was genuine only after Peter explained that the gift of the Holy Spirit had been poured out on the Gentiles "in the same manner" as the Holy Spirit had come upon them.

What was the persuasive evidence that changed their minds? Speaking in tongues, witnessing with power, and praising God.

Peter's conclusion is as appropriate for doubters today as it was for the first skeptical Christians: "So if God gave them the same gift as He gave us, who believed in the Lord Jesus Christ, who was I to think that I could oppose God?" (Acts 11:17).

God never changes. Since the apostle Peter felt it necessary to question "Who was I to think that I could oppose God?," then his position is good enough for me. What I want God to be and how I want Him to behave doesn't mean a hill of beans. What matters is what God says about Himself. The Scriptures say that God never changes. Malachi 3:6 reads, "I the LORD do not change." Hebrews 13:8 says, "Jesus Christ is the same yesterday and today and forever." As for His method of dealing with mankind, the way God sees fit to deal with each successive generation is up to Him. I respect that. And I'm glad to be part of a generation that's learning to hear His heart-cry to "be filled with the Spirit."

"Filled" sounds like past tense, but the infilling of the Spirit is an ongoing process, not a one-time event. Ephesians 5:18 says to "be filled with the Spirit;" in the Greek this means "continually being filled." The living water I've tapped into comes from a well that never runs dry. In Jesus' words,

> "Whoever drinks the water I give him will never thirst. Indeed, the water I give him will become in him a spring of water welling up to eternal life" (John 4:14).

In 1983, I had a vast reservoir of water stored securely in a tank labeled "self-will." When I was filled with the Holy Spirit, it was as though all the plugs were pulled, and I was flooded with a euphoric inner cleansing. An exchange took place. As willfulness gushed out, the power of God rushed in to saturate the one secret place I had reserved for my own personal control. Since then, the joy and the oneness with God I experienced on that occasion have lessened in intensity, but the river still flows because it's perpetual. Fresh waves of spiritual discovery splash over me repeatedly, like the ebb and flow of the ocean.

Preparation, Consecration, Service

Let's take a minute to look at how the earthly life of our Lord depicts a three-fold process, a journey that included:

1. A time of preparation
2. High points of consecration and
3. A period of day-in, day-out service to others

All of these steps were necessary for Christ to complete His earthly mission from the manger in Bethlehem to the cross in Jerusalem.

Preparation. The birth of Christ was foretold for centuries. Then, at a precise moment in earthly time, those prophecies were fulfilled. God was born in human flesh in the unlikely setting of a stable (with common, ordinary people playing major roles). That event was followed by a period where Jesus grew strong in body and in spirit, discovering and preparing for His mission. He sat under the teaching of His parents, rabbis, and other people during those years as life experiences shaped His mind and heart.

Consecration. When He was eight days old, Jesus was taken to the temple by His parents where He was circumcised and formally presented to God. As an adult, Jesus—the Christ, the promised Messiah—walked up to His cousin, John, to be baptized. (Note: John had spent years preparing for that moment but didn't know when, where, or how it would happen until he saw Jesus coming toward him.) During the sacrament of baptism, John saw the Holy Spirit come down from heaven in the visible form of a dove (Matthew 3:16). This isn't to imply that Jesus didn't communicate with the Father before this. For the most part, the unrecorded history of Christ reflects His time of personal preparation and development. The water baptism and subsequent witness of the Holy Spirit's empowerment was the beginning of His public ministry.

Service. Jesus' public ministry began on the day of His baptism. Up until then, He had performed no miracles. Even when endorsed by the Father and fully equipped by the Spirit, Jesus didn't attempt to exercise His power. See Matthew 3:17 where a voice from heaven says, "This is My Son, whom I love; with Him I am well pleased." Jesus' first order of business was to retreat for forty days to be alone with His Father and undergo a time of personal testing. Physically weak but spiritually strong, He came out of the wilderness and went straight to work.

His work still bears fruit from the seeds planted at the dusty feet of His disciples during those three short years. His ministry didn't end on the cross, or after His resurrection, or even when He ascended to heaven forty days later. He continues to carry out His mission through believers in our generation, just as He did through those who came before us—ordinary people who are willing vessels for the Holy Spirit.

Personal Application

Translating this three-step process into the present day, let's think about the different stages of our own lives. As I recount my preparation, consecration, and service, take a minute to think about how the Lord has been at work in you over the years, drawing you ever closer to Christ.

My *preparation* began in New Jersey on the day I was born. By the time I was ready for first grade, my parents had saved enough money to buy a small farm in Delaware. Dad worked three jobs; Mom was a homemaker; and my brothers and I enjoyed rural life with our calf, kittens, bunnies, and homegrown strawberries. There, Sunday school emerged as a most important aspect of my world. But my comfort zone changed when I was twelve and Dad, a civil servant with the Air Force, moved our family to Bermuda. During the next five years, my limited horizons were stretched and my values deepened. I can think of many individuals who played key roles during my years of slow, steady spiritual and emotional growth. The faces of special people come to mind—teachers who cared, summer camp counselors, a chaplain and his wife, parents who chaperoned dances, and friends.

What circumstances and influences come to mind from your younger years?

My *consecration* occurred as a baby, when my family dedicated me to God through infant baptism; later, as a teenager, when I recognized my need for a Savior and invited Christ into my life; then, as an adult, when I became a member of the church and made a public confession of my faith; and on March 31, 1983, when I fully surrendered my spirit to God. Since then, I have been baptized in a river and anointed with oil.

Does it stir your soul to reflect on times when the Lord met you in sacred circumstances? Is there a longing in you now to experience His presence in consecrated service?

My *Christian service* has become a daily challenge and adventure, and I suspect the same is true for you. If you take time to think about the ways you are already serving others, you may be delighted to discover God's power is already at work in you. If so, are you relying on the Holy Spirit from moment to moment and responding to those inner nudges and checks in your spirit?

Powerless Without Him

If ever a generation needed power for service and sensitivity to the Holy Spirit, it's ours! I'm writing this in the wake of hurricanes Wilma, Rita, Katrina, and Andrew; the tsunami in Asia; Mid-west floods; and the earthquake in Pakistan. Scenes of the devastation are vivid reminders that comfort and pleasure can turn into calamity and poverty overnight. If you and I are to be the ones who minister love to a callous world in Jesus' name, we need the boldness, the confidence, and the compassion of Christ Himself. We need the *fullness* of the Spirit, not just His presence.

> "Nation will rise against nation, and kingdom against kingdom. There will be famines and earthquakes in various places. All these are the beginning of birth pains. Because of the increase of wickedness, the love of most will grow cold, but he who stands firm to the end will be saved. And this Gospel of the Kingdom will be preached in the whole world as a testimony to all nations, and then the end will come" (Matthew 24:7–8, 12, 14).

As evil grows stronger, gains momentum, and becomes more brazen and demanding, what are we going to do about it? While some are sacrificing their lives on behalf of others, many of us are nodding our heads and greeting each other with polite hellos on Sunday morning. If there's any fight in us at all, it's to hold onto our comfortable lifestyles. I don't think this is the picture our Lord had in mind when He said, "I will build My church, and the gates of Hades will not overcome it" (Matthew 16:18).

The Carpenter from Nazareth doesn't do sloppy work. Anything He builds is built right! While the church of good intentions I just described was built with human hands, the overcoming church will be built by Jesus Himself. He's in the process even now of nailing together, piece by piece, the true church—strong enough to stand up against the evils that confront us and capable of taking the Gospel to the whole world as a testimony. When our Master Builder has completed His spiritual construction in us, we'll be strong, united, filled with the power of His love and have a heart for service.

Indwelling Versus Empowering

One of the big differences I've noticed since my baptism in the Holy Spirit is that I have a deeper sense of purpose in my life and a healthy confidence in the work I do for Jesus. In the past, my Christian service carried a lot of "what ifs" and "shoulds." Those were signs that I was trying to function on my own. I know now that I'm powerless without Him.

Just as there's a difference between knowing *about* Christ and *knowing* Christ, there's also a difference between the *indwelling* and the *empowering* of the Holy Spirit. Salvation is the First Blessing, while the empowering of the Spirit is the Second.

Paul Walker writes (*New Spirit Filled Life Bible*, p. 1851), "It should be understood that . . . 'baptism in the Holy Spirit' . . . does not refer to that baptism *of* the Holy Spirit accomplished at conversion, whereby the believer is placed *into* the body of Christ by faith in His redeeming work on the cross (1 Corinthians 12:13). Thus, no biblically oriented Charismatic ever views a non-Charismatic as 'less saved' or less spiritual than himself."

Prayer Quest

On March 10, 1983, I began my quest for empowerment with a written prayer for the gift of the Holy Spirit. In keeping with the importance of seeking the Baptizer rather than the baptism, I wrote:

I give my entire self to You, Lord—not most, not part. Empty me completely of self, and fill me with Your presence in the form of the Holy Spirit that I may live the rest of my days through Your eyes.

Later that day, I added:

> By faith, today, I believe my request for the gift of the Holy
> Spirit has been answered in a quiet and gentle, inconspicuous
> way. I thank You, Lord, and eagerly await Your work in and
> through me.

Although there was no clear manifestation that day, my prayer
was in keeping with God's will, and *by faith* I knew it had been
accomplished. Looking back, I can see that my prayer was, indeed,
answered immediately. I asked the Spirit to move in my life, and He
did. Watch how my prayer focus and desires changed in the days
that followed.

Power to Witness. On Empowerment Day Two, I cried for a
readiness to witness for God. For the first time in my life, I was
willing to move out into the world to reach lost souls.

> I seek not joy, experience, or even peace, but You, Lord—
> Your power for service in order that I may witness with ease,
> confidence, and passion instead of self-consciousness. Use
> me for effective results, not "good tries," in bringing others
> into Your light.

Compassion. Much to my surprise on Empowerment Day Three,
my heart was heavy with concern for world hunger and missionaries
who desperately struggle to feed the poor and spread the Gospel.

> Give direction, dear God, on what financial support You desire
> me to give to those sacrificially serving those who cannot help
> themselves.

Hunger for His Word. Empowerment Day Four disclosed a
growing desire to study the Word of God. Realizing I needed to be
more than just "familiar" with it, I prayed:

Lord, give me a heart-knowledge of the Bible and help me recall passages when I need them.

An interesting thing began to happen to me. The more I read the Bible, the more my prayers centered on *others* instead of on myself. The more passages I committed to memory, the more truth I learned about my own nature, which brought conviction and . . .

Confession. For someone who considered herself a "good person," I was surprised at how many sins I found to confess. But I asked for it, because I had prayed for the Lord to reveal areas of my life that needed to be addressed. Wayward thoughts and bad habits loomed over me until I laid them at His feet.

Oh Lord, how I love to tell a good joke and make people laugh, but some of them are dirty and I know that displeases You. I don't want to lose the ability to entertain people, but I want the words of my mouth to be pleasing to You. Please help.

My conscious yearning to be "right with Him" started then and continues to this day. The joy and peace of approaching my Lord in an attitude of honest remorse and repentance is so cleansing that it's something I've come to relish rather than resist. Oh, about those dirty jokes, the Lord sure does have a sense of humor. How did He help me overcome my bad habit? By blocking my ability to remember the punch lines!

Eagerness. Another thing that came out of my prayer for the gift of the Holy Spirit was an increased enthusiasm for my morning quiet time. Somewhere along the line, it changed from something I wanted to do to something I could hardly wait to do! I was truly developing a heart for God and beginning to understand how Christ must have looked forward to a daily time of undisturbed communion with His Father.

Be with me, heavenly Father, as I search the pages of my Bible. Open the eyes of my heart while I read.

Passages I had never noticed before began to jump off the page. Where I had previously skimmed over references to tongues, now I was curious.

This Thing Called "Tongues"

I was intrigued yet baffled by how many times the subject of tongues was mentioned in the New Testament. I was equally puzzled by the apostle Paul's attitude toward this mysterious phenomenon, as though it should be the rule rather than the exception to have this spiritual gift. In 1 Corinthians 12–14, Paul goes into great detail about how the church should exercise the gift of tongues and the importance of keeping it in balance. The more I learned about this heavenly language, the more bewildered I became.

Why is it that only a chosen few seem to have this gift? I'm a Christian, too, and I love the Lord just as much as anybody else.

Do those who receive the gift of tongues have some special kind of "in" with God? I felt disappointed and left out. But then I'd think, *If you can't understand what you're saying, what good is it? Besides, the Spirit moves as He wills, like the wind; some people get gentle breezes, while others get hurricanes.*

No matter how much I vacillated, I couldn't deny my fascination with tongues, so I started asking around. Most people I was brave enough to approach at church had never given it a second thought, and the few who did had never experienced it themselves. One person told me tongues was only for the original church and not appropriate for today.

I still didn't understand what God was doing in my life, but I'd come to the point of placing my absolute trust in Him. In my desire to fully yield to the Holy Spirit, my curiosity grew deeper. After all, I had vowed to relinquish every part of myself to God, and turning my tongue over to Him seemed to be the ultimate sacrifice. I thought I *had* turned over every ounce of self-will to Him, but I couldn't be sure. I needed proof. If God would grant me the capacity to speak in a language I had never learned, well, what better evidence could there be?

In 1 Corinthians 12:28–31, tongues is listed *last* in the line-up of spiritual gifts. Even so, I couldn't seem to get it off my mind. *If only I can find someone who will tell me something about tongues from firsthand experience*, I thought while pining in solitude.

And Sure Enough

It wasn't long before the subject came up at work during a coffee break. Maria, my Roman Catholic friend, had just spent the weekend at a conference in Philadelphia, and she glowed as she related her experience. I didn't know what she meant by the word "charismatic," but I caught a clue when she referred to the "gifts of the Spirit" being manifested at the conference. It was all the door-opener I needed.

It's a supernatural manifestation that allows the believer's spirit to join in perfect union with God's Spirit.

"Tongues, too?" I interrupted.

"Oh my, yes."

"But do you actually know anybody who speaks in tongues?"

"Of course. Lots of people!"

I could hardly believe my ears and tried not to look shocked as she continued.

"But it doesn't always happen right away," she said. "I know one man who received the gift of tongues when he was . . ."

Her voice faded into the background while echoes of her previous words whirled throughout my consciousness. "Lots of people . . . received . . . gift of tongues . . . not always right away." But what she said next really caught my attention.

"It happened to me as I was driving alone in my car one day. I was singing and praising God, filled with anticipation about our next Life in the Spirit seminar, when some guttural sounds began to form in my throat . . ."

"Excuse me. *You* speak in tongues?"

"Yes," she continued matter-of-factly. It never occurred to me that somebody I saw at the office every day might speak in tongues.

"I guess it's not the kind of thing you go around broadcasting." I gazed at her with newfound respect.

"No, it's not," Maria said. "It's a private, personal matter of the deepest nature. But God has a way of helping Spirit-filled believers find one another."

Maria was a gifted instructor, and I became her eager pupil. Even though we only saw one another briefly, in her presence my office became a satellite classroom for the Lord. She was always bringing me pamphlets, books, and tapes. Excitement stirred between us as she answered my many questions. There was one question, though, that my Catholic friend couldn't answer firsthand: "What do Protestants think about this charismatic stuff?"

We turned to outspoken Pam for her reaction and found that she had experienced the Holy Spirit baptism in a Methodist church service!

God had arranged for me to receive private tutoring on a daily basis from these spiritually gifted, levelheaded Christians. Between the two of them, I began to learn that the gift of tongues is a supernatural manifestation that allows the believer's spirit to join in perfect union with God's Spirit.

Biblically Sound?

I learned that some people are reluctant to seek the gift of tongues because they're not convinced that it's of God.

The Bible must be the foundation of our faith and our beliefs—not man's opinion, but the Word of God as it is written. Unfortunately, human nature would rather *challenge* the Bible than *trust* it as a guide given by inspiration of the Holy Spirit. In sharing what I discovered from researching the spiritual gifts, please don't accept what I say at face value. It would be much better for you to get out a concordance and look up all the verses you can find in the New Testament on the subject of tongues. Consider the premise of Luke 11:11–13 where Jesus asks,

> "Which of you fathers, if your son asks for a fish, will give him a snake instead? Or if he asks for an egg, will give him a scorpion? If you then, though you are evil, know how to give good gifts to your children, how much more will your Father in heaven give the Holy Spirit to those who ask Him!"

The point is this: if we ask God, the good Father, for the Holy Spirit, He will not give us something evil or harmful like an evil spirit. This passage clearly says the gift of the Holy Spirit can be received by simply asking God. Many times we make things more difficult than what they really are.

What's interesting is that the Bible doesn't tell us *if* the spiritual gifts should be used; it tells us *how* to use them. Granted, 1 Corinthians 13:8 says, "where there are tongues, they will be stilled," but this is followed by, "where there is knowledge, it will pass away." Has knowledge passed away? The whole point of this passage is not that the gifts of the Spirit will cease in this world, but that they won't be needed in eternity, and that, above all else, *love* is the greatest evidence of a true follower of Christ.

It is my understanding that there are four types of tongues:

1. *Public tongues* to strengthen the church—A language which the speaker has not learned but is recognized by the hearer or can be interpreted by someone to whom God has revealed the meaning (as in Acts 2:4–11 or 1 Corinthians 14:5, 13, 27).

2. *Private prayer tongues* to strengthen the believer—A private conversation between the individual and God. Here is how it's described in 1 Corinthians 14:2 (TLB): "But if your gift is that of being able to 'speak in tongues,'

that is, to speak in languages you haven't learned, you will be talking to God but not to others, since they won't be able to understand you. You will be speaking by the power of the Spirit but it will all be a secret."

3. ***Ministering tongues*** to strengthen others—A miraculous gift or sign where a believer has the ability to speak in a foreign language that ministers physical, emotional, or spiritual healing to the hearer. A good picture of this is Romans 8:26: "In the same way, the Spirit helps us in our weakness. We do not know what we ought to pray for, but the Spirit Himself intercedes for us with groans that words cannot express."

4. ***Warfare tongues*** to strengthen the godly warrior—A language the enemy camp can't understand and a handy tool for the believer who is waging a battle against evil spirits. According to 2 Corinthians 10:4, the weapons we fight with are not the weapons of the world. On the contrary, they have divine power to demolish strongholds.

Paul said, "I thank God that I 'speak in tongues' privately more than any of the rest of you. But in public worship I would much rather speak five words that people can understand and be helped by, than ten thousand words while 'speaking in tongues' in an unknown language" (1 Corinthians 14:18–19 TLB).

I had *no* desire for public prayer tongues. But my heart burned within me to be able to pray in the Spirit and to comprehend the meaning of Jude 20:

But you, dear friends, must build up your lives ever more strongly upon the foundation of our holy faith, learning to pray in the power and strength of the Holy Spirit (TLB).

Perfect Prayer

Maria and Pam described tongues as "perfect prayer," a prayer language undistracted by the flesh and outward influences, bypassing the mind and connecting Spirit to spirit with the heart of God. Like the gift of salvation, it's a gift from God that can be received in only one way: through faith.

> And in the same way—by our faith—the Holy Spirit helps us with our daily problems and in our praying. For we don't even know what we should pray for, nor how to pray as we should; but the Holy Spirit prays for us with such feeling that it cannot be expressed in words. And the Father who knows all hearts knows, of course, what the Spirit is saying as He pleads for us in harmony with God's own will (Romans 8:26–27 TLB).

I'm not suggesting that this passage is only for people who pray in tongues, for many have moaned on a bed of affliction or sighed out of frustration and known that their prayer was heard. But in my search to understand how the gift of tongues works, this Scripture helped me immensely. To pray in tongues is prayer from the heart that doesn't try to figure things out but transcends human intellect—prayer that is open to the very mind of Christ.

> For one who speaks in an [unknown] tongue speaks not to men but to God, for no one understands or catches his meaning, because in the (Holy) Spirit he utters secret truths and hidden things [not obvious to the understanding] (1 Corinthians 14:2 AMP).

Maria's lessons continued. "To pray in tongues is to pray with supernatural effectiveness," she explained. "It's the Holy Spirit praying for us and through us, supernaturally. When we pray in tongues, we eliminate our own preconceived answers and invite the

Lord to work in the situation according to His perfect will. We have a supernatural God, and this is a supernatural prayer language."

"Then why doesn't *everybody* want to pray in tongues?" I asked.

She was patient with me. "Probably because it's our human nature to reject things we don't understand. It's not easy for finite minds to grasp the concept of the supernatural operating in our everyday lives. Fear of the unknown is one reason."

"I think it's mostly because we insist on being in control," Pam said. "People find it difficult to surrender completely. They want to be in charge of their own destiny. Or they might be afraid they'll look foolish. In a word, *pride*."

Even though I was hungry for all that God had for me, I must admit that I was a bit apprehensive about what kind of tongue I might receive from the Lord. *Would it be a private prayer language that would take me to new spiritual heights? Or would I find myself boldly and publicly extolling God's goodness in some Asian dialect when I least expected it?*

Pride and fear, be gone, I commanded my subconscious. And in that instant, it became clear to me that God doesn't use His spiritual gifts to bring discomfort or ridicule, but to bring glory to Himself. That's when I decided that whatever God wanted for me, that's what I wanted, too.

A Real Witness

Tongues first occurred among believers when the fullness of the Holy Spirit was released on the Day of Pentecost, which is referred to as the "birthday of the church" and was clearly associated with the power to witness. It was the fulfillment of Jesus' promise to His disciples before He ascended into heaven:

"But you will receive power when the Holy Spirit comes on you; and you will be My witnesses in Jerusalem, and in all Judea and Samaria, and to the ends of the earth." (Acts 1:8).

It was the fulfillment of John the Baptist's prediction, "I baptize you with water . . . but he who is . . . more powerful than I . . . will baptize you with the Holy Spirit and with fire" (Matthew 3:11 NRSV).

When the day of Pentecost came, they were all together in one place. Suddenly a sound like the blowing of a violent wind came from heaven and filled the whole house where they were sitting. They saw what seemed to be tongues of fire that separated and came to rest on each of them. All of them were filled with the Holy Spirit and began to speak in other tongues [languages] as the Spirit enabled them (Acts 2:1–4).

The sound was so great, "God-fearing Jews from every nation under heaven" came together to see what was going on. They discovered that they could understand every word spoken, regardless of their native language. It was convincing and powerful! Then "uneducated and ordinary" (Acts 4:13), Peter began to preach. Consider his power-punch finale:

Repent and be baptized, every one of you, in the name of Jesus Christ for the forgiveness of your sins. And you will receive the gift of the Holy Spirit. *The promise is for you and your children* and for all who are far off—for all whom the Lord our God will call (Acts 2:38–39, emphasis added).

My own longing to effectively witness for the Lord grew stronger every day, but I was still shy about my faith and felt awkward about sharing it with others. I knew I had the Holy Spirit, but I also knew I didn't have the *power* of the Spirit. My heart kept telling me that there was *more*. I wanted to pray with power and to witness with boldness. More than anything, I wanted to be filled to overflowing with the Holy Spirit, but something was holding me back. I wondered if tongues might be the key to unlock the door that kept me from surrendering fully to God.

Ready or Not

Al, a coworker who was aware of my conversations with Pam and Maria, asked if I'd be interested in borrowing a tape about being filled with the Holy Spirit and speaking in tongues. *Even Al knew about these things?*

Of course, I borrowed the tape, but I didn't listen to it right away because there were some Scriptures I still needed to digest.

[Paul] asked them, "Did you receive the Holy Spirit when you believed?"

They answered, "No, we have not even heard that there is a Holy Spirit." So Paul asked, "Then what baptism did you receive?"

"John's baptism," they replied.

Paul said, "John's baptism was a baptism of repentance. He told the people to believe in the One coming after him, that is, in Jesus." On hearing this, they were baptized into the name of the Lord Jesus. When Paul placed his hands on them, the Holy Spirit came on them, and they spoke in tongues and prophesied (Acts 19:2–6).

This caused me to think. Although I had been baptized, the water baptism I had experienced wasn't the same as the baptism with fire that John the Baptist talked about. I'd repented and trusted Jesus for my salvation, but why hadn't I been taught about the work of the Holy Spirit? How could my Sunday school classes and worship services have bypassed the subject of the "power" that was available to the early church and to all whom the Lord will call? Was I living in the generation described as "having a form of godliness, but denying its power, always being instructed but never arriving at a knowledge of the truth" (2 Timothy 3:5, 8)?

The questions kept coming—questions that propelled me to the night when I finally listened to Al's tape.

Alone at Last

By 10 p.m. I was propped up in bed with pillows, reading, while Drew quietly cut z's beside me. Suddenly it dawned on me, *it's time.* I slipped out of bed, tiptoed around the bedroom and turned off lights as I gathered the cassette player and audiotape by John Gimenez of the Rock Church in Virginia. His sermon was entitled, "Have You Received?" Noiselessly, I plugged it in by the kitchen table and with trembling anticipation sat down to listen.

Will the Lord give me the gift of tongues tonight? I dared to hope. I pushed the button and turned the volume down. In rapt attention, I listened to his impassioned remarks.

He explained that when Jesus told His disciples the Holy Spirit would be coming upon them, He meant, "I'm going to give you power to *do* something, not just to have goose bumps on your goose bumps or to shake, rattle, and roll and have all kinds of good emotional feelings." Jesus was giving them the power of the Holy Ghost so they could affect the nations of the world for God's glory!

As the tape played, I learned that those who receive the power of the Holy Spirit have certain things in common:

- They hear (with ears that listen)
- They believe (with minds that are convinced)
- They desire (with spirits that are stirred)
- They pray (with voices that ask and praise)
- They wait (with bodies that are still and patient)
- They trust (with hearts that believe)

This must be what it's like to worship God in heart, mind, body, and soul, I reflected. The disciples had no comprehension of *how* God would act—only absolute assurance that He *would,* and that whatever He had in store for them would be good.

"The promise is for today!" The words on the tape jolted me, yanking my pensive thoughts back to the moment. "Available to all, but only those who have these qualities will receive and enjoy the fullness, the higher realm."

Do I have those qualities? I wondered.

"God doesn't honor unbelief," Pastor Gimenez cautioned. "You have to *believe* if you want to receive! God is the same today as yesterday . . ."

As he talked about God's transforming power and how dramatically Peter's personality changed at Pentecost, a chord tugged within me.

That's what I needed, a transformation! I prayed in a whisper, "Deliver me, Lord, from being a wishy-washy disciple, and transform me into someone who isn't afraid to speak out about the things that count—eternal things people need to know." My words and the sound of the tape melted into a blur as my whole being longed for everything that God had for me. Not a measure, but all.

"Have you received the Holy Ghost *since* you believed?" the tape broke through. "Since *you* believed?"

Not completely, I admitted.

"If you haven't, what's hindering you? Pride? Tradition? Do you want the fullness of God?" he asked pointedly.

Yes, yes! I pleaded but didn't take time to consider what might be hindering me since I wanted to hear what else he had to say.

"If you haven't received the Holy Ghost," he explained, "I'm here to tell you, this is your day, because God wants to fill you a whole lot more than you want to be filled." He made it sound so easy, so natural.

All I had to do was claim the promise and receive the Holy Spirit with the evidence of speaking in tongues.

"**God wants to fill you a whole lot more than you want to be filled.**"

"You're a candidate," his assuring voice filled the room, "if you've accepted Jesus. If you've said, 'Lord, be the Lord of my life,' this promise is for you. I don't care what you call yourself—Catholic, Lutheran, Baptist, Fundamentalist—if you're a Christian, it doesn't matter."

I must be a candidate, I cried, sitting there in the dimly lit kitchen.

"Right now, at home, in the name of Jesus, start worshipping, saying, 'I love You.' Just bow your head and receive the Holy Ghost.

This is the Gospel of Jesus Christ . . . You'll start speaking in another language as the Spirit gives utterance."

Now, I'd never heard anyone speak in tongues before, so when the people on the tape began to say things I couldn't understand, I leaned closer to the miniature speaker. I wanted to hear what it sounded like, but it was impossible to sort out the words.

"Lift your hands . . . and receive."

I lifted my hands. Well, one hand. But not too high. It felt awkward. I didn't know what to expect.

"Receive . . ."

I held my arm up a little higher, my conviction deepening. Raising the other arm, I prayed softly, "Lord, if You want me to have this gift, please give it to me. I want to relinquish myself fully, to serve You, and I want everything You have to give me. I'm open to whatever You want to do in my life."

I held my mouth open and wiggled my tongue a little, holding it out like some sort of "offering." It was almost laughable. But somehow, I think God must have enjoyed my ungainly attempt at "receiving" because He knew the sincerity behind my antics. I don't know how long I sat there with my hands dangling above my head and my mouth hanging open. The tape ran out, the service was over, and there I sat in the dark with my arms growing heavy and quiet tears of longing trickling down my cheeks.

Nothing happened. Nothing conspicuous, that is.

Oh well, I thought sheepishly, *I guess it's not for me, after all. God gives His gifts as He sees fit, and maybe I'm not supposed to have this one.*

No feelings of ecstasy, no inner flood, no hint of a new language. *No harm done,* I decided. *Nobody knows about this but God and me.* Blushing to myself, I removed the evidence and crawled back into bed.

But something had happened. I'd opened myself up to God more intimately than ever before. I'd sought Him in unknown territory, willing to appear foolish in His sight, genuinely expressing my desire for all that He had for me. And if disappointment was what He had for me that night—well, I would accept it. I had taken a major step, a step I now recognize as God's test of *"Will you still love Me if—if there's no immediate gratification—if your expectations aren't met?"*

Yes, I would still love Him, no matter what. Since my desire was for God, not simply His gifts, I could swallow the letdown. I had gained a healthy respect for His timing and His ways over mine. The Holy Spirit is not a feeling to be experienced but Truth to be reckoned with. And the truth of the matter was, little did I know that my "day of reckoning," March 31, was at hand.

"For My thoughts are not your thoughts, neither are your ways My ways," declares the LORD. "As the heavens are higher than the earth, so are My ways higher than your ways and My thoughts than your thoughts" (Isaiah 55:8–9).

Shall We Pray?

Thank You, Almighty God, for Your patience with me in my awkward attempts to know You better. Thank You for not giving me what I think I want when I want it, but giving me what You know I need when I need it most. Thank You for the way You carefully measure out Your children's blessings, not more than we can handle or less than we require.

Father, pour out Your living water on me, for I am thirsty for Your fullness. In those recesses where I harbor skepticism, feed me healthy morsels of curiosity so I won't turn my nose up at things I don't understand. Revive me, O Lord, for I am a person who needs Your power to replace my pettiness. Help me to stop running ahead of You or lagging behind. If this is a game of Hide and Seek, expose my private hiding places and meet me there.

What Can I Do For You, Lord?

Dig Into Scripture

Look up 1 Thessalonians 5:19 (a short sentence). Then read Matthew 7:7–11. As you read Jesus' words about how to ask, seek, and knock, think about what it is you desire most from Him.

God's Call: Don't Quench My Spirit

"From the beginning, the gifts of the Spirit have been controversial, often causing division among sincere believers. Rather than trying to stifle the work of the Holy Spirit, would it not be better to encourage the full expression of My gifts and work toward an understanding of what I am doing? Lay down your preconceptions and watch what I can do.

"If you are one who longs to know My fullness and your efforts to receive have not met your expectations, do not conclude that the gift of My Spirit is not for you. Do not give up, for I desire to fill you to overflowing. Persevere in seeking Me. Ask and keep on asking for more knowledge, patience, wisdom, love, and understanding, and these things shall be yours. You will find that as My nature is manifested in you, the spiritual gifts will come."

Your Response to God

I will not quench the Spirit. Instead, I will do some honest soul-searching. I may even begin to study the gifts of the Spirit, praying specifically for them as the Lord leads, and exercising the gifts He grants me.

 Seed for Thought

"A lot of good arguments are spoiled
by some fool who knows what he's talking about."

—Gene Brown

CHAPTER 7

RECEIVE THE FULLNESS OF GOD

 Seed for Thought

"A skeptic is a person who, when he sees the handwriting
on the wall, claims it is a forgery."

—*Morris Bender*

*Then Peter and John
placed their hands upon them,
and they received the Holy Spirit.
—Acts 8:17*

The fullness of the Spirit, the explosion of God's power within a human being, is not something easily grasped like plucking apples off a tree. It comes in God's good time as faith and relinquishment ripen in us.

Like pulling a sour green apple from the branch rather than waiting until it ripens into a juicy red one, we sometimes get ahead of God. Too often I find myself longing and striving for something that would have come effortlessly if I had only waited for God to reveal His plan. My unsuccessful experiment in "receiving" helped broaden my focus and move me beyond a yearning for one specific gift to a refreshing appreciation of our heavenly Father's plan for me.

Still engrossed in *The Helper*, I had come to the section on "Peace." I underlined the sentence that read, "The peace that passes all understanding is an especially precious part of [the] inheritance that not one of us can do without." I believed with all my heart that I was at peace, able to accept whatever God wanted to do with me and in me, as well as for me.

March 31, 1983

It was Maundy Thursday, or Holy Thursday—our observance of the night Jesus celebrated Passover with His disciples before His crucifixion—the Easter season. It was also my last day of work before a two-week vacation. My desk was strewn with papers when Maria came breezing into my office to proclaim, "Today's the day!"

Having no idea what she meant, I gave her a blank stare.

"I was thinking about you all the way here this morning." Enthusiasm radiated from her sparkling eyes. Excitement swirled around her like a heavenly cloak. "Today's the day!" she repeated.

"The day for what?" My question didn't dim her enthusiasm.

"This is the day you're going to be baptized in the Holy Spirit."

"Uh, oh, I don't know about that," I sputtered. "I sought the outpouring of the Spirit not long ago, and God didn't give it to me then. How can you be so sure He wants to baptize me today?"

"Because, it's the holy season." Her confidence was contagious. "Easter is the height of our faith, a season of miracles. Besides, you're about to go on vacation, you're hungry for the fullness of God, and I feel a leading to pray over you today. When God gives you a hunger, He'll satisfy it—maybe not right away, but when He's ready. And He just might be ready today! You haven't been prayed over for this gift yet, have you?"

"No, I've never been 'prayed over' for anything. What do you mean by 'prayed over,' anyway?" A fragment of hope began to stir in my soul.

"The laying on of hands," she explained. "Just like in the book of Acts. Our hands serve as channels for God's power to flow through us and into you. There really should be two of us ministering to you. Do you think Pam would be available? Would lunchtime be okay? How about 12:00?" Her plans tumbled out faster than I could follow.

But I'm Busy!

"Hold your horses." I smiled in protest. "I'm really busy today. Payroll's due, I have a hair appointment at 12:30, and I have to get everything caught up before I leave for the next two weeks. Besides, when Mr. Owens gets back, he has some dictation for me."

On cue, Mr. Owens walked through the doorway, and two of my telephone lines began ringing. Maria stood patiently by my desk until I got off the phone. Standing up and reaching for my shorthand notebook, I said to her, "See how busy I am? I truly am grateful, but I'm a firm believer in waiting on God. If He wants to baptize me today, then He'll just have to clear the way. Let's leave it like this—when 12:00 rolls around, if I'm still swamped and Pam's not available, I'll take a rain check. On the other hand, if things settle down and everything falls into place, then I'll take that as a green light from on High."

"You're absolutely right," Maria said. "Our Lord has perfect timing, and we must honor it. But," she added with a wink, "I think you'll find that the way will be clear."

Two hours later, my workload was worse than ever. The way looked anything *but* clear. Although Pam said she'd be glad to join us for prayer, the clock was ticking. I had only an hour and a half to get everything under control before noon. *Impossible*, I decided, and then another phrase pricked my thoughts: **"With God, all things are possible."**

Calling All Angels

I recalled what I wrote in my prayer journal that morning. "Help me apply myself effectively at work, Lord. I want my Christian witness to have credibility."

The emphasis in my daily devotional was on "ministering angels," and my Bible verse for the day was Psalm 91:11 (KJV), "For He shall give His angels charge over thee, to keep thee in all thy ways." The printed prayer ended with, "Lord, let Your angels effectively block me from any way contrary to Your perfect will for me" (*My 30 Day Prayer Diary*, Day 18).

So where were the ministering angels assigned to help me with this heap of work?

"You have not because you ask not."

"Please, Lord, if it's Your perfect will for Maria and Pam to pray over me today, You'll just have to send in more angels. If this isn't the right time or place, that's okay. I do need to get this work under control, and it looks like it'll take divine intervention for that! Whatever Your angels can do, I'd appreciate it."

Systematically, my hands sorted through the piles in front of me. My head cleared along with my desk as a mountain of forms, reports, and memoranda were picked up by people who suddenly needed them. Confusion dissipated as the clutter vanished before my eyes. Someone from the business office called to see if payroll was ready—and it was—so that, too, was swept out of the way. My fingers flew across the keyboard as I transcribed the last few sentences of shorthand in record time, with no mistakes. Twenty minutes to twelve. And only two minor things to finish up after lunch.

But there was still a lot of commotion. It seemed like everybody within a five-mile radius had migrated into my office for no apparent reason. My telephone lit up like a string of Christmas lights. *Seven minutes to noon, Lord*, I prayed silently. *Time is drawing near. Let me have no doubt about Your will.*

At five minutes to countdown, it was as though an unseen force swept through my office, transforming turmoil into tranquility. The phone became strangely silent, my boss left for lunch, the visitors vanished, my desk was stripped of all but one lone paper, and everything was quiet. I couldn't see any angels, but I had no doubt they were enjoying the incredulous look on my face.

I felt nervous. Excited. Scared, as though I were about to be officially summoned. *I guess this is my "green light." For God to clear the way so completely, today must be the day, after all—for something.*

In a fleeting moment amidst the previous hubbub, Pam had appeared beside my desk long enough to place a folded, well-worn paper in my hand. "Here," she told me, "read this slowly if you have a few minutes before we pray. Think of it as a love letter from God to you." When she gave it to me, I'd barely had time to glance at it; but now, faced with five whole minutes of deafening silence, I unfolded the paper and began to read:

This Thing Is from Me

*(Adapted from a message
by Laura A. Barton Snow, references from KJV)*

"My child, I have a message for you today; let Me whisper it in your ear, that it may gild with glory any storm clouds that may arise, and smooth the rough places upon which you may have to tread. It is short, only five words, but let them sink into your innermost soul. Use them as a pillow upon which to rest your weary head: 'This thing is from Me.'

"Have you ever thought of it, that all that concerns you concerns Me, too? For, 'He that toucheth you toucheth the apple of Mine eye' (Zechariah 2:8). 'You are very precious in My sight' (Isaiah 43:4). Therefore, it is My special delight to educate you.

"I would have you learn when temptations assail you and the 'enemy comes in like a flood,' that this thing is from Me, that your weakness needs My might, and your safety lies in letting Me fight for you.

"Are you in difficult circumstances, surrounded by people who do not understand you, who never consult your taste, who put you in the background? This thing is from Me. I am the God of circumstances. Thou camest not to thy place by accident; it is the very place God meant for thee.

"Have you not asked to be made humble? See, then, I have placed you in the very school where the lesson is taught; your surroundings and companions are only working out My will.

"Are you in money difficulties? Is it hard to make both ends meet? This thing is from Me, for I am your purse-bearer and would have you draw from and depend upon Me. My supplies are limitless (Philippians 4:19). I would have you prove My promises. Let it not be said of you, 'In this thing you did not believe the Lord your God' (Deuteronomy 1:32).

"Are you passing through a night of sorrow? This thing is from Me. I am the 'man of sorrows and acquainted with grief' (Isaiah 53:3). I have let earthly comforters fail you, that by turning to Me you may obtain everlasting consolation (2 Thessalonians 2:16–17).

> *"Have you longed to do some great work for Me and instead been laid aside on a bed of pain and weakness? This thing is from Me. I could not get your attention in your busy days, and I want to teach you some of My deepest lessons. 'They also serve who only stand and wait.' Some of My greatest workers are those shut out from active service, that they may learn to wield the weapon of prayer.*
>
> *"This day I place in your hand this pot of holy oil. Make use of it freely, My child. Let every circumstance that arises, every word that pains you, every interruption that would make you impatient, every revelation of your weakness be anointed with it. The sting will go as you learn to see Me in all things."*

It was exquisite, an inspired piece, but I couldn't concentrate. I was too anxious, too excited, and too afraid of the unknown that awaited me.

Oh, Lord, I prayed, *if You have something to tell me through this paper, show me what it is.* No sooner had I uttered that prayer and focused my eyes on the words, "This Thing Is from Me," when Pam walked in.

Time to Pray

"Are you ready?" she asked with a smile and a raised eyebrow.

"I guess so," I answered feebly as I got up from my desk, clutching the paper with the promise, "This Thing Is from Me," in a trembling hand.

Looking me over as we walked out together, she said, "You're scared, aren't you?"

"Absolutely! I have no idea what to expect, and it's scary."

"Fear is not of God," Pam announced. "The devil doesn't like what we're about to do, and he would do anything in his power to prevent it. The last thing he wants is for a Christian to experience the fullness of God. This fear you're feeling is a trick to scare you off. Don't fall for it. The Lord wants you to experience peace, not anxiety. Remember, God is love, and He would never do anything to hurt or frighten you. By the way, discouragement is another trick, but the Lord wants you to be encouraged. Just relax, and think about how much you're going to enjoy His presence."

Maria was standing in the hallway to welcome us into the tight 9' x 9' office, barely big enough for a desk, a chair, and the three of us. "I knew you'd come!" she exclaimed, clapping her hands like a child.

As she and Pam sat me in the chair, they counseled me further.

"Now, this is one time when you can't *do* anything," Pam said. "The only thing you can do is to sit here and *receive*. So just calm down, and get ready to open yourself up to whatever the Lord wants to give you."

"But I feel so nervous, jittery, like I'm all wound up and . . ."

"Candy, quit chattering." Pam's no-nonsense admonishment served as a balm for my frayed nerves. "Forget about your feelings. All you need to think about is that you're presenting yourself before the Lord in faith. You don't need any special training to receive His gifts, only a desire to seek Him above all else. Your emotions will settle down as you begin to experience His peace. Let us do the praying, and let God do the giving. We don't know what it is He has for you today, so try to let go of your expectations and leave it up to Him."

"Besides," Maria said, "sometimes nothing obvious happens at first, so don't be disappointed. You can be confident that God always answers the prayers of His children when they're in keeping with His will. And there's no question that it *is* His will for you to receive the fullness of His Spirit, so just trust that the Lord knows what He's doing."

"Thy will be done, right?" I asked.

"Right." Maria joined Pam who was standing behind me. "But it's actually even better if you can manage not to think at all. Try to clear your mind of all thoughts that would distract you, and turn everything over to Him."

It was time to pray. Maria and Pam stood beside opposite sides of my chair and placed their open palms on my shoulders. Folding my hands in my lap, I bowed my head, closed my eyes, and tried to clear my thoughts. Instantly, a white polar bear, of all things, popped into my mind.

But there's a reason for that. A long time ago, I heard a story about a man who accepted a bet that he couldn't stay in a white room for an hour, cleared of everything but one white chair, without thinking about a white polar bear. And what do you suppose he thought about? A white polar bear.

This is ridiculous, I fussed silently to myself. *Here I am trying to put myself in a holy attitude, and I'm thinking about a white polar bear!* It was hard not to think—to clear my mind completely. *Help me, Lord, to center my thoughts on You.*

Instantly, I realized it wasn't a matter of emptying my mind but of taking captive every thought to make it obedient to Christ (2 Corinthians 10:5).

Along with this realization came an awareness of the beauty of the prayers that floated above me. There were words of praise and thanksgiving, gratitude, and Scripture as Pam and Maria alternated in harmony, their voices orchestrated as if by an unseen conductor.

I became sensitive to their touch and was awed by the delicate balance of each hand resting upon me—lightly, but firmly. If I didn't know better, I would have thought their hands belonged to one person, not two. Their words grew quieter. Hushed and overlapping, they mixed together and blended in such a way that I could only grasp a phrase here and there. They were praying in one accord, something I had never encountered. The presence of God consumed the room.

Release of the Spirit

Finding it difficult to put into words all that occurred from that point on, I turned to my journal and asked the Lord if it would be okay to ask Him to explain what happened that day.

"Does not your spirit tell you what it is? For it is I who have directed you to ask. The Spirit searches all things, even the very depths of God. The truths revealed will be enlightening to those

who are spiritual, but to those who are unspiritual, this will seem to be only foolishness. This account is not for the benefit of the hard of heart but for those who seek after the mind of Christ."

It is written: "No eye has seen, no ear has heard, no mind has conceived what God has prepared for those who love Him"—but God has revealed it to us by His Spirit. The Spirit searches all things, even the deep things of God. For who among men knows the thoughts of a man except the man's spirit within him? In the same way no one knows the thoughts of God except the Spirit of God. We have not received the spirit of the world but the Spirit who is from God, that we may understand what God has freely given us (1 Corinthians 2:9–12; also see Isaiah 64:4).

"I was waiting there in the doorway with Maria to welcome you into the prayer closet; yet, I traveled beside you in the hallway as you approached it, speaking words of encouragement through My servant, Pam.

"Once seated, you asked Me to take your thoughts captive. Fascinated by the sound of my servants praying at the same time, you wondered if I could understand them both at once, for you could not. I reminded you that I am the One who created every living thing, giving great attention to detail—intricacies that no human eye or mind can perceive—and that if every human being were to speak in prayer at the same instant, I would hear and be attentive to each individual word. 'Nothing escapes Me,' I said.

"Gratitude swept over you for the loving attention of the two saints who stood there, freely giving of their time, their devotion, and their concern for your need, as they sacrificed offerings of praise on your behalf. Turning your attention from their words and their touch to My grace, you were able to relax. The tension went from you as you lifted your face ever so slightly.

"'I'm all Yours, Lord,' you prayed. And then you recalled Pam's instruction not to think or do anything, not even to pray—only

to receive. As I revealed that you were filling the spot I wished to occupy, your mind grasped the truth, 'I can't receive something if there's no room to put it.' It was quite natural for you to close off, even from Me, the most private part of yourself: the control center of your will. For free will is territory I have entrusted wholly to each person. Since birth, you have been the sole manager of this hidden portion of your being. I urged you to let go of the safety net—to relinquish the security of the familiar—that you may enter a deeper place of trust in Me.

"'I want to let go, Lord,' you prayed. 'I want to give this part of myself to You, but I don't know how. I don't even know what it is that I'm holding back.' You identified the reluctant spot as 'five percent.'

"Spoken words above your head caught your attention. 'Father,' said Pam, 'if there's anything interfering with Your perfect will being done here, I come against it in Your mighty name. And if there's anything in me that's not right, I confess it, Lord, and ask You to remove it.' Maria prayed likewise. You were absorbed in wonderment at their humility and insight.

"'Me, too,' you added in meek sincerity.

"Your eyelids fluttered in determination to keep them closed. However, this was not My desire for you. Just as Jesus lifted up His eyes at the tomb of Lazarus, so I planned for you to enter into this experience with your eyes wide open. You opened your eyes and looked straight ahead, not focusing on objects but aware of the bright, cheerful colors of the poster on the wall. You rejoiced in the gift of sight.

"'Yes,' I spoke to your spirit. 'As clearly as you see with your eyes, so I want you to see with the eyes of your heart.' You stared ahead, straining to catch a glimpse of Me in the colors before you. I directed your vision to the paper in your hand.

"You began to understand. This thing is from Me. You had to experience fear of the unknown that you might learn to trust Me and appreciate My ways over your own. This thing is from Me. You had to taste disappointment in your search for tongues that you might learn the importance of seeking Me above My gifts. This thing is from Me. You had to know the frustration of the inability *to fully yield yourself to Me in order to receive what only I can give. I stood ready to remove the obstacles, but first you needed to discover the futility of self-effort. 'Let Me do it,' you sensed My Spirit say. 'I am your Helper! It is by My action, not yours, that My love shall be released in your innermost being. You need not fear. Trust Me.'*

"*You needed no further encouragement.*

"'*I want to let go, to give it up,' you prayed, 'but I don't know how. I've never done it before. So, will you take it from me, Lord? Whatever the roadblock is—this five percent I'm holding back— please take it so I can know the fullness of Your Spirit.'*

"*You sat quietly, every muscle and cell utterly still. You waited, having no knowledge of how I might choose to act on your request, only believing that I would.*

"*You became aware of time. 'How long have we been here?' you wondered. Your hair appointment came to mind. I spoke to your conscience, 'What is more important, your hair appointment or your baptism? Where are your priorities?' Now contrite, you thought of your friends and their sacrifice as their fervent prayer continued. You wondered how they could think of so much to say.*

"*It was then that you heard Maria's words, 'When people look at Candy, let them see Jesus.'*

"'*Yes,' you thought, 'that's it. I want people to see You in me, Lord!' Time was no longer a factor as your desire to reflect My love, My character, and My will became your primary objective.*

"*Maria spoke again. 'I feel like she should praise God. I think she should pray and praise Him herself, out loud.'*

"*You knew what was expected of you and needed no further invitation. There was no hesitation in your response. I cherish those few childlike words of praise offered to Me from your lips that day. The angels rejoiced in the unity of Spirit among the three of you. 'I love You, Lord. I love You, Lord. Thank You, Lord.' Inexperienced at praise, you found your limited vocabulary inadequate to express the joy that was welling up within you.*

"'*Hallelujah,' an angel whispered in your ear.*

"'Hallelujah,' you repeated. It was a good word, a praise word—a universal word of adoration, rich and satisfying. You liked the way it felt to say it. So you said it again. And again. And again. Your voice became a whisper as you digested the true significance of praise. You were experiencing the wonders of exemplary praise, heartfelt worship.

"It was My good pleasure at that moment to release the power of My Spirit within you. Flooding the innermost parts of your soul so that your fondest expectations might be exceeded, My love flowed uninhibited, racing to touch every cell, every thread of your being. It was My delight to transform your restricted language into fluent praise and glorious adoration, magnifying the very essence of My love. The sounds that spilled from your lips were an outward sign of the great exchange taking place within you—the exchange of your will for Mine."

From My Perspective

The uniting of my spirit with God's Spirit, this consummation, is difficult to describe. There's no adequate way to explain what it feels like to have "rivers of living water" flowing through you. But I'll try.

It was a marriage between my being and Christ, a vast awareness of the magnitude of His unlimited authority and power, and a new appreciation for the depth of His mercy and grace. It was perfect love. And the words, "This Thing Is From Me," will be forever etched in my being.

People have cautioned me not to dwell on the experiential aspect, for God is not in the business of dishing out thrills, but since my whole "self" was affected, I can't in good conscience leave out the part that has to do with the physical realm.

As I savored the meaning of the word "hallelujah," my tongue did an unexpected turn, and the word changed to an unfamiliar combination of vowels and syllables. My awareness grew to a mild warmth, a tingling energy that built within the pit of my stomach. Then my voice reduced to puffs of air passing through my lips as I consciously engaged my vocal chords to attach sound to the whispers.

The warmth in my stomach expanded, growing in intensity, seeping upward and outward, spreading ever so gently. Then came the *release*. The fullness of the Spirit exploded in regions of my body where only a trickle had been before. It was a deep, gushing sensation. I felt the love and energy of God flooding through me, saturating areas in me I didn't know were there. It traveled down my arms and hands to my fingers, and down my legs and feet to my toes. Then it hit my nose with a tingling that could only be described as joy. No part of my body was unaffected.

Tears trickled quietly down my face. My tongue surrendered in praise. My hands, no longer folded in my lap, lifted slowly upward, reaching to embrace the source of this incredible, indescribable joy. My ears heard gladness as my voice mixed with Pam's and Maria's, praising God in the Spirit. Strangely enough, my emotions didn't go wild; instead, I experienced a profound calm. I was at complete peace, with my feelings internalized more deeply than I'd ever known possible. Love, I guess, isn't noisy. The wave of ecstasy came softly, crested for a time, and then receded. I was left with weak knees and a buoyancy as I stood up.

"He's so wonderful!" I said over and over again. "I never knew what God's love was until now!" Hugging was in order. As I latched onto Maria and Pam, I couldn't thank them enough.

Coming Down to Earth

How do you come back down to earth after something like this? Well, the first sign of re-entry for me was a need to know what time it was. I was surprised to find that all of this had taken place in a span of less than fifteen minutes.

We said our good-byes and went our separate ways. I was aware of the tappety-tap of my heels in the hallway, but it was as though I had a cushiony cloud under my feet. *This must be what they mean by walking on air*, I thought. My face was flushed and felt like it glowed with radiant beams like artists draw. I wondered if anyone would notice. Al, the friend who had loaned me the tape on tongues, was in his office just down the hall.

"Something wonderful has happened to me," I announced as I stood in his doorway.

"I can see that from looking at you," he said. "Would you like to come in and tell me about it?"

The Spirit gave me a boldness I'd never known before. Al listened intensely as I shared my experience in a way that would have made any babbling brook proud.

"It's obvious that something magnificent, something beautiful, has happened, all right." He paused. "You realize, Candy, you'll never be the same." I started to disagree, but I knew he was right. Touched by the power of God, I was forever changed.

"I never knew what God's love was until now!"

Al thanked me sincerely for stopping by. I thanked *him* for letting me borrow the tape which played a significant part in my experience. As I left his office, he said, "I'm so happy for you."

And then he added, "Maybe someday I, too, can have what you've found."

I was changed, all right. I'd just shared my faith, and it wasn't work; it was a thrill to share what the Lord had done in me! Now, I ask you, isn't that what Christian witnessing is all about? Reflecting Christ's love and joy so clearly that others will see it and want to embrace it themselves? Although I don't know if Al ever received the infilling of the Holy Spirit, I do know that he was actively seeking a closer walk with God and that I planted a seed of faith in him that day.

Remembering my hair appointment, I excused myself and glowed right on down the hallway, out the door, and into my car, arriving at the hairdresser's shop right on time.

Still Me

The shampoo was a real treat and appropriate follow-up to the inner cleansing I'd just had. I found myself being pampered inside and out. Looking at myself in the mirror, I could see that, although I was forever changed, I still looked "normal." I was still me. And right away I realized how important it was not to become so heavenly minded that I'd be no earthly good.

At the hairdresser's, it felt strange to be back in the real world where ladies discussed things like Easter outfits, recipes, and taking the puppy to the vet. I had a lot of sorting out to do, and until I became better acquainted with how to handle my experience, I thought it best to keep my spiritual enthusiasm under wraps. So, while the beautician trimmed my hair, our conversation centered on kids and diets. The small talk served a good purpose, helping to bring me back to where I needed to be, in tune with the familiar world.

So Much to Learn

Back at work that afternoon, Pam had some more wise counsel for me. "Be careful," she said, "about who you share this with. People don't usually understand spiritual things, so pray for wisdom before you tell anybody about your experience—especially about tongues."

I listened as she paraphrased Matthew 7:6. "You don't want to cast your pearls before swine," she said. "Sometimes people don't want to hear. Not only could you be wasting your time, but some may be offended or try to tear what you're telling them to shreds."

"Your advice comes a little late," I told her. "The first thing I did when I left you was tell somebody . . ."

I explained how I'd bubbled over at Al and how receptive he was. "On the other hand, God gave me the prudence to keep my lip zipped at the beauty shop." Even though I hadn't consciously *prayed* about either situation, it was apparent I had *responded* to the Spirit's leading. Even so, I resolved to pray for the Holy Spirit's guidance before telling anybody else.

"Now that I've experienced this prayer language, I never want to lose it," I said, with the sinking feeling that it might have been a one-time occasion.

"God doesn't give His gifts, then take them back," Pam said. "He's opened up improved lines of communication between you and His Spirit. All you have to do is use the gift He gave you. Just keep practicing your 'tongue' and experiment with it. Pray in the Spirit every day, and you'll find your 'vocabulary' will grow. It's a voluntary thing. You can turn your heavenly language on and off just as easily as you do any prayer. At first you may have only a couple of phrases, but if you keep exercising your gift, your prayer language will become fluent. You're like a baby learning to talk. As long as you keep on praising Him and using your gift, you'll never have to worry about losing it."

Test of Credibility

"There's another thing I ought to mention," Pam said. "There may come a time when you'll wonder if your new language is genuine. You may think you're making it up yourself and suspect it's not real. Satan will try to discourage you and cause you to doubt."

"But I *know* this is real! There's no question in my mind about that!"

"You know it *now*," she said. "I'm talking about later on when the glow starts to fade. You're on the mountaintop today, but you'll have to come down to the valley sometime. That's when the devil will try to steal your gift. He despises tongues, not only because he can't understand what you and God are saying to each other, but because he knows your new gift of a heavenly language contains tremendous power. If he can convince you it's not genuine or not of God, he can get you to deny your gift. Unfortunately, some people fall for his trick and, as a result, a powerful prayer life and untold blessings are missed.

"Here's a test you can use if you ever wonder about the validity of your gift of tongues or its source: Just ask yourself, 'Am I closer to my Lord Jesus Christ as a result of praying in tongues or not?' Remember, you're known by the fruit you bear."

To the Reader

The apostle Paul said it well:

> When I came to you, brothers and sisters, I did not come proclaiming the mystery of God to you in lofty words or wisdom. . . . *I came to you in weakness and in fear and in much trembling*. My speech and my proclamation were not with plausible words of wisdom, but with a demonstration of the Spirit and of power, so that your faith might not rest on human wisdom but on the power of God (1 Corinthians 2:1, 3–5 NRSV, emphasis added).

And what about you, dear friend? Have you discovered His power and the resources available to you through faith?

Does your spirit tell you that it's genuine? That people like us can actually know the reality of the power and the glory of God inside our mortal bodies, within our human emotions and finite minds? I'm not trying to persuade you, entice you, or push you into desiring the baptism of the Holy Spirit. I've told my story for one purpose: awareness. Too many dedicated Christians today don't know that they can have this kind of relationship with God.

God is pouring out His Spirit around the world today. He knows we need His power. Apart from His help, how will we be able to cope, stand firm and, yes, even overcome all the obstacles bombarding us these days?

The security blanket of the familiar is becoming more soiled all the time, yet we hold tightly to it. We resist having it washed in "rivers of living water" where the currents of faith move swiftly and run deep. We're afraid of losing control and being carried away. But if those of us who dare to enter into this life-changing relationship hold tightly to the Gospel of truth, we will find ourselves wrapped by strong hands in the spotless garments of divine security and everlasting peace.

If You Yearn

If you find that your are hungering for your own personal discovery of God's power through the infilling of the Holy Spirit, I think it's safe to say, "You shall have it." If you're yearning for this gift, it's because God Himself has given you that desire—proof that the Spirit is already at work within you. And whatever God gives us a desire for, He'll be faithful to supply in His good time as we diligently seek Him.

How He chooses to supply a desire is a completely different matter. There's no *one* method, formula, or procedure because the Lord deals with each person on an individual basis. He knows the best way for each of us to experience the manifestation of the Holy Spirit.

From what I can tell, we have two requirements to meet in order to receive this gift:

1. We have to ask in total submission.
2. We have to believe that the gift of the Holy Spirit is for us.

Do not, I repeat, *do not* seek an "experience" or expect your baptism to be just like mine. There is no right way. For me, receiving the baptism involved other people and the laying on of hands. For others, it means meeting God alone in the privacy of their bedroom. Still others find that the Spirit rushes in like a mighty wind, filling a crowded room where everyone begins to praise and worship in one accord.

You are unique to God. And you can be sure that He'll find a unique and personal way to reveal His fullness in your life. Don't limit Him by setting up your own expectations. He has surprises in store for you that are much better than anything you could dream up on your own.

Consider my impatience just prior to the outpouring of the Spirit—right in the middle of Pam and Maria's prayer. Remember how time-conscious I became? How concerned I was about how long it was taking? If the two of them hadn't been praying so fervently and sincerely at that moment, I'd have probably quipped something like, "Amen, thank you ladies; I appreciate your effort, but it looks like nothing's going to happen." But something did happen, shortly afterward. If I had given in to my impatience and called it quits, they would have stopped praying prematurely, and I'd have missed the blessing.

The choice is ours—to wait on the Spirit or walk out on Him. Never assume that it's "not for you." The fullness of the Holy Spirit isn't given to a chosen few; the fullness of the Spirit is lovingly distributed to all who ask, believing.

I have no idea how God plans to minister to you, but I do know that as we seek Him the best we know how, Christ Jesus will teach us individually and disburse His gifts in unique and personal ways. We have only two guidelines—faith and hope.

Rhema and Logos

This is a good time to remember Romans 10:17: "Faith comes by hearing and hearing by the Word of God" (NKJV). The Word comes to us in two ways: in the form of the written Word, the Bible or *logos* that we read for ourselves or hear when spoken aloud, and the *rhema* (ray-mah) Word of God that comes when the Spirit speaks to our hearts and minds. Another way of understanding the difference is that *logos* is the message; *rhema* is the communication of the message.

Individual experiences of the baptism of the Holy Spirit are as varied as snowflakes. Sometimes the Spirit is manifested through tongues, but sometimes not. Reactions range from tears to holy giggles to visions or a blinding light. Some see nothing out of the ordinary, while others jump up and leap for joy or fall to their knees in adoration. And then there are the quiet ones the Holy Spirit stirs gently with no outward sign except a bountiful crop of good fruit.

Here are a couple of interesting examples of people I know who received the gift of tongues.

Anne Receives

My friend Anne read the first edition of my book three times and was really hung up on the whole concept of tongues. The first time through, she said it didn't make any sense to her. The second time, she became curious. After the third time, she had a strong desire to have the gift herself.

Maria loaned her a tape by Francis Frangipane in which he demonstrated a variety of tongues. Anne was resting in her bedroom on a Sunday afternoon, listening to the tape. At one point, she thought quite simply, *I can do that.* So she opened her mouth and sweet sounds rolled off her tongue. She said she felt more close to God in that moment than she had in her whole life. Although she only received one "phrase" in her prayer language, she used it mightily in her prayers.

I saw an interesting change in her disposition after that—a softer, more sensitive Anne.

Maria's Son

Several years later, Maria moved to Florida, and I had the privilege of visiting when her son received the infilling of the Holy Spirit. After we prayed for him, Frank said he felt the presence of God and that "something happened," but there was no evidence of the manifestation of tongues. She kept encouraging him to speak whatever sounds the Lord gave him.

I was skeptical about Maria's coaching at first, especially since the first thing he said was "A." But I figured the Lord had used her as a vehicle in my own spiritual blessing, so I kept an open mind. She prompted him to keep repeating A A A A A A A.

After a while, she asked if there might be a different sound the Lord was giving him. When he nodded, she said, "Okay, then, Frank, go ahead and say it." Imagine my amusement when he said "B." Maria and I looked at each other and smiled, but she encouraged him to repeat it. "B B B B B B B," he said. Then came—you guessed it, "C C C C C C," and it was all I could do to hold back my snickering.

But then Maria suggested to Frank, "How about combining the sounds?" So he complied. At first it was the standard "A B C," but then he began sounding out the vowels and consonants differently, "Ah Bah Sah," and stringing the sounds together, "Abba Sa . . ." Suddenly, it was as though a verbal dam broke, and he was speaking in fluent tongues.

Right Relationship with God

So, as you can see, there is no one "right way" to receive the infilling of the Holy Spirit. It's all about God's grace, our faith, and a right relationship with Christ.

There are people who think they're not good enough, not worthy. We will never be worthy. Only Jesus is worthy, and the baptism is His gift to us (Acts 2:38–39; 10:45). Like salvation, we can accept or reject it. It's not something that can be earned, just received in childlike faith.

Some put it off, thinking they will seek God for this some other time. They may doubt if it's real or think it's okay for others but not for them. They may be afraid of what people will think. But today is the day, now is the time. Tomorrow is one of the devil's favorite words. And what does it matter what others think if we are hungering and thirsting for more of Jesus?

Others are afraid they would be making up a language or copying someone, but if your heart is sincere, Jesus wouldn't let you make up a language even if you could. If you ask Him for bread, you get bread (Matthew 7:9-11), because Jesus is waiting, willing, and able to feed His hungry child. When we speak in tongues, it is Spirit to spirit—Christ's Spirit giving the utterance through us.

If you are hungry for a closer walk with the Holy Spirit, carve out a block of time to honestly evaluate your relationship with the Lord and delight in how He has brought you to this point in your faith. Let God bring to your remembrance times when you may have thought He had let you down, only to discover later that He was with you all along. *Enjoy Him!* As you become more accustomed to discovering Christ's presence right where you are, in your circumstances and in your faith, you'll become more aware of and receptive to each personal invitation He extends to you.

If you find you are impatient or discouraged, here is some wisdom from *My Utmost for His Highest*, April 27, that may help you identify a potential problem:

> There is nothing easier than getting into the right relationship with God, unless it is not God you seek, but only what He can give you. If you have only come as far as asking God for things, you have never come to the point of understanding the least bit of what surrender really means. You have become a Christian based on your own terms. You protest, saying, "I asked God for the Holy Spirit, but He didn't give me the rest and the peace I expected." And instantly God puts His finger on the reason—you are not seeking the Lord at all, you are seeking something for yourself.

If you are hungry for a closer walk with the Holy Spirit, carve out a block of time to honestly evaluate your relationship with the Lord and delight in Him.

Love Sandwich

Never forget that the most important thing of all is *love*—loving God first and then loving one another. It's interesting to note that the love chapter, 1 Corinthians 13, is sandwiched between Paul's instruction on the spiritual gifts (chapter 12) and a specific teaching on the gifts of prophecy and tongues (chapter 14).

The meat or substance of the sandwich is love which represents all nine elements of the fruit of the Spirit. Each of the other eight elements of the fruit (joy, peace, patience, kindness, goodness, faithfulness, gentleness, and self-control) are by-products of love.

As we move into the next chapter, we'll see how the fruit of the Spirit can break through the calloused shells around our hearts. Once the fruit becomes a priority in our lives, we are wide open to receive the manifestations of God's power (the gifts of the Spirit) and a changed life.

The gifts of the Spirit are like the bread surrounding the sandwich. Look it up for yourself as you dig into Scripture in the lesson at the end of this chapter.

1 Corinthians chapter 12 = a slice of bread
1 Corinthians chapter 13 = the substance of the sandwich
1 Corinthians chapter 14 = the other slice of bread

The fruit of the Spirit is the manifestation of God's character and nature, while the gifts of the Spirit manifest God's power and anointing.

Shall We Pray?

According to Your riches in glory, may I be strengthened with power through Your Holy Spirit so that You, O Christ, may dwell in my heart through faith, as I am rooted and grounded in love. May I have the power to comprehend, with all the saints, what is the breadth and length and height and depth, and to know the love of Christ that surpasses knowledge, so that I may be filled with all the fullness of God. Now to You who are able to accomplish abundantly far more than all I can ask or imagine, to You be glory in the church to all generations, forever and ever. Amen.

—Ephesians 3:16–21, personalized

WHAT CAN I DO FOR YOU, LORD?

DIG INTO SCRIPTURE

Read Romans 12:1–21 regarding personal responsibility and what it means to offer your body as a living sacrifice to God. Meditate on the words of Psalm 51:10.

The Sandwich Challenge
- Read 1 Corinthians chapter 12 (a slice of bread), asking the Lord to speak to you about your role in the body of Christ and how He wants to work through you to build it up.
- Read 1 Corinthians chapter 13 (the substance of the sandwich), asking the Lord to show you areas where you are pleasing Him and where you can improve in loving others.
- Read 1 Corinthians chapter 14 (the other slice of bread), asking the Lord to refine or expand your comprehension of the gifts of prophecy and tongues.

GOD'S CALL: RENEW YOUR MIND

"The plans I have for you, My child, are good, acceptable, and perfect. It is My pleasure to create in you a new heart with a renewed mind, that you might honor Me and obey My commands. I want only what is best for you. To present yourself as a living sacrifice for My service should not be a chore but a joy. Rest. Rest in Me. The renewal I have planned for you cannot be accomplished through striving but through your relinquishment. Refreshment and renewal will come in equal measure to your ability to surrender yourself to Me. Then will the Holy Spirit create in you a pure heart and renew a steadfast spirit within you."

YOUR RESPONSE TO GOD

Dear Lord, I present my body to You as a living sacrifice. My initials on this line _____ (or a special place in my Bible or journal) indicate my sincere desire for You to renew my mind so that I, in turn, can control my will, actions, and emotions in ways that are pleasing to You.

 SEED FOR THOUGHT

Formula for living:
Keep your chin up and your knees down.

—Author Unknown

 SEED FOR THOUGHT

"When a Christian is in the wrong place,
his right place will be empty."

—*T. J. Bach*

CHAPTER 8

PRUNED TO FLOURISH

 SEED FOR THOUGHT

"I am only one, but still I am one.
I cannot do everything, but still I can do something;
and because I cannot do everything,
I will not refuse to do something I can do."

—*Helen Keller*

"I am the true vine and my Father is the gardener.
He cuts off every branch in me that bears no fruit,
while every branch that does bear fruit he trims clean
that it will be even more fruitful."

—*John 15:1–2*

We're known by the fruit we bear, good or bad. Plentiful crops of good fruit don't just happen; somebody has to prune the trees. Just as unhealthy or excess branches can drain strength from a tree, so can stubborn character defects rob us of the spiritual fruit we need to mature us. Galatians 5:24 assumes those of us who belong to Christ Jesus have "crucified our sinful nature with its passions and desires." That's strong language. Pruning, like crucifixion, is painful. The fears, self-centeredness, and other aspects of our sinful nature must be removed.

For quite a while now, God has been sawing away at an obstinate branch of timidity I've had since childhood. During the ten years it took me to write this book, I told only a handful of people about my Holy Spirit baptism because I was afraid most wouldn't understand. I didn't want to risk rejection or ridicule.

Back in 1983, I knew I'd have to tell my husband. Although Drew and I had never kept even the slightest thing from one another, I was in no hurry to let him in on this. *How will he take it? Will he like the new me? Will he feel intimidated? Will he understand?*

For several days, I secretly exercised my new prayer language—not only during my regular quiet time but in the shower, the car, the back yard—anywhere I could be alone. Then came our vacation to Georgia, and there went my privacy.

Of course, just as prayers don't need to be spoken aloud, the same is true for tongues. But I was fascinated by this language I had never learned, so I kept it to a soft whisper. Within inches of each other for a whole week, I wondered if Drew might be pressing an ear against the bathroom door of our motel room, curious about my hushed conversations with God. If he did, he never mentioned it.

Our destination was Augusta and the practice rounds of The Masters golf tournament. The setting was flawless. It was like heaven on earth. The plush grass was so meticulously groomed I had to touch it to see if it was real. Azaleas were blooming at their peak, while pools of sparkling water complemented the sunshine, fresh air, and gentle breezes. The beauty almost made me dizzy.

That first evening, in an intimate setting of candlelight and soft music, it was perfectly natural for our conversation to turn toward the beauty of God's creation. The time seemed right to talk about my spiritual awakening.

"Something has happened to me that you need to know about," I said.

"What's that?" Drew leaned forward with interest.

"Well, you know how important my personal devotions have been to me over the past month or so. I've been learning how to become more intimate with God and . . ."

I was able to tell Drew everything, not with apprehension but with joy. "So, hon, now that you know, what do you think?"

"I knew it was coming," he said, gazing across the tiny table, love radiating from his eyes.

His reaction amazed me—especially since we'd had little or no discussion about the baptism in the Holy Spirit or the subject of tongues.

"You what? You knew it was coming? How could you possibly know?"

"I guess I didn't exactly *know*," he said. "It's just that I've been watching you, and I'm not surprised."

I had his enthusiastic endorsement! Still curious about his observations, I asked, "Have you noticed any change in me?"

"No. Well, yes. I do see a difference in you—but it's a good difference. It's as though all the best parts of you are even better."

From that point on, we talked of how we appreciated each other and why. It was better than our honeymoon. Our love overflowed, growing in intensity with each word of affirmation. Holding hands across the table couldn't begin to express the closeness we felt. At that special moment, it was as though God reached down from heaven, lifted us from our seats, and deposited us on the dance floor where we wrapped our arms around each other.

Drew held me with a tenderness that reached into my very soul. As we moved to the melody of the music in the dimly lit room, he caressed my hair. Never before had Drew been so openly affectionate, so deeply romantic. Although the music continued, our dancing slowed and stopped. He held me close and lifted my chin, kissing me so thoroughly that I was aware of nothing but an overwhelming love for him and for the God who brought us together. Never had I known so clearly what it meant to be *one in the Lord*.

God was teaching me that spiritual gifts aren't for our own satisfaction or self-advancement; their purpose is to help us love and serve God and others.

> If I had the gift of being able to speak in other languages without learning them, and could speak in every language there is in all of heaven and earth, but didn't love others, I would only be making noise. If I had the gift of prophecy and knew all about what is going to happen in the future, knew everything about *everything*, but didn't love others, what good would it do? (1 Corinthians 13:1–2 TLB)

Becoming Fruit Inspectors

Drew is a "fruit inspector." He knows what it means to "taste and see that the Lord is good" (Psalm 34:8). Quietly observing my baby steps of obedience in following God, he must have had some unspoken questions: *Will Candy's spiritual search include or exclude me? Will she still value my opinion or will she feel she has all the answers? Will she be able to balance day-to-day responsibilities or will she be overwhelmed?* God is love. Drawing closer to God didn't take me away from my husband; it drew me closer to him.

Religion by itself, on the other hand, has been known to divide and separate. It might not be a bad idea to ask ourselves occasionally, *Is what I'm doing legalistic or loving? Do I focus more on regulations than on relationships? Am I more concerned about myself or others? Is what I'm doing drawing me closer to or further from friends and family?*

Bad fruit sometimes comes wrapped in packages of materialism, greed, or gluttony. So in addition to battles of the mind and the spirit, we must constantly be alert to battles of the flesh. Preoccupation with money and the things money can buy robs us of the things money can't buy, like walks in the park and snuggle time. Today's "golden calf" comes in all shapes and sizes. Do we really need *another this*, or a *bigger that?*

> But when you follow your own wrong inclinations your lives will produce these evil results: impure thoughts, eagerness for lustful pleasure, idolatry, spiritism (that is, encouraging the activity of demons), hatred and fighting, jealousy and anger, constant effort to get the best for yourself, complaints and criticisms, the feeling that everyone else is wrong except those in your own little group—and there will be wrong doctrine, envy, murder, drunkenness, wild parties, and all that sort of thing (Galatians 5:19–21 TLB).

How to Grow Good Fruit

In contrast to the list of negatives that threaten to undo us, God calls us to grow wholesome fruit that will make a difference in our day-to-day relationships and in our well-being as individuals.

"Since we live by the Spirit, let us keep in step with the Spirit" (see Galatians 5:22–25) by developing these nine character traits:

- Love
- Joy
- Peace
- Patience
- Kindness
- Goodness
- Gentleness
- Faithfulness
- Self-Control

In our society of instant expecttions, we may be impatient with ourselves when these characteristics ripen slowly. But the fact is, the fruit of the Spirit begins as a seedling and continues to grow daily as we receive nourishment from the Vine. Then, and only then, do we find these attributes replacing our old, self-centered nature.

LOVE in a Medicine Cabinet

In our first year of marriage, Drew and I had a lot of adjusting to do. We faced numerous challenges:

- Combining families (with his two teens making way for my semi-spoiled three-year-old).

- Remodeling the house to accommodate our blended family (paint brushes flying, carpenters knocking out walls and windows, electricians climbing over plumbers).

- Getting acquainted (since we'd only known each other seven weeks before tying the knot).

As you might imagine, there were times when Drew and I didn't see eye-to-eye. We tried several methods for resolving our differences, but the one that worked best was the love chapter. I typed the words of 1 Corinthians 13:4–8 (TLB) on a card and taped it to the back of my medicine cabinet mirror for quick reference; then, whenever our opinions clashed, I'd race into the bathroom and point out the areas where *he* was falling short.

Love is very patient and kind,

never jealous or envious, never boastful or proud,

never haughty or selfish or rude.

Love does not demand its own way.

It is not irritable or touchy.

It does not hold grudges

and will hardly even notice when others do it wrong.

It is never glad about injustice,

but rejoices whenever truth wins out.

If you love someone

you will be loyal to him no matter what the cost.

You will always believe in him,

always expect the best of him,

and always stand your ground in defending him.

All the special gifts and powers from God

will someday come to an end,

but love goes on forever.

I typed the words of 1 Cor. 13:4–8 on a card and taped it to the back of my medicine cabinet mirror for quick reference.

Then it would be Drew's turn to read the love chapter. Somehow, he always managed to come up with at least two or three shortcomings for *me* to work on. Disagreements don't last long when both sides look at themselves in the light of God's love.

Sometimes for a wedding gift I'll write the words in calligraphy, along with the name of the bride and groom and date of their wedding, and attach these simple instructions to the back of the frame:

1. Place in a conspicuous location.
2. In case of controversy, open eyes and read.
3. Discuss.
4. Kiss and make up.

Love is the umbrella that covers all the other fruits. Notice that joy, peace, patience, and the rest are practical expressions of love that not only benefit marriage but spill over into every area of life, including the workplace.

Unexpected JOY

By nature, I'm a compliant person who tries hard to please others. This tendency can lead to what is known as "doormat Christianity." God doesn't want us to be doormats; He wants us to be *overcomers*. Learning to say "no" to people who take advantage of us requires some work, but I'm getting better at it.

I used to work for an over-critical boss. I tried to win him over, but no matter what I did, my efforts never seemed quite good enough. At times, he'd provoke me to anger or tears. I would think of all kinds of ways to get even, but I knew retaliation would only make things worse.

Maybe I should confront him. No, others with more influence have tried, and he hasn't changed. I can file a complaint, but who wants the added stress?

Eventually, I realized that God was using this situation to strengthen my character. Although I couldn't change my employer's critical nature, I *could* change my reaction to his criticism. I found the King James Version of 1 Corinthians 14:38 helpful. Although written for a different situation, the words spoke to my need and even made me chuckle from time to time: "If any man be ignorant, let him be ignorant." I chose to emotionally distance myself and to disagree with his opinions of me.

I will not allow myself to be yanked around emotionally. I will do my job, and I will do it well. I will be pleasant, professional, and diligent. Outwardly, things had not changed. Inwardly, however, I was free! Free to be my best self. In reality, I was living out a biblical principle:

You slaves must always obey your earthly masters, not only trying to please them when they are watching you but all the time; obey them willingly because of your love for the Lord and because you want to please Him. Work hard and cheerfully at all you do, just as though you were working for the Lord and not merely for your masters, remembering that it is the Lord Christ who is going to pay you, giving you your full portion of all He owns. He is the one you are really working for (Colossians 3:22–24 TLB).

At the end of a particularly stressful but productive week, I lingered for a moment by the office door to appreciate my surroundings and savor a deep sense of accomplishment. Everything was in order. Papers had been filed, letters mailed, phones answered, and reports assembled. People who needed a listening ear had found someone who cared. Problems had been solved. As I left the building, a gust of fresh air swept my satisfaction to an even higher level. I was exhilarated and buoyant.

Where does this kind of joy come from? I asked the Lord. *And why should I feel this way today, of all days?*

He reminded me of Nehemiah 8:10, "The joy of the LORD is your strength."

It means so much when someone says, "I appreciate you," but those words rarely come when we need them. Instead, those of us who do our work "as unto the Lord" (even if we're slaves) can experience fulfillment because the Lord provides strength for the task and joy when we least expect it. Sometimes, peace comes the same way.

PEACE Under Pressure

As a mother, anything that affects my daughter affects me. When Kim finds peace in the midst of turmoil, I feel as though her breakthrough is my own.

There was a time when only one thing stood between Kim and her Delaware teaching certificate—the reading portion of the national test.

After taking it six times, she was still three points shy of the magic number. Although she overcame her learning disability in college, this hurdle had her stymied.

Opening yet another set of negative results that came in the mail, she burst into tears and fled to her room. I followed her to offer consolation.

"You have another year and a half to go, hon."

"I know, Mom, but I want to get this reading test behind me. How will I ever pass? I don't even know which questions I got right and which ones I got wrong. It's like a guessing game that I always lose."

"God hasn't brought you this far to let you down. You know you've been called to teach. You have a God-given ability to reach students with empathy that others don't have. Don't be discouraged, honey. Remember how frustrating it was when you were in special ed and we had to work so hard to help you learn? But you *did* learn. What seemed like a disadvantage then is an advantage now. You're using those techniques to help your own special ed students. I know you're under pressure, but God won't let you down."

"Do you think He's trying to teach me something?" Kim asked.

"Maybe. Whatever it is, it's between you and God. Why don't you pray about it?"

Composure was written all over her when she faced the next testing session. She didn't have to tell me she'd prayed; it showed. Ironically, the odds were against the outward peace she exhibited. She had a sore throat, and a friend had kept her up late the night before so she didn't get much sleep.

On top of that, there was this obnoxious guy who distracted her before and during the test. He introduced himself to Kim by bragging about how he was working on his doctorate. She tried to distance herself from him but, wouldn't you know, his assigned seat was right beside hers. They had to share a table, and just as the test was about to begin, he reached over and helped himself to one of Kim's pencils, whispering, "Mine isn't a number two." Then, after breaking the point, he took the second of her three pencils. She finally spoke up and told him to ask the proctor for help. He thumped and fidgeted during the whole test, bumped the table each time he marked an answer, and flipped pages noisily.

"But you know, Mom," Kim said afterwards, "it didn't bother me because, as we began, the proctor opened the door and a ray of bright white light came into the room. It was as if God said, ***"See, I'm here with you,"*** and He covered me with His peace. I can't explain it, but all my anxiety and irritation just disappeared, and I was able to concentrate in spite of the distractions."

The test results came back, and Kim only improved her score by one point—not enough.

Although Kim had been working as a Special Education teacher for some time and got rave reviews from students, parents, and her administrators, she had one last chance to take the test. If she failed again, she would not be permitted to teach in the state of Delaware. We submitted her name to prayer chains and intercessory groups and clung to Philippians 4:6–7 like a lifeline.

Don't worry about anything; instead, pray about everything; tell God your needs and don't forget to thank Him for His answers. If you do this you will experience God's peace, which is far more wonderful than the human mind can understand.

His peace will keep your thoughts and your hearts quiet and at rest as you trust in Christ Jesus (TLB).

Don't worry about anything; instead, pray about everything.

This time when she came home, she felt optimistic and said the questions seemed "easy." She made up her mind to leave the results with God, saying, "It is what it is, and if I don't pass, it must mean the Lord had something better in mind."

Three months later, the envelope came. She not only passed, but with flying colors!

Since then, Kim's career and self-confidence have blossomed. In addition to changing the lives of her students, she mentors other teachers, was named Teacher of the Year in 2004 for her school, and is awaiting the results of her national boards—a feat some equate to earning a second master's degree. As all-consuming as the process can be, Kim sensed the presence of Christ throughout and feels she did her best. Although the results won't be back in time for me to report a "happy ending," she saw a mental picture of the word "CONGRATULATIONS" on the monitor when the proctor announced the test was concluded.

I would like to tell you that Kim floats through her pressure-packed days peacefully. In fact, some days she does. But as a working wife and mother of two preschoolers, she struggles with perfectionism. Sometimes, the slightest thing out of order drives her crazy. She's working on that.

And isn't that the way it is for all of us? Just when we think we've overcome a major obstacle in our lives and found peace, another trouble spot pops up to torment us. But the promise of peace under pressure is real. God is teaching us daily how to be an overcomer in our trials (whether external or internal) and how to practice patience.

PATIENCE That Pays Off

"Dear God, please give me patience, and give it to me *now!*" Sound familiar?

Patience doesn't grow on trees. It hides its roots deep in the soil of faith and hope where it can't be seen for the *longest* time. Then, just when you think you have a sprig of patience to point to, the Master's pruning shears snip it off. There's no easy way to develop this particular fruit.

Writing the first edition of *Fruitbearer* taught me more about patience than anything I can recall. How glad I am that it wasn't published in its original form. The Lord knew it would take years for me to refine my writing skills, learn to handle rejection, appreciate the value of relinquishment, test my faith, practice what I preach, and establish credibility. He knew that I needed time and experience to develop pure motives and get rid of false humility so I could give Him the glory. I'm working on a fiction series now, and believe me, the

Lord has His hand on it. Not a day goes by that I don't turn to Him for wisdom and direction. Truly, apart from Him I can do nothing.

My friend Joyce Thomas says, "God may delay the answers to our prayers in order to enlarge our capacity to receive." She knows what it's like to pray for things to get better, only to have them get worse. Joyce, whose husband died in a plane crash thirty-five years ago, leaving her to raise two infant daughters to adulthood on her own, is one of the most composed Christians I know. She made an important discovery: "Sometimes, when you're really desperate, when the clock is running out and you're about to give up, God brings the answer at *five minutes to midnight.*"

Another friend writes, "I never pray for patience but for endurance; to me, patience means the 'grind your teeth while you wait' syndrome. With endurance, you abide in God's love and hang on until the trial is over." Patience endures. It doesn't complain.

> Is your life full of difficulties and temptations? Then be happy, for when the way is rough, your patience has a chance to grow. So let it grow, and don't try to squirm out of your problems. For when your patience is finally in full bloom, then you will be ready for anything, strong in character, full and complete (James 1:2–4 TLB).

Patience knows how to relinquish control and how to wait. Patience understands the meaning of the words hope, trust, and perseverance.

KINDNESS We Can Measure

The best definition of kindness I can find comes from a book published in 1974 entitled *Spirit Fruit* by John M. Drescher (see Recommended Resources):

> What then is kindness? Kindness is love in little things. It is respect for the feelings and personhood of another. It is thoughtfulness put in action. It is the kind of spirit which

builds togetherness and love in situations which could be explosive. Kindness brings blessing and good feeling in the places where bitterness and ill will would flourish.

What is kindness? Kindness is helping another in need. It is consideration of the relationships between persons. Kindness is conversation which centers on the good qualities of others. Kindness avoids speaking evil. Kindness reaches out to others in trouble or suffering. Kindness supports others. Kindness gives a helping hand or healing touch in time of trouble. Kindness refrains from words which will hurt another or cast doubt on character. Instead it will speak kindly and hope for the best.

Someone in our choir suggested that we adopt a family for Christmas. We learned of a young woman with small children whose husband was in jail. Each choir member carefully selected and wrapped gifts which we put into gigantic leaf bags for delivery. None of us knew the woman or had any idea how she would react to our initiative. I was elected to make contact with her.

"Don't let her be offended, Lord," I prayed as my car turned onto the dirt road and neared the deteriorating mobile home. My timid knock on the rickety door was answered by a slender, tall woman with long, light brown hair, expressive eyes, a pale complexion, and a look of confusion on her pretty face. Some sort of explanation tumbled out of me as I inched the cumbersome packages onto the doorstep and paused for her reaction. She was hesitant, but accepted the unexpected gifts graciously, a humbling experience for us both. Her deeply touching letter of thanks to the choir was the beginning of a relationship that blossoms to this day.

Shortly after our first encounter, Dawn and her children began attending worship services. The choir continued its holiday mission for her family until they became self-sufficient. One Christmas, prompted by the Holy Spirit, I tucked Evelyn Christenson's book, *What Happens When Women Pray* (see Recommended Resources), into the bag of presents. As a result, Dawn committed her life to Christ.

She and I have become intimate friends, true sisters in Christ. By an uncanny coincidence, we wore the same size. At a time when there seemed to be no way out of her troubles, my nearly new suits and dresses gave her the boost she needed to attend and graduate from college. What I felt was a small kind deed, she saw as a gift of hope.

Any kindness I've shown her has been returned to me tenfold through her prayers and the satisfaction I have from knowing I played a small part in helping her find the Lord. Oh, how He transformed her. Dawn has had an emotional setback since her grown son was killed in an accident. The last time we spoke, she told me she didn't "feel close to God" but still trusts Him and knows He is restoring her emotionally. If our church had not extended kindness to her years ago, would she be able to draw on this assurance today?

Kindness is measurable. If you want to test the level of your kindness, rank yourself on a scale of 1 to 10: How kindly do I treat those who are unkind to me? How quick am I to forgive? When I die, how many acts of kindness will I leave behind for people to remember?

The *Chicago Tribune* published this touching tidbit:

A mother asked her six-year-old what loving kindness meant.

"Well," the child said, "when I ask you for a piece of bread and butter and you give it to me, that's kindness. But when you put jam on it, that's loving kindness."

GOODNESS That Counts

John Drescher describes goodness as "love in action" and says that it deals primarily with the motives of our speech and conduct. I agree.

If goodness had a face, I think it would look like Mother Teresa. If goodness could talk, perhaps it would tell us the most important thing in life is relationships. Goodness considers others more important than oneself.

When I think of goodness, another face comes to mind—the face of my mother. She was an encourager, the kind of person others wanted to be around. Her words were spiced with nuggets of wisdom or "just common sense" as she called it. She enjoyed doing things for people like baking cakes, knitting sweaters, and writing personal notes with each Christmas card. Mom never wanted a lot of fanfare or accolades for her generosity. Her joy came from quietly doing good, setting an example of unselfishness, and sowing seeds that have grown into cherished memories. Mom taught me how to practice love in action.

Twelve years ago, her health failed and Hospice was called in. Dad was exhausted from trying to be at Mom's bedside round-the-clock, so I decided to stay overnight. I made a bed for myself on the floor next to her and tucked myself in. Mom's discomfort had increased, and she could only rest for about half an hour at a time. Her needs were simple but frequent—a sip of water, a visit to the bedside commode, or a request to turn over her tape of Tennessee Ernie Ford hymns. I cherished the opportunity to pamper the one who used to pamper me.

Beyond giving of myself, I wanted to give her something else to lift her spirits above the anguish of dying—something to show how much she meant to me. So, eight days before her death, I poured out my heart to Mom in blue ink on pink parchment. It was a special letter, punctuated with tears that splashed on a few words here and there, confirming my love, devotion, and appreciation.

"I wrote you a letter," I told her, "but it might make you cry, so you may want to read it later."

"Honey, I don't have to read it to know what it says."

"How can you know?" I asked. "I just wrote it."

"I just know," she answered. "Put it over there on the counter."

Within a few days her eyes began to cloud over, and she couldn't read it if she wanted to.

"About that letter," I said, "would you like me to read it to you? I think I can get through it without choking up." Again, she declined with a knowing smile.

"I understand," I fibbed. "Maybe it was for my own benefit; it was probably good therapy for me to put my feelings on paper. I read it to Kim that night, and we both had a good cry which led into one of those rare mother-daughter talks like you and I used to have."

Although Mom never got to see or hear the contents of my letter while she was living, a portion of it was used during the memorial service as an illustration of her deep, abiding faith.

Then, on the day of her burial, I tucked it into my purse thinking I might read it privately over Mom's grave. I whispered to Dad at the end of the service, "I want to read my letter before we leave." He promptly announced, "Candy wants to read a letter." Suddenly, I was standing in front of the microphone, sobbing my way through it.

"I was going to come up and help you read it," Drew said, "but I was too choked up myself."

My uncle had to take an anxiety pill. "The only thing that saved me," he said afterward, "is that I couldn't hear."

Mom was a sensible woman. She didn't wear her religion on her sleeve to be scrutinized; she wore it in her heart to be read. Ah, that explains it. Mom didn't need to read my letter because the goodness I described in it was written on her heart:

> You yourselves are our letter, written on our hearts, known and read by everybody. You show that you are a letter from Christ . . . written not with ink but with the Spirit of the living God, not on tablets of stone but on tablets of human hearts (2 Corinthians 3:2–3).

Goodness, like faithfulness, is not only developed daily but is most evident in the face of difficulty.

FAITHFULNESS That Can Be Trusted

My experience with the organized church is probably the best illustration I can give of a time when God used difficult circumstances to increase my faithfulness—to teach me what it means to be steadfast, loyal, devoted, unwavering, trustworthy, dependable, and true. For about ten years, our congregation went through a series of trials and tribulations that helped me appreciate what James meant when he said we should welcome tough times:

> At the time, discipline isn't much fun. It always feels like it's going against the grain. Later, of course, it pays off handsomely, for it's the well-trained who find themselves mature in their relationship with God (Hebrews 12:11 MSG).

Faithful people don't run from problems; they address them with kindness, conviction, and truth. When our church troubles first began, I came home in a huff, ready to go shopping for a new preacher.

Faithful people don't run from problems.

"Whose church is it?" Drew asked candidly. "Is it Rev. ____'s church, or is it God's church?"

"God's," I admitted, the wind knocked out of my sails.

"If all the people who feel like you do were to leave, what do you think would happen to God's church?" he asked. "Wouldn't it be better to stay and speak up for your convictions?"

That was the beginning of my education in faithfulness. During the years of turmoil that followed, our pews gradually emptied as others left to find new church homes, but we stayed. This is not to imply that those who left were unfaithful. Perhaps God used the situation to call them to a different place for a different purpose. Sometimes, like a mother eagle that removes the downy feathers from the nest and exposes the thorny twigs to encourage her offspring to move on, the Lord employs uncomfortable situations to move us forward spiritually.

In my case, it seemed clear that the Lord not only wanted me to stay among the thorns, but He challenged me to become involved in clearing them. My opinions were heard as an elder, at choir rehearsal, in Sunday school, and on the pastor nominating committee. Oddly enough, the minister whose theology upset me so greatly turned out to be the one under whose pastorate I experienced the most spiritual growth. Our tactful confrontations forced me to dig into the creeds and confessions of the church and search the Scriptures with newfound purpose. Because of him, I learned to say what I believe.

It was during those tumultuous years that I discovered *The Helper*. Would my search for the Holy Spirit have been so intense had everything been status quo at my home church? I wonder.

Numerous ministers have come and gone since then. During the transition, both clergy and congregation had more than their fair share of hard feelings, misunderstandings, and tears. When our congregation gained the nickname of "the church with no pastor," we began to do some serious soul searching and praying. In response, God sent us a pastor with a shepherd's heart—a man who knows how to care for a scattered flock.

I'm glad I stuck around. Today, I look forward to the sermons, the pews are filling up, and the people are seeking Bible studies and opportunities to grow. We've even added a new education wing and fellowship hall. (Funny how we tend to measure success by attendance and buildings, but God looks on the heart.) Best of all, the Lord has used the ups and downs to shape my character and faithfulness. I am better balanced and more well-rounded as a Christian than I would have been had I left in a huff.

Oh, the benefits of faithfulness that gently influence our churches, our families, our communities, our workplaces, and our friends.

GENTLENESS That Speaks Without a Word

Our Sisters in Christ group had an interesting occasion to employ gentleness during our study of *The Helper*. We were discussing the chapter entitled, "He Convicts Me of Sin," when Sonja said softly, "I'm hung up on this chapter. I used to be a sinner, but now I'm a Christian and don't have a problem with sin anymore."

Lynn and I, who were responsible for leading the group, looked at each other for clues on how to respond. Sonja, who was emotionally unstable, had just been released from the psychiatric unit of the hospital, and her condition was delicate. Exercising gentleness (meekness), neither of us could bring ourselves to explain that we are all sinners who continue to fall short of the glory of God. Sonja was just beginning to feel good about herself. One of us suggested she skip over that chapter for the time being. After the meeting, Lynn and I prayed that the Holy Spirit would teach her in His own good time and way.

Several months later, to our great amazement, Sonja stated quite frankly, "We're all sinners, you know." God had revealed this to her without a word from us.

We prayed that the Holy Spirit would teach her in His own good time and way.

To discover the strength of gentleness is humbling, indeed. Blessed are the meek who place their confidence in God and take responsibility for their own actions.

SELF-CONTROL Sums It Up

This is the area I need to work on the most. The point was driven home recently while I was preparing my speaker's information sheet. To accent my speech topics, I began using "Fruit of the Spirit" word art to decorate the page. There I was, having a great time with artistic placement of the words love, joy, peace, patience, kindness, goodness, faithfulness, gentleness. I was smiling at how far I'd come in these areas and rejoicing that the Lord had given me Galatians 5:22–23 as my life verse . . . when I realized I had come to the bottom of the page and there was no room for the word self-control. My first and very telling reaction was, *Oh well, guess I'll just have to leave it out.* Oooohooo. Leave it out? I don't *think* so!

All of us have our own personal temptations. For me, these days it's overeating. For others, temptation comes in the form of alcohol or drug abuse, sexual desires, stealing, compulsive spending, raging tempers, gossiping, or perhaps procrastination.

While some people think the best way to handle temptation is to yield to it, others realize that people who struggle with similar temptations can help each other overcome them. This is the stuff support groups like Alcoholics Anonymous are made of. I believe one of the reasons for the success of twelve-step programs is that they admit their powerlessness and understand they need a "higher power." (Of course, the name of my "higher power" is Jesus.)

The fruit of self-control does not come from our own determination; it comes from the Holy Spirit who works within us to change our desires and establish our steps. As we respond to the Holy Spirit's internal tugs and reminders, we find ourselves exercising control over not only our appetites and impulses but also over our thoughts and actions. In my struggle to shed unhealthy pounds, my self-control is not as well-developed as I would like, but the Lord is teaching me a whole new approach to nutrition, holding me accountable to Himself and to others, and helping me to make significant progress.

God will not take over the management of our physical bodies. He holds us responsible for our own deeds in the flesh. We must decide whether to obey the Lord and rely on His help or quench the Spirit and suffer the consequences. When I eat too much, I get fat, but the issue is deeper than an expanding waistline. It could be a matter of life and death:

> Do not be deceived: God cannot be mocked. A man reaps what he sows. The one who sows to please his sinful nature, from that nature will reap *destruction*; the one who sows to please the Spirit, from the Spirit will reap *eternal life*. Let us not become weary in doing good, for at the proper time we will reap a harvest if we do not give up (Galatians 6:7–9, emphasis added).

Self-control: What a fitting summary of all nine fruits of the Spirit. For unless we commit our desires, our actions, our emotions, and our motives to God and exercise self-control, we cannot effectively and consistently walk by the Spirit.

Have you noticed how the attributes of the Spirit are intertwined? They are not isolated from each other but all represent elements of a singular fruit: LOVE.

Rotten Apples

By contrast, the god of the world of rotten apples spreads a tempting feast, but when his tasty-looking morsels are digested, they reap destruction: stolen joy, broken relationships, and rotting flesh.

> "Watch out for false prophets. They come to you in sheep's clothing, but inwardly they are ferocious wolves. *By their fruit you will recognize them.* Do people pick grapes from thornbushes, or figs from thistles? Likewise every good tree bears good fruit, but a bad tree bears bad fruit" (Matthew 7:15–17, emphasis added).

Testing the fruit of our lives and deeds is essential. Unfortunately, not everything that is done in the name of religion is of God. Abuse of spiritual gifts is not uncommon, and the gifts of the Spirit have been misused and misunderstood, often by people who mean well. Even the Scriptures have been used as a club to drive noncompliant people out of the church. Things can go wrong in even the best of churches. Satan will get a toehold wherever he can—in our seminaries, our schools, our homes, and our places of employment. That's why we have to carefully inspect work that's done in the Lord's name to see if it bears good fruit.

Sisters in Christ

Our Sisters in Christ group learned the hard way that the devil is a worthy opponent. We also learned not to give him more credit than he's due.

Our home Bible study and prayer group was about a year and a half old when we got into some heavy discussion about deliverance and the power of the evil one. Our talks about Satan's power scared one woman so much that she stopped coming to our meetings. At other times, what started out as sincere prayer concerns somehow turned into avenues for gossip. Unrealistic expectations—usually petty—became fertile soil for hurt feelings. Broken confidences became a stumbling block to openness.

It appeared that Satan was winning. Our group had begun with three women, grown to twenty-three, and was back to three. It looked as though our fellowship would be divided and destroyed.

But God had other plans. He used our failures to teach us to center our conversation around Jesus' victory instead of satanic matters, to speak the truth in love, to forgive, to grow in grace, to keep confidences, and to depend on the Lord instead of on each other.

Over the years, our meetings have changed from once a week to once a month and back to weekly again. There are times when meetings are suspended completely, but the fellowship is still growing. Some members have relocated and initiated Bible studies in their new communities. Although there may only be three of us at some of our meetings, I have a list of 140 women who have been a part of our group at one time or another. That's a lot of sisters!

Lives are changed in our meetings, and decisions are made—to follow Christ, to change careers, to pursue a degree, to reconcile a troubled marriage, to take the plunge as a missionary, to seek professional counseling or medical attention, or to replace suicidal thoughts with hope. Women who come weighed down with problems are encouraged to put their troubles in a heap by the door; then, after we have spent two hours focusing on Christ, they're free to pick them up again on their way out. Often they discover that their problems aren't worth picking up at all, they're lighter than they seemed before, or they've mysteriously disappeared as we prayed or read Scriptures.

I can't count the valuable lessons that I have learned personally through my involvement with Sisters in Christ. Here's one example of how God took what might be considered bad fruit and turned it into something good.

In my desire to lead the group, I had unknowingly given Satan a foothold by trying to be everything to everybody. It's called the "Savior Syndrome," where you feel personally responsible for fixing everyone's problems, and it's a sure-fire path to burnout and an inflated ego. To stay off that destructive path, I learned to point hurting people to the One who can really help them. A pastor once told me, "God can even use your mistakes." I try to remember that whenever I slip into my old habit of thinking I have to have all the answers.

The devil despises home-based fellowship groups. He hates it when two or three believers get together with Christ in their midst. Groups like Sisters in Christ have been able to overcome Satan's interference by allowing the Lord to do the leading. They recognize the truth of Psalm 127:1, "Unless the LORD builds the house, its builders labor in vain." How can we know if God is leading? By His nature. Consider these words from my journal:

"The Spirit of God is known by qualities of orderliness, gentleness, and lovingkindness. Test your leadings by how much of My nature is revealed. Ask yourself questions that will open your eyes to what is happening.

"Are there numerous obstacles that throw you into discord and confusion? Is your plan rigid and unbending, void of adaptability to changing needs? Then your leadings are not directed by My Holy Spirit. Are you being influenced by those who are quick to judge or criticize? This is an indication of superficial love. Are you being pressured to make a hasty decision? My leading is determined prayerfully, not by the demands of the loudest voice, whether it be someone else's or your own.

"Fellowship plans originating from the throne of grace are visions to behold. Doors open unexpectedly, ushering in opportunities for compassion. Details effortlessly work themselves out with minimal effort on your part. Prayer is not only studied and discussed, it is practiced. Love, joy, peace, faith, and hope reign when I am leading the group.

"True, you can expect to encounter obstacles that appear to frustrate your efforts to come together in My name, for the enemy works tirelessly against the fellowship of believers. When this happens, wait upon Me. I will open a way. Then, when you see the path I have cleared, you may walk in fellowship with confidence."

Beware

Not all spiritual seekers who desire fellowship are Christians. People who are led by an "unholy spirit" may seek fellowship for the sole purpose of leading us astray. Discernment is essential.

False teachings and trappings are everywhere. Often they are cloaked in packages that appear to be harmless or entertaining, so well-disguised that we may not recognize them. Contrary to public opinion, ignorance is *not* bliss. Don't be fooled. Educate yourself by reading books like *Satan's Evangelistic Strategy for This New Age*, by Erwin Lutzer and John DeVries (see Recommended Resources). Visit a Christian bookstore and ask for materials that can give you an in-depth biblical perspective on:

- *Mind control practices such as hypnotism, ESP, and Transcendental Meditation.* While the science of hypnotherapy is a respected profession, open minds that are not focused on Christ are vulnerable. How can we truly know what a therapist believes? Be very careful about seeking this method for your problems.

- *Fortunetelling and spiritism.* If you're tempted to dabble in occultic practices like tea leaves, tarot cards, palm reading, crystals, and Ouija boards, don't! The Scriptures denounce these things. Look up passages under sorcery and witchcraft in a topical Bible; you might find it interesting to see what Isaiah 47:13 has to say about horoscopes.

Satan is having a heyday with the naive and misled citizens of the world. He knows his time is short, and he's pulling out all stops so that he might even deceive the elect, if that were possible (Mark 13:22).

Satan's deceptions are not innocent! If they are allowed to infiltrate fellowship groups, there will be real chaos. They must be renounced by anyone who chooses to follow God—especially those who seek the baptism in the Holy Spirit. The human body can become a spiritual battlefield for those who openly invite good and evil to occupy the same space. God's glory and Satan's destruction are simply not compatible.

This is no time to blindly accept any teaching just because people sound like they know what they're talking about. In this day and age, we need discernment like never before. Find out for yourself what the Bible says about these subjects.

Like the wicked queen's luscious-looking apple in *Snow White*, Satan's wickedness is sugar-coated on the outside but saturated with deadly poison on the inside. Don't fall for his tricks! If you have been involved in any way with false teachings and practices, this is serious business.

> Be self-controlled and alert. Your enemy the devil prowls around like a roaring lion looking for someone to devour. Resist him, standing firm in the faith (1 Peter 5:8–9).

God didn't mince words when He admonished the people about the dangers of pagan practices (Deuteronomy 18:9–13). His message has not changed. False teachings are still an abomination to Him.

To cling to doctrinal error is to invite a spiritual tug-of-war. There is no such thing as having "the best of both worlds" where the kingdom of God is concerned (Joshua 24:15–24). Anything that even hints of evil must be deliberately and soundly rejected. "Submit yourselves therefore to God. Resist the devil, and he will flee from you" (James 4:7 KJV). We face enough battles on the *outside* without asking for trouble on the *inside*.

How do we resist the devil? How do we stand firm in the faith? Here are some practical suggestions.

Steps to Victory

1. Make a choice: for God and against Satan. Say NO to anything that you know isn't of God. Avoid the tempter's territory. "Have nothing to do with the fruitless deeds of darkness, but rather expose them" (Ephesians 5:11).

2. Pray for God to set you free from any unwelcome spirits that have controlled you. Ask Him to fill the empty places in your life with His Holy Spirit. Those who are deeply in bondage would be wise to seek professional help from Christian counselors or a reputable deliverance ministry. Ah, but you ask, how does one go about finding a reputable deliverance ministry? Sadly, there are many that cause more harm than good. If only I could give you the name of a reliable pastor around the corner. Here is a web site you may find informative: *www.christian-faith.com/spiritualwarfare/healingdeliverance.html.*

    Jesus said of Himself, "The Spirit of the Lord is upon Me; He has appointed Me to preach Good News to the poor; He has sent Me to heal the brokenhearted and to announce that captives shall be released and the blind shall see, that the downtrodden shall be freed from their oppressors, and that God is ready to give blessings to all who come to Him" (Luke 4:18–19 TLB).

3. Show you mean business by studying your Bible and memorizing the Scriptures. "The whole Bible was given to us by inspiration from God and is useful to teach us what is true and to make us realize what is wrong in our lives; it straightens us out and helps us to do what is right. It is God's way of making us well prepared at every point, fully equipped to do good to everyone" (2 Timothy 3:16–17 TLB).

4. Actively seek the fellowship of others who can help strengthen you. You need to be around God's people. Find a Bible-believing church and get involved. "Let us not neglect our church meetings, as some people do, but encourage and warn each other, especially now that the day of his coming back again is drawing near" (Hebrews 10:25 TLB).

Remember, "Submit yourselves . . . to God. Resist the devil, and he will flee from you. Come near to God and He will come near to you. . . . Humble yourselves before the Lord, and He will lift you up" (James 4:7–8, 10).

The Fruits of Our Labor

The fruit of the Spirit is not simply for our own satisfaction and spiritual development but for the good of others.

In the end, "The only thing that counts is faith expressing itself through love" (Galatians 5:6). It sounds like a lot of work to grow a good healthy crop of spiritual fruit. Sure it is—anything of value is worth working for. But sometimes the best "work" we can do is to simply *abide*, as taught in John 15. And then there are those times when God tells us to ***take heart, and get moving.***

When the harvest is ripe, there is only a brief time for the crop to be gathered. If the farmer can't work fast enough, the crop is lost and wasted, left to rot on the vine or to be plowed under. We are called to a labor of love—a labor of urgency.

If you have any encouragement from being united with Christ, if any comfort from His love, if any fellowship with the Spirit, if any tenderness and compassion, then make my joy complete by being like-minded, having the same love, being one in spirit and purpose. Do nothing out of selfish ambition or vain conceit, but in humility consider others better than yourselves. Each of you should look not only to your own interests, but also to the interests of others (Philippians 2:1–4).

Walk a Mile With Me
(Charles L. East)

If you have learned to walk a little more sure-footedly than I,
Be patient with my stumbling then and know that only as I do
    my best and try
May I attain the goal for which we are both striving.
If through experience, your soul has gained heights which I as
    yet in dim-lit vision see,
Hold out your hand and point the way, lest from its straightness
    I should stray.
And walk a mile with me.

"The harvest is plentiful but the workers are few. Ask the Lord of the harvest, therefore, to send out workers into His harvest field" (Matthew 9:37–38).

Shall We Pray?

Lord of the harvest, we can see from the signs around us that the harvest is plentiful, and there are so few of us to do Your work. I am willing, but I feel so inadequate. And while I may never have had formal theological training, I am convinced that You can and will teach me everything I need to know to be an effective worker. Thank You for providing friends, mentors, and pastors who know and love the Scriptures. Count me among the faithful servants who are motivated and empowered by Your Holy Spirit to do my unique part in Your harvest field.

*W*HAT CAN I DO FOR YOU, LORD?

DIG INTO SCRIPTURE

Read Galatians 5:13–25 again (the tendencies of the flesh versus the fruit of the Spirit). Read also John 15:1–17.

GOD'S CALL: LIVE BY MY SPIRIT

"As you read the 15th chapter of John, dwell especially on verse five. Write these words on your heart: "I am the vine; you are the branches. If you remain in Me and I in you, you will bear much fruit; apart from Me you can do nothing." Is there a voice of condemnation telling you that you are not doing enough for Me? That is not My voice. For My voice does not condemn but beckon. You see, what I require is that you enjoy My company and grow into My likeness. The work that you do for Me is not the primary but the secondary consideration. Christian service is the overflow that comes from abiding in Me. If I were to give you a word of caution it would be this: Take care not to let any service, regardless of how noble, receive a higher place than the time spent nurturing your relationship with Me."

YOUR RESPONSE TO GOD

Spend 15 minutes each day alone with the Lord. Reserve 21 days on your calendar to do this. During those 15 minutes, review your day to evaluate the fruit that comes from this time. Ask the Lord to spotlight the fruit He wants to increase in you. Record your progress in your journal. Note what you did right, what you did wrong, and what you want God to help you change.

 SEED FOR THOUGHT

You don't need to know where you're going
if you know God is leading.

—*Author Unknown*

CHAPTER 9

EXPLORE YOUR CALLING

SEED FOR THOUGHT

"To know that even one life
has breathed easier because you have lived—
that is to have succeeded."

—*Ralph Waldo Emerson*

The hour has come for you to wake up from your slumber,
because our salvation is nearer now than when we first believed.
The night is nearly over; the day is almost here.
—Romans 13:11–12

God showed me through a dream how He calls ordinary people to affect society. When I woke up, I knew this was no ordinary dream. The details were so vivid and dripping with symbolism, I was perplexed. The images lingered in my mind and intrigued me. *What am I supposed to do with this dream?* A consuming desire to capture the details on paper provided the answer: ***Write it down.***

The Dream

The setting was a university campus. Although the surroundings were new to me, I seemed to know the place well. There was a lot of commotion. People were moving with purpose, briskly bound for diverse destinations.

I was responsible for guiding a small group of rookie students to their respective classrooms. Cutting through the crowd, they followed me like ducklings trailing their mama.

When we arrived at the first classroom, I gave each student my undivided attention while the others waited patiently in the wings. I fielded their questions and impressed upon each one how individualized their lesson plan would be. Then, before moving on, I pointed to the instructor and said, "You'll never have a better teacher. Although you may find His style a bit unusual, even unpredictable, He is truly a Master Teacher!" I repeated this process seven or eight times until each one was situated where he or she belonged.

Then, with the satisfaction of a mission accomplished, I was free to roam around. The crowd was still thick, and I blended in along the fringe feeling delightfully inconspicuous. I was under no pressure, with no particular goal—just an intense desire to explore. As I roamed the corridors, peering into busy lecture halls, libraries, study areas, and classrooms, the crowd gradually dissipated until the halls were clear. Eventually, the doors to all the rooms closed.

I was alone and blanketed by an exhilarating silence. It was a majestic, peaceful atmosphere. *Good,* I thought, *I've got the place all to myself.*

Innate curiosity drew me to the bottom step of a nearby staircase. The banister was sturdy, highly polished, and mammoth—a fitting complement to the wide and winding hardwood stairs. *Everything here is so solid,* I noticed, *and so old. This place must have been around for eons.* The inside of the building smelled fresh and sweet like spring air and fine furniture polish, not at all stuffy. Leisurely, I climbed one ancient step after another.

At each landing, I meandered through numerous corridors, poking my head into well-stocked closets and vacant but thoroughly equipped laboratories. Up, up, up I went until I found what had to be the top floor. This time, there were no hallway doors to open, only a spacious corridor with brilliantly buffed floors that seemed to stretch out a mile in front of me.

And then I saw the magnificent doors in the distance. They reached from floor to ceiling, from east to west. Ornately and exquisitely carved, it was as though they had been personally fashioned by Michelangelo. They conveyed a sense of grandeur and power. I felt a sort of "calling" to move toward them. I just had to see this masterpiece up close, maybe even touch it.

Once again, I was acutely aware of being alone—not another soul in sight. It was eerie, but reverent, like being in an empty church. *Maybe I shouldn't be here,* I contemplated. By then, I had reached the doors.

Within my grasp were two perfectly matched bronze handles on a door that must have been at least ten feet tall. I felt like Alice in Wonderland. They were so big; I was so small. To my delight, I discovered a little recessed spot at the bottom of each handle, just right for my outstretched fingers. At my slightest touch, the stately doors inched open, and I peered through them. The sight was breathtaking.

It was as though I had opened the doors to another country— another world. Spread out before me was a gigantic, open-air auditorium, an amphitheater big enough to host a Billy Graham crusade or the Olympics! Although it was dark, I had no trouble scanning the countless plateaus of vacant, cushioned seats.

It was then that I saw them—a group of men dressed in business suits way down in front on the stage. They were standing around a long table that looked like a judge's bench. Several of them leaned over the table with their heads together like military officers studying a map or planning battle strategy. The others reclined in easy conversation or thoughtful reflection.

One of the men stood head and shoulders above the rest. He was extraordinarily handsome with a deeply bronzed complexion that seemed to almost glow. His imposing posture implied gentle but strong leadership, and there was an aura about him that radiated power and authority. I had no doubt that he was the one in charge.

Whatever these men are doing, I decided, *it must be important— and confidential since they are so far removed from everybody else.* A shudder ran down my spine. *I don't belong here. I've gone too far. I'm out of my league!* Gripped by a holy fear, I turned quickly to slip out unobtrusively, but I bumped into something that made a noise—just a little sound, but it echoed from every wall! Had they heard it? Had they seen me? Glancing over my shoulder, I saw that they were all looking up at me.

I'm in big trouble now. My thoughts raced. Calling on every ounce of energy, I strained my body forward and sped down the endless hallway, certain that someone was chasing me. Faster and faster I ran, gaining momentum as I finally reached the stairs. No slowing down! My feet barely skimmed the steps as I ran down them.

My heart throbbed and pounded at the thought of being grabbed by my pursuer. *I shouldn't have been snooping around where I didn't belong*, I groaned as I ran. I was guilty, and I knew it. In my mind, I could see a fierce, rough hand clutching my neck—and wringing it. No doubt I would be dragged off and punished without mercy.

And then I heard him. ***"Candy, Candy,"*** He called. *He knows my name!* I gasped. Sneaking a glance back, I saw Him—their leader, the one with all the power. Although I had a thousand questions, I had to get away. With a new burst of energy, I surged ahead, but not fast enough.

He tackled me around the waist. Down I went, but He was gentle, soft, and tender, as though His arms were padded with feather pillows. My body folded in half like a floppy rag doll in slow motion, and an unexpected sense of peace flooded my soul.

I was reluctant to look into the face of my captor, but I knew I had no choice. Slowly, I turned my head and found myself gazing into understanding eyes. In that instant of eye contact, all fear vanished, and my questions no longer seemed to matter.

What did matter were His words. ***"Come,"*** He said. ***"You're to be a part of this. Come. I have something important to show you."***

Then I woke up, without a hint as to what the "important thing" might be.

What Could It Mean?

It would be years later before I would understand. Erwin Lutzer, senior pastor of Moody Church in Chicago, summed up my dream succinctly in his radio broadcast of August 23, 1992, when he said, "Life is like a college entrance exam. The things we do here on earth will have consequences all throughout eternity."

The interpretation came to me in the form of a series of questions:

- Could the students in the dream be friends and acquaintances who have come to learn heavenly truths?

- Could the Master Teacher to whom I led them be the Holy Spirit who so expertly customizes our life lessons?

- Could the various classrooms represent the choices we have to make? When all the doors closed and I found myself alone, does it mean that there will be doors that open for others that are closed to me?

- Could the ancient, highly polished staircase represent the solid, sturdy foundation of the kingdom of heaven, indicating that faith is based on substance, not wishful thinking?

- Could my solitary ascent to the top floor depict a private spiritual search?

- Could the numerous corridors with their many doors and well-supplied rooms imply new opportunities that await us? Perhaps it indicates a season of inner exploration and discovery.

- Could the magnificent doors portray the majesty and grandeur of Almighty God, and could the little recessed places in the handles illustrate the access made possible by the nail-prints of Christ?

- Could the men I saw be Jesus meeting with a group of angels or heavenly saints?

- Could I have glimpsed the war room of heaven where they were poring over a map of Christian households in preparation for a strategic, global mission?

- Could my panicky flight illustrate how sinful humanity cannot stand in the presence of holiness?

- Could it be that the One who pursues me and calls me by name knows everything about me—and you?

- Could the feather-pillow "capture" represent the surprise and relief we experience when we find ourselves embraced by Christ's forgiveness and love?

- Could His invitation to *"Come, you're to be a part of this"* mean that Jesus personally invites us to participate in His unfolding plan in these uncertain days?

The Master says to us, *"Come, I have something important to show you."* I believe that "important thing" is our part—our role, our calling. Unfortunately, we often perceive a Christian calling as too difficult, or we're fearful because the future is unknown. So we run from it with all our might, preferring the comfort zone of tradition. Or we may be enthusiastic about Christian service and plunge in, eagerly trying to "help God out," only to discover that pride has rendered us ineffective.

Instead, He calls us to sit under the teaching of the Holy Spirit and learn how to live fruitful lives. If we harbor ill feelings toward others or allow ourselves the luxury of smug attitudes, we cannot be in league with God. But as we begin to rest in His loving arms and look full into His wonderful face, He lifts us up and calls us out. The Lord may not always let us know where He is leading us, and we may not understand the path of service He's chosen for us, but one thing is certain—*we who believe can follow Him anywhere, unafraid.*

"Come, I have something important to show you."

Peter Comes to Mind

Remember when Jesus asked Peter three times if he loved Him (John 21:15–17)? Each time Peter answered, "Yes, Lord," the third time adding, "You know all things."

Jesus does, indeed, know all things. He knew that Peter, in his humanity, wasn't capable of the kind of unconditional devotion that would be required of him as the rock upon which Jesus would build

His church. But He also knew that Peter's love and loyalty were authentic and that the Holy Spirit would help him fulfill his calling. Christ affirmed Peter's love by giving him an assignment—to feed His lambs and take care of His sheep, and Peter did.

Do we love Jesus? If we answer like Peter, "Yes, Lord, You know that I love You," can we in good conscience refuse to do what He asks of us?

Are we willing to develop an intimacy with Him, to follow Him unconditionally and sacrificially when His words, *"I have chosen you,"* speak to our hearts?

> "You are My servant; I have chosen you and have not rejected you. So do not fear, for I am with you; do not be dismayed, for I am your God. I will strengthen you and help you; I will uphold you with My righteous right hand" (Isaiah 41:9–10).

At the office, Maria breezed in, bubbling over from another charismatic conference.

"One day we'll have a Spirit-filled conference right here in Sussex County and . . ." She paused and smiled. "You'll have a part in it. Yes! You'll be the one to greet the people and . . ." I could see her mind turning. "You'll coordinate it, too."

"Who, me? I can't do that. I've never even *been* to a Christian conference. I don't know anything *about* conferences."

"So much the better!" My panic-stricken face did nothing to curtail her enthusiasm. "That way you won't have any preconceived notions. You'll be totally dependent on the Holy Spirit."

Within three months, Maria's "prophecy" was confirmed.

What in the World is "Heptad?"

There we were in 1984—Maria, five other Christians, and me—all from different church backgrounds. If not for Maria's clear direction from above, it would have been the blind leading the blind. But God was at the helm, and our mission was clear—to determine the feasibility of hosting a conference. Our goal was to promote unity in the body of Christ and to make people aware of the Holy Spirit's activity on the Delmarva Peninsula (all of Delaware and portions of Maryland and Virginia). The seven of us talked, prayed, and adopted the name *Heptad* to describe ourselves—a Greek word for "group of seven."

The number seven occurs frequently in the Scriptures, especially in Revelation, and is the number of perfection or completion. According to *Today's Dictionary of the Bible*, the seven branches of the golden candlestick; the seven trumpets and the seven priests who sounded them; the seven churches, seven spirits, seven stars, seven seals, seven vials, and many others sufficiently prove the importance of this sacred number.

Heptad went to work. We identified seven objectives, invited a speaker and a Gospel singer, made plans for small group discussions and a children's ministry, printed 7,000 brochures, ordered thirty dozen donuts, and hosted the first of seven annual outdoor picnic conferences. The last two years we moved indoors and hosted dinner theaters with full-length performances (lights, sound, costumes—the works).

But that first year, not knowing what kind of attendance to expect, I asked the Lord how many people to plan for. I was sure I heard Him correctly when He said, **"Plan for many."** How many is many? To God, apparently *eighty* was many, since that's how many came with their picnic lunches (to go with our 360 donuts). Hmm, maybe God wasn't thinking about donuts but the number of lives that would be touched by Heptad over the years.

The Holy Spirit moved powerfully among those who came. Throughout the day, we learned and laughed, prayed and praised.

"This was wonderful! Let's do it again," the people said. So, each year, guess who served as coordinator and greeted the people, even after Maria moved to Florida? Yes, I did—the one with no experience, the one who said she didn't know how. During Heptad's nine-year existence, more than 500 people developed a clearer appreciation for Christian unity as the Holy Spirit drew us together to praise God, to focus on Christ, and to embrace His priorities. God called me to do something I didn't think I could do, and then He gave me on-the-job training to do it.

I learned a lot about presumption through Heptad.

The second year, in a radio interview, the announcer asked what we would do in case of rain, and I boldly proclaimed over the air, "God wouldn't rain on His own parade!" I knew the minute the words were out of my mouth I shouldn't have said that. In fact, it did rain—a gentle drizzle, forcing us to huddle together under the cover of a pavilion. God will be God, and I found that God can have a successful picnic conference, even in the rain.

There are dozens of other Heptad stories and fond memories. In the end, when the Lord called me to other responsibilities, it was as hard for me to give up my role with Heptad as it was to embrace it in the first place.

Where You Come In

God is ready to assume responsibility for anyone who fully commits his or her life to Him. If you look for evidence of God's power in your life, you'll see it. If you allow the Lord to stretch you beyond your comfort zone and trust Him to do what you can't possibly do in your own strength, you'll experience a sense of freedom you've never known. Offer yourself to God, and see what He will do.

"But I have nothing to offer," you may say. Nothing to offer? How about your prayers? They don't have to be eloquent to be effective, just sincere.

Perhaps you feel that your church isn't "feeding you." Then try giving instead of taking. As you draw daily from the well of the One who built the church, offer yourself as a light to your congregation. Pray for renewal, asking God to let it begin with you. I learned long ago that worship "is not about me." It's about honoring God.

Offer a few hours a week to volunteer at a neighborhood shelter for the homeless. Visit a nursing home. Ask if any of the residents are lonely and would appreciate having someone sit with them for a few minutes to talk, read, or listen.

Don't get hung up looking at the big job; just follow instinctively wherever the Lord may lead. When you sense that He's calling you to a job that seems too big, ask yourself, "Can I handle this moment? This very moment?" That's all that matters, anyway—the present moment and how we respond to it. According to the promise of Philippians 4:13:

> I have strength for all things in Christ Who empowers me [I am ready for anything and equal to anything through Him who infuses inner strength into me] (AMP).

Remember, the main objective is what Christ can do *through* you.

> "I am the vine; you are the branches. If a man remains in me and I in him, he will bear much fruit; apart from me you can do nothing" (John 15:5).

From My Journal

Of all the things I've written in my prayer journal, I think this Thanksgiving entry is my favorite. What began with a passage from Isaiah and a prayer ended as a metaphor for today's church:

> O LORD, You are our Father.
>> We are the clay, You are the Potter;
>>> we are all the work of Your hand (Isaiah 64:8).

I see Your hand at work in our lives, Lord—shaping, molding, stretching, smoothing, and on occasion pinching us through the circumstances of our lives—fashioning us according to Your plan.

I am thankful for the difficulties of my life, for without them I would not grow in character or have the strength of conviction I have developed.

I am thankful that You have placed within me such a hunger for truth and a willingness to respond to Your call.

I am thankful for the resources You have given me; the blessings are abundant. Even when I had little, You made it seem like a lot.

I am thankful for friends, for family, and for fellowship. I am thankful for whatever lies ahead, whether it be difficulty, hardship, or joy, for I know that You are in all things.

"I, too, My child, am thankful—thankful to have obedient children who are willing to do My bidding regardless of the consequences. You need not fear when discouragement comes or in times of distress, for My ways are perfect and all things are taking shape in the manner I have foretold."

Looking up from my journal, my eyes were drawn to the scattered pieces of a jigsaw puzzle someone had left on the coffee table. As new thoughts formed in my mind, I wrote them down.

Jigsaw Puzzle Metaphor

"Consider the jigsaw puzzle. The box of many pieces has been poured out and appears as a pile of misshapen tokens. First, they must be turned face up, then sorted—likes with likes.

"Each lone piece of the puzzle does not see its relation to the next, nor does each joined segment know how it will fit together with other sections to complete the finished puzzle. I alone see the completed picture, for it was by My design that it was created. So it is with you, with your loved ones, and with the church.

"This is the meaning of the jigsaw puzzle: The numerous pieces poured out are the many people who have been called to worship the living God in spirit and in truth. Notice that none are alike. The turning right side up is the desire of each person to draw near to Me, to seek Me with their whole heart, mind, and strength.

"The sorting according to like pieces illustrates the variety in how My people worship—some through different denominations,

some apart from the organized church. There are many groupings, but all belong to the larger picture. All have distinct differences, but all are required. This is how the true church, the body of Christ, comes together. At first, are not the pieces united one at a time? And later, as large segments fit together, is not the picture more quickly recognized?

"The pieces do not move by themselves. They are moved by a hand. It is My hand you see now, drawing the members of the body of Christ together. As major splits are joined, as differences of opinion over trivial matters are resolved, as wounds are healed through love, as My hand draws together in harmony those who know Me, the true church will be more quickly readied.

"The Bride: That is the title of this puzzle. And not one piece shall be missing."

Our Place in the Puzzle

There's a place in that puzzle for you and me. In fact, just like the way jigsaw puzzles are made, with no two pieces the same, your piece is also very special. Nobody can fill your space but you. Only you have your face, your size and shape, your attitudes, talents, background, hopes, and dreams. Where do you fit in? Right where you are. Right where God has placed you, with your own measure of faith and opportunities to share it.

My earnest prayer is that the One who was and is and is to come will continue to guide you into a deeper understanding of His love and your calling. As my heart stirs, I sense words flowing from an inner voice . . .

"There is a saying, My beloved, 'opportunity knocks but once,' but I tell you that My Spirit never tires of knocking. I stand at the door of your heart, tirelessly awaiting permission to do My best work in you. Every day you have the opportunity to respond to My call. Continuously, I plant wisdom in your mind. You can act on these thoughts and discover My will for you, or you can *reject them and stray from the path. Each time you respond to the opportunity to reflect My character, My voice grows clearer and your joy grows fuller. But with each lost opportunity, your sensitivity to My call diminishes. You are presented this day and every day with opportunities to pursue your faith to its fullest. Waste them not, but open your heart to receive the blessings of joy that await you as you embrace your calling."*

Embracing the Call

Over the years, God has planted many good thoughts in my mind and provided lots of opportunities to hear His voice. Responding to the promptings and circumstances that He orchestrated has enabled me to recognize my calling as a writer, publisher, and speaker.

As you reflect on some of the ways God has directed my path, think about your own heart's desire and how He may be working in your life to prepare you for a specific task, how He gives courage for the next step, and how He brings others alongside to help. See if you can think of examples of divine providence in your life—times when it seems that God Himself directed people or events in advance to meet a need.

It's been said that *God doesn't always call the equipped, but He always equips the called.* Another saying is, *God doesn't call the qualified; He qualifies the called.*

Writer

In 1984, as I was journaling a conversation with God, I had a clear word from the Lord that I wasn't sure I wanted to write down: ***"You will write a book, and it will bless many."*** With a vivid recollection of the 30 dozen donuts we bought for the 80 people who showed up for the first Heptad conference, again I wasn't sure what "many" meant to God. The whole idea caught me off-guard, but I wrote the words and proceeded to pepper my journal with whiny "But Lord" questions.

"But Lord, what would I write about?"

"Write about your spiritual journey."

"But Lord, who would want to read such a thing?"

"Write with your friends and family in mind, in the same chatty style as your Christmas letters."

"But Lord, how do I do this? Where do I start?"

"Write your experiences as they happen. I will bring helpers alongside as you progress."

What an exciting prospect for a novice. It appeared that God and I were entering into a partnership with clearly defined roles. It would be His job to teach me how to write and open doors for publication, and it would be my job to put words on paper. Although only time would tell if this idea really came from the Lord, I believed with all my heart it was an assignment from above. If it didn't pan out, it would be for lack of trying on my part.

Diligently, I began writing. My words resembled tossed salad: good ingredients, but all jumbled up. In no time I had 300 pages which were speedily rejected by kind publishers who, no doubt, rolled their eyes and shook their heads at my inexperience. Their tactful suggestions encouraged me, however, and I see now that this was the Lord's gentle way of getting me to seriously study the craft of writing. Then came opportunities to attend Christian writers conferences where I gained not only knowledge but lifelong friendships and prayer partners.

After rewriting all 300 pages three times on my IBM Selectric typewriter, a godly mentor introduced me to the wonderful, fearful world of computers. Not knowing much difference between software and hardware, I taught myself WordPerfect for the text pages and learned just enough about CorelDraw to design a basic cover. Since I wasn't having any luck with royalty publishers, I painstakingly studied self-publishing books and learned the requirements of ISBNs, bar codes, and how to comply with printing industry standards. Equipped with the skills to "do it myself," I obtained quotes from local printers and—voila—I had a book in my hand.

It was a fearful thing to release my personal spiritual journey into the hands of the world. After all, some of the people in my church and family didn't know about my personal encounter with the Holy Spirit. But now in this third printing, I am sharing my faith with joy and confidence because I know that "He who began a good work in [me] will carry it on to completion until the day of Christ Jesus" (Philippians 1:6).

In fact, it is because of the Lord's track record in moving me through assignments far beyond my ability that I could embrace my current "God-sized" project—a spiritual fantasy thriller series for ages 9 and up.

God's call to write fiction came to me while I was reading the first J. K. Rowling *Harry Potter* book. About halfway through the book and wondering where she was headed with it (would it turn out to be an allegory?), I entertained a fleeting thought: *Somebody should write a Christian book that's just as much fun to read.*

Immediately, three words pierced my mind. **You do it.**

By then, I knew whose Voice that was. But how did I react? By replaying the same old broken record. *"But Lord . . ."* After all, I didn't know anything about writing fiction. Gently, He reminded me of all the other things I didn't know and how He had shown the way.

So, during my last two years of full-time work as a secretary, I threw scribbled notes about characters, plots, and settings into a folder. Then, after retiring, I thought I'd better research how to write a novel and came up with the title, *Gavin Goodfellow and the Lure of Burnt Swamp.*

Ecclesiastes 3:1 says, "There is a time for everything, and a season for every activity under heaven," and this was *Gavin's* time. I knew I should buckle down and get serious, but I didn't realize how seriously until I mentioned the vision for the book at a meeting of Delmarva Christian Writers' Fellowship. It was Diane Cook's first visit. She's an award-winning journalist and dramatist I had heard about and respected from a distance for years but never met until that day.

The premise of *Gavin Goodfellow* appealed to her and led to a stimulating discussion over lunch. With her tremendous, God-given gift for creativity, I realized she would be an invaluable resource for brainstorming. A deep friendship was born that day, and we began meeting monthly to examine the possibilities and organize the project.

You would think that was enough, but God had even more helpers in the wings. In January 2003, I was accepted as one of eight serious writers for a three-day mentoring session with Nancy Rue, a respected author of young adult books. My manuscript was affirmed, and the group has since bonded into a dedicated critique and intercessory group. We call ourselves the "Writeen Crue."

Marlene Bagnull, organizer of the mentoring event and director of the Greater Philadelphia and Colorado Christian Writers Conferences (see Foreword), provides ongoing encouragement and training to keep me up to speed.

But the Lord didn't stop there. He connected me with Linda Windsor, a friend of Diane's who is a well-published novelist in both the general and Christian markets and who lives just forty-five minutes away.

When Linda heard that I planned to self-publish, she insisted I pursue the royalty route first and helped me put together a proposal. As difficult as it is to find an agent, three expressed interest!

So, now I have an agent, and book one is finished! Oh, how tempting it is to let fear and insecurity overtake me. But God has brought me this far, and with the kind of support that has come to me as naturally as breathing, I would be a fool to doubt Him. Time will tell if a royalty publisher will offer me a contract or if it is God's will for me to publish *Gavin* independently, but every day I press on toward the goal before me—no matter how daunting it may seem. Talk about being out of my comfort zone!

At this stage of my life, it's fun to look back and realize that my favorite subjects in school were typing, English, and art. Apparently the Lord began preparing me as a secretary, author, and artist from an early age. It's also interesting to note that my first full-time job was with a printing company.

Publisher

Who would have thought when I was eighteen and pasting up ads at Dover Graphic Associates that one day I would have my own publishing company? It's all interconnected. Five years after

Fruitbearer was in print, I had become proficient at self-publishing and I saw a need. It is hard (if not close to impossible) for beginning authors to get their manuscripts published.

My pen flew over the pages of my journal in 1998 as instructions flowed from Lord on how I was to develop a business to help others publish independently. A year later, Fruitbearer Publishing was born, a home-based office committed to transforming rough manuscripts and humble ideas into attractive publications. Our motto, "Small Seeds for a Great Harvest," is based on Zechariah 4:10 (TLB), "Do not despise this small beginning, for the eyes of the LORD rejoice to see the work begin." The Lord has prospered the business so much that I am training apprentices to help with the workload.

Speaker

Public speaking is another area where the Lord knew I would need on-the-job training, especially since I would much rather *be* the audience than stand in front of one. But God knew that my self-consciousness would fade as I began accepting invitations to speak. So Jesus took me by the hand, in a sense, and marched me down the hall at Delaware Tech to address a class of secretarial students.

"Nervous" isn't strong enough to describe how I felt as I stood before twenty-eight young women to share my career story as an executive secretary. I experienced all the symptoms—sweaty palms, knocking knees, trembling hands, pounding heart, shallow breathing, churning stomach, and a quivering voice.

But something happened in the middle of my talk. As I related my successes and failures, I realized I had valuable information to share—knowledge that could help them when they graduated and entered the workforce. Somehow, I was able to move beyond "me" to "them." The question was no longer *What will they think of me?* but *How can I help them?* The transformation began as I became audience-centered and God-reliant instead of self-centered and self-reliant. The students and I connected. As they nodded in agreement and leaned forward in their seats, I became more relaxed and animated. I'll never know if they were really interested or just felt sorry for me.

Regardless, it gave me confidence. Once or twice I even got them to laugh. By the time I left the classroom, I was energized and eager to try it again.

Telling budding secretaries about my professional career was one thing. Faith-sharing was another. For years, I retained a timid streak in front of audiences, but God gave me valuable insight to impart and provided a variety of platforms. During those times, I leaned heavily on this Scripture:

> For the Holy Spirit, God's gift, does not want you to be afraid of people, but to be wise and strong, and to love them and enjoy being with them. If you will stir up this inner power, you will never be afraid to tell others about our Lord (2 Timothy 1:7–8 TLB).

This passage has come to life for me. After years of meaningful speaking engagements with affirmative feedback, I no longer tremble in front of an audience, whether it's a small gathering or a packed auditorium. Why? Because I have testimony after testimony of how my Lord has sustained and guided me, strengthened and encouraged me, and lifted me up and called me out. As a graduate of CLASServices and member of Word Warrior Ministries Traveling Light speakers' network, I actively seek opportunities to share my faith. My transformation may have been gradual, but it is real. Armed with increased confidence, my challenge now is to continue to depend on God for every word that comes out of my mouth and not rely on past successes.

To Go or Not to Go

For more than a decade, God taught me how to say "yes!" to opportunities that groomed me for His work. Now, it appears that He's teaching me how to say "no." There's a season for all things: a time to go and a time to say "whoa." Sometimes, it can be just as important to "not do" as it is to "do."

Even when we know God is calling us to a particular direction of service, it's not always easy to know which way to turn or when.

Yet, our heavenly Father often provides helpful hints to keep us aimed toward the goal. The key to successful service is that we rely on God's power, not our own. This passage from Zechariah 4:6 has become my theme song:

"Not by might nor by power, but by My Spirit," says the LORD Almighty.

My first clue that I was relying more on my own might than on His Spirit was a *time crunch*. Friends and family began to caution me that I should slow down, but I kept pressing on—filling up every evening on my calendar, making appointments with friends over lunch, squeezing in breakfast meetings, extending my day from 5:30 a.m. until midnight, planning seminars—and praying for supernatural strength so I wouldn't let the Lord, my family, my friends, my boss, or the church down. For a long time, it worked. But every minute of every day was so tightly committed that there was no room for the unexpected.

Illness was my second clue. The flu hit me in February 1993 when I was pulling out all the stops and going full speed. It kept me out of commission for a month. Then, of all things, I had a tonsillectomy the following spring that took me out of the loop for another month. For the previous ten years I'd become so accustomed to the Lord telling me, **"Not yet,"** for my book that I didn't hear Him say, **"Now!"** until He put me in a quiet place (twice) where I could hear Him better. By the way, I had also become negligent with my morning devotions during this time. From my bedridden vantage point, the Lord reminded me that the book He had called me to write was still incomplete.

After ten years of writing and rewriting, *Fruitbearer* was still in rough draft form. Even my best chapters needed a major overhaul. So I spread loose pages of the manuscript all over the bed, matching good stuff with good stuff and throwing the excess in a pile on the floor. Inspiration flowed. From the very beginning, I had prayed that this book would be written and published in God's perfect time (not by my manipulation) and to His glory (not so I could say, "Look what I did"). The third indication that it was "time" for the book was how easily the pieces started fitting in place.

From February through April that year, my snail's pace manuscript came together like iron filings to a magnet. In August, I was even able to take a hand-bound draft of my "book" to a Christian writers conference where I presented a workshop on self-publishing. In my talk, I stressed how important it is to "do what you can with what you have." As I held up my homemade book, my thrill at seeing *Fruitbearer* becoming a reality was tempered by another area in me that God had targeted—*fear of success.*

Between February and October, for 240 days, inspiration and motivation accelerated steadily. Then, as I raced toward a self-imposed deadline to get the book to the printer, the Lord put on the brakes.

Computer problems and a family emergency brought the work to an unexpected halt. I had to chuckle that, so close to the "finish line," God was giving me a fresh lesson on how to "run with patience."

The hardest part of accepting God's call may not be embracing the challenge; sometimes it's letting go of the familiar.

The delay also helped me confront a problem I didn't realize I had. Deep inside, I was afraid to let go of the manuscript that had been safe at home and under my control all those years. *Once it's in print, you can't take the words back.* I was apprehensive about the doors that a published book might open. *My boundaries will expand. What if I have to travel to big cities, maybe even alone since Drew doesn't like to fly?* The Lord knew my deep need for affirmation and guidance, so He arranged for me to meet a circle of friends at the writers conference who not only played a vital role in fine-tuning the manuscript but helped me come to grips with the need to fully embrace my calling as an author and speaker—regardless of where it might take me.

Letting Go of the Familiar

My friends' wise counsel and encouragement got me back on track. But the hardest part of accepting God's call may not be embracing the challenge; sometimes it's letting go of the familiar. Often, the Lord requires us to *stop* doing something—even something worthwhile that we enjoy, or possibly something He had previously called us to do—to make way for a new assignment or direction.

I learned during my month-long illnesses that I wasn't as indispensable at work as I thought and that most of my pressing personal responsibilities weren't so important, after all. While other people could do most of those things, only *I* could write my story.

Once I was convinced that God wanted me to put my book on the front burner, other things had to go to make room for uninterrupted writing time. It was up to me to identify and pare down the activities and relationships that drained me of time and energy. It became clear that I could let go of just about everything except my immediate family, close friends, full-time job, and commitment as an elder in our church. The hardest thing for me to relinquish was my alto seat in the choir.

"Sad news," I announced to the rest of the choir members as we donned our robes for the Sunday morning service. "I'm going to have to take a leave of absence from the choir to work on my book."

All the choir members were understanding—except for John, the director, who tried his best to dissuade me. But during the service, the Lord spoke to me three times: through the second hymn, the Scriptures, and the sermon.

Back in the choir room after the service, John picked up where he left off. "Let me play the devil's advocate for a minute," he said.

"John," I smiled, "you can play devil's advocate all you want, but nothing you say is going to change my mind. All through the service, God has been confirming this is something I have to do."

His attention shifted to how other members had moved away or couldn't attend. He began naming them. "And now with Candy on sabbatical, maybe this is God's way of saying, 'Wake up! I have something to say to you.'"

Whoa! Was that another confirmation, or what? "John," I said, "you don't know this, but you have just uttered the very Scripture my book is based on!"

"What?" He looked dumbfounded.

"Yes, the Bible verse that motivated me to write the book is Revelation 3:2, 'Wake up! Strengthen what remains and is about to die, for I have not found your deeds complete in the sight of My God.'" I patted him on the shoulder. "See what I mean about confirmation? And out of your own mouth, of all people!"

Debate closed. God had settled the matter with humor, and I was officially off choir duty for a season.

Do You See Your Calling?

According to Oswald Chambers, "My contact with the nature of God will shape my understanding of His call and will help me realize what I truly desire to do for Him." Don't worry about putting a label on your calling. Remember how the Lord once cautioned me, **"Seek not to name your gift but to use it wisely"**?

Labels can be interpreted differently by different people. (The word "evangelist," for example, may bring a certain image to your mind that is different from my perception.) The important thing is not *what* you are called but *that* you are called. The key to discovering your calling is to test whether your heart is beating in time with the heart of God or if it's out of sync.

Here are some questions to ask yourself to see if you're in tune with His calling:

- Do I have desires in my heart that I sometimes realize in retrospect were planted there by God (Psalm 37:4)?

- Do I experience freshness and joy in the work that I do for God as I discover that He has already provided all I need (2 Corinthians 9:8)?

- Do I seek the Lord because I enjoy His presence, or do I pray only when I need or want something? Do I enjoy the fellowship of congregational worship, or do I go to church because I think I should (Psalm 95:1–7)?

- Is it becoming more important to establish intimacy and oneness with Him and less important for me to know why God allows things in my life (Proverbs 3:5–6)?

- Has it become easier to say "no" to things that squander my time or energy and take me away from the work God is calling me to do (Hebrews 12:1)?

- Am I searching His Word for direction with a sincere heart (Psalm 119:105)?

- Have I looked at my circumstances and considered what God may want to accomplish through them (Romans 8:28)?

- Do I desire to pursue the spiritual gifts and put them into action (1 Corinthians 12:4–31; Ephesians 4:1–6; Romans 12:6–8)?

- Do I have a trustworthy circle of born-again friends who can give me objective feedback about my spiritual growth and other activities (Proverbs 11:14)?

- Am I diligent in using the talents and abilities God has given me (Ecclesiastes 9:10)?

- When faced with a decision, do I wait until I have peace about it or do I just react (1 Corinthians 14:33)?

- Do I welcome the Lord's rod of correction with a teachable outlook (Revelation 3:19)?

- Am I a light to those around me who are walking in darkness (Matthew 5:16)?

Are you getting the idea of how to discover your calling? Let God guide you in other questions to ask yourself. Basically, there are three elements to consider. Does what you're doing:

1. Give you a sense of fulfillment and inner joy?
2. Produce the fruit of the Spirit in your life?
3. Benefit others?

If so, God's will for your life—His call—will become evident as you serve Him daily.

For God's gifts and His call are irrevocable. [He never withdraws them when once they are given, and He does not change His mind about those to whom He gives His grace or to whom He sends His call] (Romans 11:29 AMP).

Shall We Pray?

Dear Father in heaven, don't let me flounder. Increase my devotion to prayer and cause me to be watchful and thankful. Teach me to recognize Your presence—and Your will—in my circumstances. Open doors for Your message, and give me the boldness I need to share the Good News of Christ. Teach me to be wise in the way I act toward others, and help me to make the most of every opportunity. In short, make me worthy of Your calling.

*W*HAT CAN I DO FOR YOU, LORD?

DIG INTO SCRIPTURE

- 2 Thessalonians 1:11
- Ephesians 4:1–16
- 2 Peter 1:3–11
- Romans 8:28–30
- John 15:16
- Matthew 25:21–29

GOD'S CALL: FOLLOW ME

"As your faith increases, so will My power increase within you—power to do what is right. Although you may repeatedly falter in your performance, remember that I am the One who will make you worthy of your calling and will fulfill by My power every good resolve and work of faith. This, then, is your calling: To know Me, to love Me, to be filled with My Spirit, and to do good works which I have prepared in advance for you to do. To discover your calling is to respond to My invitation to follow Me. Will you?"

YOUR RESPONSE TO GOD

If your answer is yes and you sincerely desire to discover your calling, write a prayer of commitment in your own words. Ask the Lord what will draw you closer to Him and bring His will for you into focus. As you discern His answers, record the words in your journal or a place where you can refer to them later. This will serve as a reminder of your promise and His faithfulness.

 SEED FOR THOUGHT

A lot of kneeling will keep you in good standing.

—Author Unknown

CHAPTER 10

STAND FIRM!

The devil is never too busy
to rock the cradle of a sleeping saint.

—Author Unknown

So be on your guard, not asleep like the others.
Watch for his return and stay sober . . .
protected by the armor of faith and love,
And wearing as [your] helmet
the happy hope of salvation.
—1 Thessalonians 5:6–8 TLB

A spiritual battle is raging all around us. If ever we needed to respond to God's call, it's now!

I first sensed this urgency more than twenty years ago when I began my spiritual journey. Last week someone asked me if I thought these devastating hurricanes meant the end was near. And how can educated Americans actually believe it would be beneficial to remove the Ten Commandments from public buildings? If Christ has not returned as of this writing, His delay only intensifies our need to strengthen what remains.

Our heavenly Father is warning us to prepare today, just as clearly as He warned Noah. Do we hear Him? Read the Spirit-inspired words recorded by the prophet Jeremiah. Let them register deep in your soul, for we have come to a critical fork in the road of our spiritual journey:

This is what the LORD says: "Stand at the crossroads and look; . . . ask where the good way is, and walk in it, and you will find rest for your souls. But you said, 'We will not walk in it.' I appointed watchmen over you and said, 'Listen to the sound of the trumpet!' But you said, 'We will not listen.' Therefore hear, O nations; observe, O witnesses, what will happen to them. Hear, O, earth: I am bringing disaster on this people, the fruit of their schemes, because they have not listened to My words and have rejected My law" (Jeremiah 6:16–19).

A book entitled *Racing Toward the Mark of the Beast* by Peter and Paul Lalonde (see Recommended Resources), presents carefully documented evidence that shows why this generation, unlike any before it, is capable of fulfilling crucial end-times prophecies. In the last chapter entitled "Where Will You Stand?" they state, "We must choose which side we will be on. Those who reject God will grow closer and closer to a very subtle but real decision to join forces with the spirit of antichrist."

We will come up against scoffers who say, "Where is this 'coming' He promised? Everything goes on as it has since the beginning of creation." Their very words are a fulfillment of prophecy recorded in 2 Peter 3:3–4. Check it out. And read the rest of the third chapter of 2 Peter where it says:

> But do not forget this one thing, dear friends: With the Lord a day is like a thousand years, and a thousand years are like a day. The Lord is not slow in keeping His promise as some understand slowness. He is patient with you, not wanting anyone to perish, but everyone to come to repentance.
>
> But the day of the Lord will come like a thief. The heavens will disappear with a roar; the elements will be destroyed by fire, and the earth and everything in it will be laid bare.
>
> Since everything will be destroyed in this way, what kind of people ought you to be? You ought to live holy and godly lives as you look forward to the day of God and speed its coming. That day will bring about the destruction of the heavens by fire, and the elements will melt in the heat. But in keeping with His promise we are looking forward to a new heaven and a new earth, the home of righteousness (2 Peter 3:8–13).

Perseverance

> Lay aside every weight, and the sin which doth so easily beset us, and . . . *run with patience the race that is set before us*, looking unto Jesus the author and finisher of our faith" (Hebrews 12:1–2 KJV, emphasis added).

But we are not alone in that race. Unlike the fig tree that withered and died for not bearing fruit, we are to nurture others along the way with the fruit our Savior has cultivated in us. We must remain persistent in our efforts so we won't miss Him. James counsels us to:

> Be patient, then . . . until the Lord's coming. See how the farmer waits for the land to yield its valuable crop and how patient he is for the autumn and spring rains. You too, be patient and *stand firm, because the Lord's coming is near* (James 5:7–8, emphasis added).

The farmer can't hurry the growing process; he must wait for his crops to ripen. He doesn't take a summer vacation and wish for a good harvest because he knows his diligence is required in the field during the growing season. As we wait patiently for Christ's return, there is much we can do to get ready for the sweep of the sickle. Christians, like farmers, must live by faith, anticipating the day when they will reap a harvest for their labors. Live as if Christ could come today! Work faithfully to build His kingdom, for when the time is ripe, He *will* return—just as He promised.

The Time *Is* Ripe

People are hurting, and we fruitbearers have the healing salve they need. Unsuspecting and unprepared souls will have to face a time of terror and trouble that will inhabit the world with unprecedented force—worse than anything humanity has ever experienced, even worse than the Nazi holocaust—and we have the Word of Truth that can help them find their way to safety.

Those of us who know Christ are secure in Him. But what about unbelievers who don't have that comfort? People we pass on the street? Our coworkers? Our neighbors? Our friends? Our family members? We have relationships with these dear souls who may look fine on the outside, but what if they're spiritually dying inside? Yet, conditioned by political correctness and diversity-driven courtesy, we bury our seeds with small talk and withhold vital information that could save them from destruction. We have Good News to share!

The Holy Spirit once told me, *"You cannot share the joy of the Lord with your mouth closed."* That seems clear enough. If you want to share the joy of the Lord, you must *talk* about Him. Faith comes by *hearing* (Romans 10:17). Talk with somebody about the signs of the times and Bible prophecy. Even if they disagree, get your friends and family thinking. Give them an anchor to which they can cling.

"Take these words not lightly, My child. Every believer must take responsibility for communicating the Gospel if it is to be spread to the ends of the earth. Speak of those things you know to be true. Be not timid about the way I have touched you personally, and be not ashamed of the bold and wondrous things My Spirit is doing today. Do not be embarrassed to ask questions. In this way, you and others will grow stronger. In this way, the Scriptures will come forth in power to strengthen the remnant of believers.

"You must be willing to become vulnerable one to another for My name's sake. Let there be no shame in declaring yourself to be a follower of the One who is the Beginning and Ending of all things. Let your mouth speak with joy and conviction. Take care, though, not to wear My name as a badge that might cause others to see you as belonging to an elite club. Rather, show yourself to be My follower by your example of loving compassion for the unlovable, peaceful understanding for the troubled, and joyful hope for those who seek encouragement. If you do not tell them, those who need to know will remain ignorant of the victory that can be theirs. How will they hear if you do not tell them?"

"You cannot share the joy of the Lord with your mouth closed."

If an act of kindness comes to mind (to call someone, to send a card, to visit a neighbor, to buy a gift, to say a prayer), act on the idea as if it came from God—it very well may have. Don't let the opportunity slip away. The need may be immediate. Perhaps that single act of kindness or compassion will be the key that opens the door to discussion about the hope of Christ.

If you have a desire to start a Bible study or prayer group, jot down the steps you'll need to set the ball in motion, and then take that first step. As you allow God to move you step-by-step to the point of no return, you'll look back one day and be amazed at what He's done through you.

Even if you feel your level of commitment is meager, tell God you're willing to do *something* for Him and watch to see what opportunities He provides.

You may be inspired to write a letter to someone you love; if so, ask God to help you choose the words. A friend once told me she feels some of the most important words we will ever write may never be published. A well-placed letter can have life-changing potential for those near and dear to us.

Use your creativity to reach your circle of friends, family, and acquaintances. Remember, the Lord has commanded us to share our faith, so let us stay firmly rooted in Christ and speak up about what He has done for us.

Do you lack confidence, feel hesitant, or uneasy? The Holy Spirit will give you the right words and produce in you the boldness you need to be an effective communicator of the Gospel. I know; He does it for me all the time. I'm always saying to Him, "But Lord . . . ," and He's continually saying back to me, *"But Candy . . . My grace is sufficient."* As we grow in the grace and knowledge of our Lord, He works around our limitations to accomplish His will.

What seems like a simple act of obedience today could play a critical role tomorrow in helping our friends and families avert unseen danger. Let me illustrate.

Bird in the Road

One quiet morning, I was driving to work and saw a robin in the road, perched in the middle of the other lane, nonchalantly pecking at some food as I drove by. *That's not smart, little bird*, I thought.

A truck sped toward me, aimed right at him.

"Get out of the way!" I shouted, looking in my rear-view mirror. But he was still there eating. He hadn't heard me. I was too far away.

As I rounded a curve, putting the bird out of view, I wondered if he would hear the rumble of the approaching wheels. Could he escape at the last minute? It didn't appear so. My heart sank as I considered the probability—a thud and feathers flying, another vulnerable creature struck down because sudden destruction caught him unaware.

If only I could have run up to him and waved my arms to get his attention. If only I could have gotten close enough to warn him of the impending danger.

If I feel this alarmed about a bird in the road, how much more should I be alarmed about my family and friends? "Lord, let me get close enough to warn them! Give me the courage I need to speak the words that burn within me. Let me recognize the opportunities You give me to witness to them."

Our instructions for dealing with different types of individuals are clearly spelled out in Jude 22–23:

> Be merciful to those who doubt; snatch others from the fire and save them; to others show mercy, mixed with fear—hating even the clothing stained by corrupted flesh.

The Lord is calling us to work not only in good times or when it suits us but also during difficult times. As we respond in obedience to His call, relying on His help to get us through each day, we will be able to trust Him at ever-deepening levels.

God allows the fiery darts of Satan to target, refine, and purify us, just like He allowed His servant Job to be tested. Even Christ, who was sinless, had to go to the cross to fulfill the divine plan. We shouldn't be surprised to find ourselves facing trials and afflictions of every kind, for Satan knows his time is short and he's pulling out all the stops. When our time of trial comes, our hope lies in the fact that God is in control and that there is purpose in our suffering. With nothing to be gained from whimpering about our woes, our victory lies in heeding God's call to *do what we can with what we have.*

Up and at 'Em

In everyday language, our Lord is calling us to, *"Wake up! Get dressed! There's a battle raging!"*

Wake up from your sleep . . . Christ will show you the light! So watch your step. Use your head. Make the most of every chance you get. These are desperate times! Don't live carelessly, unthinkingly. Make sure you understand what the Master wants (Ephesians 5:14–17 MSG).

Consider this journal entry:

"You are soldiers in holy battle. Seek your orders from Me and be faithful to carry them out readily and precisely. There will be wars and rumors of wars, internal and external, but the battle is Mine and has already been won. Victory will be realized through the faithfulness of My people executing their assignments until I come.

"The land is marked with strategic prayer stations. When the cries of My children are as one voice, then will the trumpet sound.

"Your redemption is indeed drawing near. Look around you, though. Look upon the faces of the multitudes who are not yet prepared. Look upon those who have not yet heard the way to safety. Sound the alarm! And usher the handicapped into the shelter of My Word. There are many innocents who are blind and deaf, who do not see the danger. You can lead them to safety.

"Do not complain that your assignment is too great, for I am not sending you into battle unprepared but fully dressed in the armor of God to rescue these little ones. You go not onto the battlefield alone, but with hosts of heavenly angels to guard and protect you. The mission entrusted to you is great, but I have chosen you for the task and you will prove faithful, for you will be relying on My strength and not your own.

"Be alert and self-controlled. Above all, be joyful! For the Lord your God is strong in battle and mighty to save."

Dressed in the Armor of God

Years ago, Dr. Charles Stanley (In Touch Ministries, Atlanta, GA) taught on the armor of God (Ephesians 6:13–17). He challenged listeners to mentally put on the armor of God, piece by piece, before getting out of bed each morning. For seven days, I followed his instructions meticulously.

First, I put on *the belt of truth.* The promise of the Scriptures is that the Truth will set us free, and if the Son sets us free, we are free indeed (John 8:32, 36). The truth is, I'm a child of God and nothing can touch me that He doesn't personally allow for a good purpose, whether I understand it or not. The truth is that the Holy Spirit who is in me is greater than Satan or anything else in the world (1 John 4:4).

Next, I put on *the breastplate of righteousness* which protects my heart and emotions. When I make a choice to walk in His ways and not my own, the Lord takes responsibility for covering my tender and unpredictable feelings with His consistent righteousness.

Then, I put on *the sandals of the gospel of peace.* Wherever I walk, God's peace—the peace that passes human understanding—goes with me. For this to happen, I must watch where my feet take me and see that my steps are pleasing to Him.

The fourth piece of armor is *the shield of faith.* This shield deflects the enemy's fiery darts. They fizzle on contact and bounce off, but the protection is only effective if I pick up the shield and use it. We can thank the Lord for giving us the precise amount of faith we need at any given moment.

The fifth article is *the helmet of salvation.* This guards my head—my mind and my intellect—all my thought processes. This is where the battle begins, in the mind. But 1 Corinthians 2:16 says I can have the mind of Christ! As I entrust the safety of my thinking into His care, the mental games of the enemy or temptations of the flesh are easier to recognize and to reject, especially in the early stages.

Finally, *the sword of the Spirit*, which is the Word of God, is at my disposal to cut away the devil's foothold. It is living and active, a double-edged weapon that is just as effective for offensive strategies as it is for defensive maneuvers.

Now, fully dressed in the armor of God, I prepare for battle by praying in the Spirit which builds up my faith and lifts me beyond my sin and circumstances. As I intercede for others, God targets them with His power and their lives are touched—sometimes tangibly, sometimes imperceptibly—but they're always affected to some extent.

After a full week of carefully and consciously dressing in the armor of God, I evaluated the results. My perception of reality had undergone a paradigm shift. Even difficult days seemed effortless. Instead of my problems being troublesome, they became challenges to overcome. Hard work became satisfying, not stressful. It was as though I had a secret weapon that brought excitement and purpose to even mundane tasks. What joy! But this daily experiment was time-consuming and took a lot of concentration.

All good habits, like brushing our teeth, are developed by daily discipline. If we get lazy and miss a day, we notice a difference. In the same way that good hygiene becomes less time-consuming as we make it part of our normal routine, I found the exercise of dressing in God's armor didn't need to be a tedious procedure.

Dress Me, Lord

"Oh, Lord," I wrote in my journal, "what if I forget to put on the armor one day? Will I be entering into the world unprotected and vulnerable? Will I have to do this every morning for the rest of my life in order to experience this kind of victory?"

"You have known the benefits of applying this protection piece by piece through the eyes of faith. If I were to say to you, 'Armor of God,' could you picture yourself fully dressed in it?"

"Yes, Lord. It's like seeing a photograph of a warrior in full battle garb with a shield in one hand, a sword in the other, a helmet and vest—everything in place. I can see the whole outfit. I can even see my own face peering out from under my helmet."

"Good. Now stand up and let Me dress you for continuing battle. Stand, My child, and I will prepare you."

I felt a little silly, but nobody was in the house to laugh at me, so I stood up. Like a little girl, I stood there in the bedroom waiting to be dressed. In my mind, I could see a leather apron being placed around my waist, invisible hands tying the cords in back, drawing it snug against my abdomen.

Then the image of a breastplate lowered over my head, coming to rest on my shoulders with thick leather straps. It was heavy. I was surprised to notice it not only covered my chest but had a panel to protect my back as well. This surprised me, because I had always heard that a Roman breastplate covered only the front, teaching that Christians weren't supposed to turn and run. But the Lord reminded me, **"I AM your rear guard."**

Anticipating the "sandals" would be next, I lifted my left foot off the floor. Nobody saw me wobble in stork-like fashion to be fitted by the Master's hand. Nobody saw me put that foot down and raise my right one for the same treatment. When both sandals were in place, I experienced a pervading sense of peace and mission.

A shield was placed in my left hand. It was big and bulky, too heavy for me to hold at first. But my mind's eye caught a glimpse of Jesus lifting one corner of it off the floor. With His assistance, it was feather-light and stable. Faith is like that.

In that moment, an uncommon stillness blanketed the room. The absence of sound was broken by distant musical chords of great fanfare as the Lord encased my head with an elaborate helmet. Ornately decorated, it felt like it weighed more than all the other pieces combined. For a moment, I thought I would collapse beneath the weight of it, and my eyes flew open. The sight of the room brought me back to the present. My mind was crystal clear. The vision continued. When I peered out from inside the helmet, my peripheral vision was obstructed by blinders. Unable to see to the right or to the left, I could only look straight ahead. Only at the Lord. *Single-minded, that's what He wants me to be.* How easy it is to let the world distract me if I take my eyes off Christ even for a moment.

After tracing His face with my thoughts, I moved slowly toward the dresser where I reached out to receive the sword He offered, the written Word of God. As I picked up my open Bible, all my burdens lifted! The heavy armor was suddenly light, the weighty responsibility well-balanced.

My dad always told me I had a good imagination. Maybe so. But when it comes to spiritual warfare, imagination isn't much ammunition against the forces of evil. Faith is. Returning to my journal, the account closed with these words.

"Through faith you are already dressed in My armor, for I have dressed you and go with you each day into battle. Never will I forsake you. I am always by your side. Pray in the Spirit and practice My presence. For My kingdom is at hand."

Safe!

The people of our generation are caught in the crossfire of a spiritual battle. Even in the midst of chaos, however, the Lord offers us tranquility, hope, and courage to persevere as we interpret the signs of the times. While our bodies may bruise and age, our souls are safe in Jesus Christ, the only reliable refuge. But the promises of the Scriptures are not automatic. We either choose to embrace or ignore them.

How can we know if we're saved? If you're among those who have tried to embrace the Gospel but wonder if your conversion "took," here's a verse that should help:

> Single-minded, that's what He wants me to be. How easy it is to let the world distract me if I take my eyes off Christ.

This is how we know we are in Him: Whoever claims to live in Him must walk as Jesus did (1 John 2:5–6).

What does it mean to walk as Jesus did? It means we go through our days depending on our heavenly Father, just as Jesus did. Salvation is a gift from God that comes one way—by grace *through faith*, not by works, so we can't brag about it (Ephesians 2:9). God is sovereign. The same chapter goes on to say:

> We are God's workmanship, created in Christ Jesus to do good works, which God prepared in advance for us to do (Ephesians 2:10).

Only one thing can separate us from His love—a hardened heart. Even the worst cases of pride, rebellion, apathy, and the like can be softened if the owner will grant God permission to crack and peel the crusty outer shell.

If you want to believe but just don't know how and really mean it, get on your knees and be honest with God. People who pray, "I don't know if You're real or not, but if You are, then somehow, some way, prove Yourself to me," often discover the Bible they once thought dull has suddenly come to life.

Let the living Christ speak to your deepest need. Invite Him to meet you where you are and reveal Himself to you. His invisible hand will come down from heaven to lift you up. Lay your burden at His feet—whether it be doubt, guilt, emptiness, anger, sin, fear, or pain—and give Him your life. You'll never be sorry. A simple but earnest prayer, "Come into my heart, Lord Jesus," is all it takes. Do it now.

Why the Urgency?

"The end of all things is near. Therefore be clear minded and self-controlled so that you can pray," the Bible says in 1 Peter 4:7. Jesus is sending a strong, clear warning for those who have ears to hear it:

> "Watch out! Don't let My sudden coming catch you unawares; don't let Me find you living in careless ease, carousing and drinking, and occupied with the problems of this life, like all

the rest of the world. Keep a constant watch. And pray that if possible you may arrive in My presence without having to experience these horrors" (Luke 21:34–36 TLB).

In *The Message* this passage reads,

"But be on your guard. Don't let the sharp edge of your expectation get dulled by parties and drinking and shopping. Otherwise, that Day is going to take you by complete surprise, spring on you suddenly like a trap, for it's going to come on everyone, everywhere, at once. So, whatever you do, don't go to sleep at the switch. Pray constantly that you will have the strength and wits to make it through everything that's coming and end up on your feet before the Son of Man."

Get right with God *now*, even in your shopping habits, that you may be among the steadfast believers counted worthy to receive His protection. These are comforting words for all who trust and obey Christ:

"I will also keep you from the hour of trial that is going to come upon the whole world to test those who live on the earth" (Revelation 3:10).

As we express a willingness to become co-laborers with Christ, we may stagger under the weight of what He asks us to do or to face. The needs are so vast, the days are so treacherous, and we're so few and ill-equipped. But God still calls ordinary people to do extraordinary things! Never forget what David said when he faced Goliath:

"It is not by sword or spear that the LORD saves; for the battle is the LORD's" (1 Samuel 17:47).

Days ago, the following message came to my e-mail inbox from James W. Goll, Encounters Network (*www.JamesGoll.com*), and it seemed a fitting way to close:

The ebb and flow of revival throughout church history has often been compared to that of the waves of the ocean. The tide comes in and out with subsequent waves of activity in between. Such it is with God's manifested presence and this wonderful thing called "revival," "the move of God's Spirit," and even "city transformation."

We don't want to settle in and passively become the stewards of the "best of the past." We must press into the heart of God and cry out for a fresh outpouring of His grace in our time!

Just today I learned that George Barna has a new book titled *Revolution* (see Recommended Resources) about a group of people who are more interested in producing fruit for the kingdom of God than clinging to comfortable Christianity. Imagine my surprise to find he drew his conclusions from surveying "grassroote believers" and that more than 20 million adults indicate they are committed to living their faith and making God the top priority.

Shall We Pray?

We cry out for a fresh outpouring of Your grace in our time, O Lord, for Your mercy and sustaining grace. In exchange for fear, give us Your peace. Replace any complacency in us with a passion to serve You. Empower us by Your Holy Spirit so that we may stand firm, for we want to be overcomers. Thank You for waking us up and strengthening us. Show us creative, practical, loving ways to inspire others to keep their eyes on You. Do whatever it takes to turn us into people who watch and long for Your appearing, prepared to take our place in the Third Great Awakening.

As the fruit of Your Spirit blossoms and new buds begin to sprout, yank out the weeds that threaten to choke Your righteousness in us—even though it will be painful. Between now and the day of Your return, stir up the gifts which are in us so that we may bear good fruit—fruit that will last. *Even so . . . come, Lord Jesus!*

WHAT CAN I DO FOR YOU, LORD?

DIG INTO SCRIPTURE

Study these passages of Scripture as though your life depended on them:

- 2 Peter 3 (the Day of the Lord)
- Ephesians 6:10–18 (the armor of God)
- The book of Revelation, chapters 1, 2, and 3 (Jesus' letters to the churches)

GOD'S CALL: STAND FAST

"When the trumpet sounds, will you be among those who watch and long for My appearing? Or will you be distracted by earthly things and hope I don't notice? Will you listen for My voice and respond to My call? Or will you ignore My warnings and do your own thing? Will you stand firm and unwavering in your devotion to Me? Or will you be ashamed of Me and My words? Truly I say to you, 'I am coming soon. My reward is with me, to repay according to everyone's work. I am the Alpha and the Omega, the first and the last, the beginning and the end'" (Revelation 22:12 NRSV).

YOUR RESPONSE TO GOD

_____

_____

_____

_____

 SEED FOR THOUGHT

"The seeds sown in the good soil stand for those who hear the message and understand it; they bear fruit, some as much as one hundred, others sixty, and others thirty."

—*Matthew 13:23*

About the Author

CANDY ABBOTT has been writing and speaking since 1983. Retired after 35 years of service as an executive secretary, she now devotes her time to writing fiction, giving inspirational speeches, running Fruitbearer Publishing (a home-based independent publishing business), directing Delmarva Christian Writers' Fellowship, serving as executive director of Mothers With a Mission, and enjoying her husband, three grown children, and four grandchildren. A Spirit-filled conservative evangelical, Candy is active in the Georgetown Presbyterian Church where she and her husband are ordained elders. Her contributions to the body of Christ are best exemplified by Sisters in Christ, a non-denominational Bible study she co-founded that has been discipling women for more than 30 years.

She was named "Writer of the Year" at the 2003 Greater Philadelphia Christian Writers Conference.

Fearless when following the leading of the Lord, especially in her writing, Candy is tackling the challenge of telling a teen nerd's story (think Charlie Brown meets Harry Potter) who must save his hometown in a spiritual battle of good versus evil. The Bible-based *Gavin Goodfellow* trilogy holds much promise, and book one is already being used in Christian schools.

But young adult fiction is only part of Candy's literary calling. In addition to *Fruitbearer,* her credits as a contributing author include the following anthologies: *Chicken Soup for the Prisoner's Soul; Chicken*

Soup for the Volunteer's Soul; Chicken Soup for the Christian Woman's Soul; God Answers Prayers; For Better, For Worse; The Heart of a Father; Touched by Angels of Mercy; Stories for a Woman's Heart; Stories for a Teen's Heart 2; and *My Turn to Care.*

Candy enjoys her role as public speaker and workshop presenter. She is a CLASServices graduate, a lifetime member of ISN Works, and a charter member of Southern Delaware Toastmasters. Candy's speaking ministry is blossoming. Why not consider her for your next event?

P.O. Box 777 • Georgetown, DE 19947
302.856.6649
www.fruitbearer.com
info@fruitbearer.com

SEED FOR THOUGHT

"So let us not become tired of doing good; for if we do not give up, the time will come when we will reap the harvest."

—*Galatians* 6:9 (TEV)

 SEED FOR THOUGHT

[Jesus said,] "Well, I'm telling you to open your eyes and take a good look at what's right in front of you. These Samaritan fields are ripe. It's harvest time! The Harvester isn't waiting. He's taking his pay, gathering in this grain that's ripe for eternal life. Now the Sower is arm in arm with the Harvester, triumphant."

—*John 4:35–36* (MSG)

RECOMMENDED RESOURCES

Devotionals

31 Days of Praise: Enjoying God Anew by Ruth and Warren Myers, Sisters, OR: Multnomah Publishers, Inc., 1994.

Come Away My Beloved by Frances J. Roberts, Uhrichsville, OH: Barbour Publishing, Inc.,1970, 2002.

The Helper by Catherine Marshall, Grand Rapids, MI: Baker Books, 1978, 2001.

My Utmost for His Highest: An Updated Edition in Today's Language by Oswald Chambers, edited by James Reimann; authorized by the Chambers Publications Association, Ltd. Grand Rapids: MI: Discovery House Publishers, 1992.

Hearing God's Voice

The Beginner's Guide to Hearing God by Jim W. Goll, Ventura, CA: Regal Books, 2004.

Dialogue With God by Mark and Patti Virkler, Gainesville, FL: Bridge-Logos Publishers, 1986.

The Elijah List, an online newsletter with prophetic words and prophecies. Visit *www.elijahlist.com.*

How to Hear from God: Learn to Know His Voice and Make Right Decisions by Joyce Meyer, NY, NY: Warner Faith, 2003.

How to Listen to God by Charles Stanley, Nashville, TN: Thomas Nelson, Inc.,1985. Other resources available from In Touch Ministries, P.O. Box 7900, Atlanta, GA 30357, *www.intouch.org*.

Intimate Friendship with God: Through Understanding the Fear of the Lord by Joy Dawson, Lincoln, VA: Chosen Books, 1986.

John Paul Jackson's courses (Streams Ministries International) which are taught all over the U.S. and in several other countries. The first course is called *Streams Course 101: The Art of Hearing God*. Visit *www.streamsministries.com* for teaching schedules.

Personal Growth

God In You: Releasing the Power of the Holy Spirit in Your Life by Dr. David Jeremiah, Sisters, OR: Multnomah Publishers, Inc., 1998.

Experiencing God by Henry T. Blackaby & Claude V. King, Nashville, TN: LifeWay Press, 1993, 1997.

Living Beyond Yourself: Exploring the Fruit of the Spirit by Beth Moore, Nashville, TN: LifeWay Press, 1998, 1999, 2000 .

Power in Praise by Merlin R. Carothers, Plainfield, NJ: Logos International, 1972.

Revolution by George Barna, Ventura, CA: The Barna Group, Ltd., 2005, *www.barna.org*.

Satan's Evangelistic Strategy for This New Age by Erwin Lutzer and John DeVries, Wheaton, IL: Victor Books, 1989.

Spirit Fruit by John M. Drescher, Scottdale, PA: Herald Press, 1974.

What Happens When Women Pray by Evelyn Christenson, Colorado Springs, CO: Cook Communications, 1997.

The Lord's Return

Escape the Coming Night, a dramatic narrative on the book of Revelation by Dr. David Jeremiah, Wheaton, IL: Tyndale House Publishers, 1971.

Racing Toward the Mark of the Beast by Peter and Paul Lalonde, Eugene, OR: Harvest House Publishers, 1994.

Speaker/Writer Training

CLASServices (CLASS stands for: Christian Leaders, Authors & Speaker Services) is a complete service agency for both the established and aspiring Christian speaker, author, and publisher. Focusing on the Christian community, CLASS finds, trains, develops, educates, and nurtures raw talent. When the person is ready, CLASS helps launch them through their speaker's service and through providing publishing assistance. Visit them at *www.classervices.com* or contact them at P.O. Box 66810, Albuquerque, NM 87193-6810, 800-433-6633.

Traveling Light Speaker's Network, a Division of Word Warrior Ministries, Inc. Word Warrior Ministries is dedicated to facilitating outreach opportunities for Christian performers and speakers to evangelize through the Word of God. To schedule a speaker or inquire about training, contact Diane Cook at 4102 Pearsons Corner Road, Dover, DE 19904, 302-734-0572.

Write His Answer Ministries. Marlene Bagnull's writing and speaking ministry includes Bible studies, books and tapes, At-Home Writing Workshops (a correspondence study program), seminars, and editing and mentoring services to Christian writers. She directs both the Colorado and Greater Philadelphia Christian Writers Conferences annually, and her web site contains a wealth of information for both aspiring and seasoned writers: *www.writehisanswer.com*.

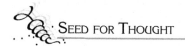 SEED FOR THOUGHT

Then Jesus said, "God's kingdom is like seed thrown on a field by a man who then goes to bed and forgets about it. The seed sprouts and grows—he has no idea how it happens. The earth does it all without his help: first a green stem of grass, then a bud, then the ripened grain. When the grain is fully formed, he reaps—harvest time!"

—*Mark 4:26-29* (MSG)

ruitbearer
What Can I Do For YOU, Lord?

- *Did you borrow this book? Why not order one for yourself so you can highlight and underline?*

- *Is this your book? Consider ordering a copy for a friend or relative—or for your church or local library.*

RDER INFORMATION

Available your local bookstore, Amazon.com, or Ingram
ISBN 978-1-886068-07-0

For autographed copies or bulk discounts, contact
Candy Abbott
P.O. Box 777, Georgetown, DE 19947
302.856.6649 • FAX 302.856.7742

www.fruitbearer.com
info@fruitbearer.com

THER BOOKS BY CANDY ABBOTT

MY 30-DAY PRAYER DIARY

This handy diary is was created as a companion to *Fruitbearer: What Can I Do for You, Lord?* by Candy Abbott. It is patterned after the prayer diary by Catherine Marshall and Leonard LeSourd that Candy used in her journey to become better acquainted with the Holy Spirit. Come near to God, and He will come near to you (James 4:8) is a promise from His holy Word. By committing yourself to thirty days of prayer, you are intentionally drawing near to God, and you can do so in confidence, knowing that He is drawing near. Many of the topics addressed in this diary will be familiar, probably all of them, but each time these areas confront our spirit, we may be in a different frame of mind or circumstance. The blank portion, "My Prayer Requests" and "God's Answers" can be used to record your own personal spiritual journey or prayer concerns for others. If the Holy Spirit speaks to your heart, capture His words and date the entry so you can reflect on them later. The Word is alive in those of us who believe. Give the Holy Spirit freedom to search areas you may have resisted before.

SPIRIT FRUIT: A CANDID CALENDAR FOR FRUITFUL LIVING

This perpetual calendar will tickle your funny bone, make you think, and strengthen your spirit. A light and unexpected approach to biblical and everyday truths, *Spirit Fruit* will become your daily friend and be a good conversation piece for the whole family . . . year after year.

FEELINGS: PRAYERS FOR WOMEN IN A WACKY WORLD

A TO Z EMOTIONS DEVOTIONS

Are your emotions soaring heavenward one minute and splashing for survival the next? This devotional will keep you anchored in Scripture so you can hear God's voice and heed His call, whether you're sinking or swimming. Each "feelings" page begins with "Lord, I feel _____," followed by a real-life situation, a relevant Scripture, and the Lord's perspective. Try it yourself. Half of the pages are lined for you to journal your own feelings.

MOURNING BREAKERS: A DAUGHTER'S REFLECTIONS ON HER MOM'S HOMEGOING

Tears may flow in the night, but joy comes in the morning (Psalm 30:5).

If you are grieving the loss of a loved one or helping someone through their final days on earth, this brief personal experience devotional is a proven resource for caretakers who are seeking an anchor. Find your joy in the mourning.

GAVIN GOODFELLOW: THE LURE OF BURNT SWAMP

What do twelve-year-old dyslexic Gavin Goodfellow, prophetically-inclined Uncle Warney, mother-daughter witches from London, and a tattooed New Age guru have in common? Burnt Swamp—where flames from a mysterious underground fire have been smoldering for ten years. The battle is on for dominion of the swamp and possession of an ancient diary that holds clues to release or destroy the evil that dwells beneath the surface. Will Gavin respond to the Holy Spirit and embrace his God-given calling? Or will Bea Daark and her mum unleash forces that lure Gavin and the sleepy town of Ashboro deep into bondage?

Book One of the Burnt Swamp Trilogy

"Just when I thought the best fantasy-mystery-adventure books had already been written, I found *Gavin Goodfellow*. NOW you have the best! Not only is the story deliciously strange and can't-put-it-down intriguing, but Gavin and the challenges he bumps into are as real as you are. And at the center of it all, there's God—like you've never experienced God before. So follow Gavin and his cousins, Molly and Eric, into Burnt Swamp and be prepared for the journey of your life!"

—Nancy Rue, award-winning author
of youth and adult fiction

OTHER BOOKS BY CANDY ABBOTT

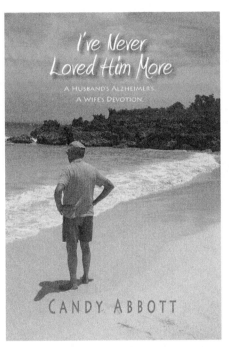

I'VE NEVER LOVED HIM MORE: A HUSBAND'S ALZHEIMER'S, A WIFE'S DEVOTION

I've Never Loved Him More is one wife's story of what it means to live out her vows, "in sickness and in health." As her husband's caregiver in his struggle with Alzheimer's, this story takes the reader through discovery, acceptance, adjustment, and battle against the ravages of what is often seen as a soul-crushing disease. Armed with faith, humor, and a history of spiritual victories, Candy demonstrates how she is loving her way through the mind-maze that would steal her husband of four decades. Displaying peace under pressure, she never pretends to have the answers as she navigates unfamiliar waters while also dealing with her own health issues, financial uncertainty, and more. She finds strength in her faith, family, friends, and the kindness of strangers. She engages Scripture, prayer, and spiritual support to combat this disease, weapons which can inspire others who are fighting chronic illnesses. Far from depressing, this is a worthwhile, helpful read for anyone struggling with anything.

SEED FOR THOUGHT

God will have the final word. And it will be good.

—*Author Unknown*

Made in the USA
Middletown, DE
12 February 2022

61028063R00159